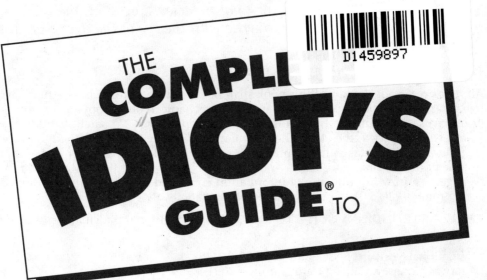

Surviving Anything

by Patrick Sauer and Michael Zimmerman,
produced by BookEnds, LLC

ALPHA

A Pearson Education Company

This book is dedicated to Survivor—not the television show, the band—because both of us authors try to write with the eye of the tiger every time our pens touch paper.

Copyright © 2001 by BookEnds, LLC

International Standard Book Number: 0-02-864174-4
Library of Congress Catalog Card Number: 2001089687

03   02   01   8   7   6   5   4   3   2   1

Interpretation of the printing code: The rightmost number of the first series of numbers is the year of the book's printing; the rightmost number of the second series of numbers is the number of the book's printing. For example, a printing code of 01-1 shows that the first printing occurred in 2001.

Printed in the United States of America

Note: This publication contains the opinions and ideas of its authors. It is intended to provide helpful and informative material on the subject matter covered. It is sold with the understanding that the authors and publisher are not engaged in rendering professional services in the book. If the reader requires personal assistance or advice, a competent professional should be consulted.

The authors and publisher specifically disclaim any responsibility for any liability, loss, or risk, personal or otherwise, which is incurred as a consequence, directly or indirectly, of the use and application of any of the contents of this book.

Publisher
Marie Butler-Knight

Product Manager
Phil Kitchel

Managing Editor
Jennifer Chisholm

Acquisitions Editor
Mike Sanders

Development Editor
Lynn Northrup

Production Editor
Billy Fields

Copy Editor
Susan Aufheimer

Cartoonist
Brian Moyer

Cover Designers
Mike Freeland
Kevin Spear

Book Designers
Scott Cook and Amy Adams of DesignLab

Indexer
Angie Bess

Layout/Proofreading
John Etchison
Mary Hunt
Ayanna Lacey
Stacey Richwine-DeRome

Contents at a Glance

Contents

Appendixes

Foreword

The Complete Idiot's Guide to Surviving Anything is a great survival encyclopedia!

I found the authors' style to be a refreshing and entertaining read. They interject humor throughout the text, enticing the reader to learn more. Covering survival in each of the global climates is just the beginning. This book goes on to provide valuable tips on how to survive a natural disaster, man-made disaster, and even *man*.

As a global survival expert and author of several books on the subject, I was pleased to see the first three chapters address the human factor of survival. Although many issues have a part in one's ability to stay alive under adverse conditions, I am a firm believer that our will to survive plays a major role in the outcome. After all, how can we explain why some individuals thrive in less-then-optimal conditions while others perish under ideal circumstances? During these early chapters the authors discuss such subjects as our will to survive and what it takes to be a survivor, and both subjects force the reader to process these potential issues.

When pondering such matters I often reflect on my early education as a wannabe USAF Survival Instructor. I spent six months surviving under the harshest conditions imaginable, followed by another six months learning how to teach these skills to others. On our first month-long venture I found myself in over six feet of snow in sub-zero temperatures and forced to go four nights without sleep and five days without food. My mind began to drift and I found it difficult to even accomplish the simplest of tasks. When the trip was over I had lost 25 pounds and gained a true appreciation for the harsh realities of survival. Approximately 75 percent of my class quit for one reason or another. What motivated some of us to stay while others gave into the psychological stress? Our will to succeed or survive was the key.

Although I believe the will to survive is the most influential factor in staying alive, learning some basic survival skills can have a major impact on your odds of success and comfort. After helping the reader understand the human factor and how to survive the various global climates, the authors present a variety of survival skills for such situations as surviving a hijacker, train crash, plunging elevator, volcanic eruption, earthquake, and even derailment of an amusement park ride. There's even a section on how to deliver a baby, and based on my experience, I can definitely see how this might fit into a survival text.

Like the *Encyclopedia Britannica, The Complete Idiot's Guide to Surviving Anything* will provide you with valuable insights on surviving almost any challenging situation. But unlike the *Encyclopedia Britannica*, this book provides its information in an informal yet enjoyable format.

Gregory J. Davenport

Gregory J. Davenport is a global survival authority and owner of Simply Survival, a wilderness education program (www.simply-survival.com). He is the author of *Wilderness Survival* (Stackpole Books, 1998)and *Wilderness Living* (Stackpole Books, 2001).

Introduction

Surviving anything ... what does it mean?

Is it possible to survive *everything?* There hasn't been a breakthrough in cryogenics or cloning allowing us to survive forever, has there? We all have to check out sometime, don't we?

Technically ... yes, but along the way, the cosmic curveballs that come down the pike can be unfathomable and that's when the will to survive is the only thing that will keep us going. It's been said that life is a joke and we're the punch line, but it's laughing in the face of extinction that makes survivors. *The Complete Idiot's Guide to Surviving Anything* won't help you survive run-of-the-mill catastrophes. It won't help you cure a broken heart, regain losses in the stock market, or make peace with the in-laws before they sit down at your house for a Thanksgiving feast. It will, however, help you get through those unforeseen life-or-death scenarios by offering practical how-to advice on diverse topics such as ...

➤ Handling hijackers.

➤ Battling bears.

➤ Finding fish and other sources of food.

➤ Avoiding asteroids.

➤ Mastering mountains and deserts.

Survival is tough. *The Complete Idiot's Guide to Surviving Anything* is designed to help you combat those rough moments of life, because it's a jungle out there ... and you'll need this book in case you ever *do* find yourself in a jungle out there.

What You'll Learn in This Book

The Complete Idiot's Guide to Surviving Anything features advice, trivia, facts, and ideas on becoming a survivor. Although it may seem like the only book you will ever need, it shouldn't be adhered to as though you're attending classes to become a Green Beret. The following five parts will take you on a whirlwind survival tour that's a lot more exciting than those pale television imitations:

Part 1: "I Will Survive," is a primer on what it takes to become a true survivor. It deals with mental toughness, CPR, smoke signals, and the most important dinner-table discussion question of all: Would you eat your best friend to stay alive?

Part 2: "Wilderness Survival," takes you from the comfort of your living room to the hairiest of jungles, the coldest of tundras, the driest of deserts, and the thickest of forests. It includes ways to find shelter, food, and water, and what to do when giant mammals are looking to have you for dinner.

Part 3: "High-Tech Survival," doesn't cover man-eating robots because they don't exist ... yet. It does cover what to do with technology gone awry, like flaming cars, rampaging trains, plummeting airplanes, and the ever-popular towering inferno.

Part 4: "Natural Disasters," deals with the hellacious weather calamities, one or all of which you face, depending on where you hang your hat. The wrath of Mother Nature can be extraordinary, but with this book and a little luck, we can all ride out the storm with our feet up and a cold beverage ... a hot one during blizzards.

Part 5: "Getting Away from It All," takes you to the four corners of the globe (how can a globe have corners?) where you'll survive a coup, rot in a foreign jail like a pro, defend yourself against dangerous attackers, live through roller coaster mishaps, deliver a baby, and learn how to save lives in the wild through ice rescues and rudimentary surgical procedures. How many all-inclusive resorts can guarantee that?

More for Your Money!

In addition to all the explanation and information, this book contains other tidbits to enhance your attempts to survive anything. Here's how you can recognize these features:

SOS

In these boxes you'll find warnings and alerts to any pitfalls you might encounter. Ignore them at your own risk!

Tactical Terms

These boxes give you definitions to clear up the more obscure terms, because surviving and educating are not mutually exclusive.

Survival Kit

In these boxes you'll find "insider" pearls of wisdom to give you a leg up on a diverse range of topics ranging from alligator attacks to deadly mudflows.

Adventures of a Lifetime

In these boxes you'll find first-person accounts, often-told anecdotes, and interesting yarns from the world of survivors.

Acknowledgments

Patrick Sauer: I would like to thank all of the sources (listed in the back) for the book, because the topics covered a wide swath. I would also like to thank John Talbot; Jessica Faust for having the guts to start a company; Mike Zimmerman for pinch-hitting; Dad for medical tidbits; Matt Bender for the quicksand deconstruction; Myron and Callen for spending two years saving the world in a tropical paradise; Bob Topel for actually reading one; Kim for helping me survive more than I think she realizes; and Mom for surviving more bad hands than any good soul deserves to be dealt.

Mike Zimmerman: I'd like to thank the above-mentioned Ms. Faust and Mr. Talbot for the same reasons, and Mr. Sauer for welcoming me aboard. Other thanks for other reasons go to Christine McGinn and Greg Emery, without whom I would be wrong about a lot of things. Thanks also to Indiana Jones, James Bond, Bugs Bunny, and all those other dudes who make this stuff look easy. I officially dedicate my work on this book to Julia, the new and exciting woman in my life who motivates me to survive a little while longer to see how this whole thing plays out.

Special Thanks to the Technical Reviewers

The Complete Idiot's Guide to Surviving Anything was reviewed by several experts to ensure you get the most accurate information possible. Our thanks go to the following people: Christopher Effgen, owner of the *Disaster Center* Web site (www. disastercenter.com); Eric Carlson, airline pilot; John Byorth, editor at *Hooked on the Outdoors* magazine; David Alloway, author of *Desert Survival Skills;* Andy Vietze, managing editor of *Down East: The Magazine of Maine,* co-author of a guide to eco-travel called *Adventures,* and author of articles about the outdoors for a variety of magazines; Will Woodard, survival writer and author; Christine Bauer, registered nurse; Alex Fernandez, fireman; Christine McGinn, M.D.; and the National Academy of Railroad Sciences, at Johnson County Community College, Overland Park, Kansas—director, Andy Burton.

Trademarks

All terms mentioned in this book that are known to be or are suspected of being trademarks or service marks have been appropriately capitalized. Alpha Books and Pearson Education cannot attest to the accuracy of this information. Use of a term in this book should not be regarded as affecting the validity of any trademark or service mark.

Part 1

I Will Survive

For some of us, every day is a lesson in survival. Just getting through work and life is enough to challenge even the toughest. But what if you were to face some dangerous, unforeseen obstacles? Do you have the mettle to stare down a charging grizzly, look a hurricane in the eye, or escape a towering inferno?

Read the chapters in this part to not only discover whether or not you have the mettle, but to know what that truly means. Learn the skills of a true survivor—first aid, smoke signals, how to assemble a lifesaving kit, and how to recognize a self-actualized person. And once you know the basics, you'll be ready for anything.

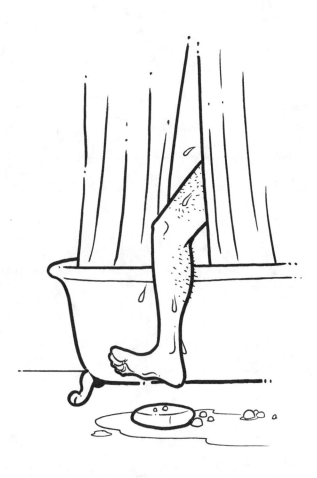

Chapter 1

The Will to Survive

In This Chapter

➤ Your survival depends on *you*

➤ The importance of mental toughness

➤ Learn the healing powers of maggot therapy

➤ Start packing your survivor's kit today

I will survive.

Not only is this one of the finest disco records ever recorded, it is also the motto of this book. Everybody now, say it strong, say it proud, three … two … one:

I will survive.

Three little words strong enough to change the course of human destiny. It doesn't matter what challenge you encounter—be it physical, emotional, psychological, animal, environmental, or extraterrestrial—declaring to yourself that you *will* survive is the most important step to recovering from the perilous situation in which you find yourself.

The Will of the People

Take a moment to think of the toughest challenge you ever faced, and be honest. It doesn't have to be a fistfight with a Yeti, escape from a swarm of killer bees, or a battle with advanced cyborgs bent on world domination. Think of the scariest situation you ever faced: the death of a loved one, the loss of a job, or being lost in the forest with no food. No matter what your dilemma, survival depended on your grit and determination. Whether you were conscious of it or not, you made the choice to fight another day. The bottom line: If you *decide you will survive,* the chances are infinitely greater that you will.

This book is about looking the most frightening situations in the eye and beating them. It doesn't cover everyday tragedies like death, bankruptcy, divorce, disease, or depression; but at the core, all misfortunes share one truth: It is up to you to survive. Granted, there are illnesses that can't be defeated, but the will to survive can stave off their ultimate outcome for years. This is not a feel-good platitude either, because the will to live is our strongest natural instinct and helps people overcome the most unimaginable calamities.

How Tough Are You Mentally?

Here's an unscientific test to see if you have what it takes to be a survivor. A strong mental attitude will do a lot more for a neophyte who gets shipwrecked on an island than a lifetime of studying what to do by someone who can't overcome panic.

Think of how you handle stress and answer the following questions honestly:

SOS

Don't underestimate mental toughness. Research has shown that when it comes to emergencies, individual situations matter less than the fortitude of the individuals themselves. It always boils down to Hamlet's basic question of the human desire to live: *To be or not to be?*

➤ Do you have the ability to make quick, firm decisions or are you wishy-washy when the pressure is on?

➤ Are you able to think on the fly, improvise, and adapt to unfamiliar situations?

➤ Do you take sensible risks or do you always go by the book?

➤ Are you cool-headed? Do you remain calm and collected? Do you panic? Make mountains out of molehills?

➤ Are you patient and/or logical? Or are you impetuous and irrational?

➤ Do you acknowledge your fears, weaknesses, worries, and deficiencies and try to confront, control, and/or overcome them? Or do you ignore them and hope they will simply never come up?

➤ Are you able to "read" people; to become a uniter and not a divider?

➤ Do you have a strong, innate common sense?

➤ Do you like who you are? Not in a cocky, arrogant way, but do you have an unshakable self-confidence?

Survival Kit

The simplest way to develop a survivor's outlook is to start living by the sentence that best sums up how to approach life: Hope for the best, but prepare for the worst.

If you've honestly answered these questions, you have a basic idea of how well you will survive anything. If you go to pieces because the copier is broken and you have a report due in 10 minutes, you won't come up with an alternative solution or assess whether the situation is remotely life-or-death. In intense circumstances, like being in a hijacked plane, your personality traits will be magnified and a survivor's outlook could mean the actual difference between life and death.

If you don't trust me, read the opening line to the *U.S. Army Survival Manual:* "Many survival case histories show that stubborn, strong willpower can conquer many obstacles."

Under fire, American GIs take cover somewhere in Germany during World War II.

(Photo courtesy of the Franklin D. Roosevelt Library Digital Archives.)

Saving Yourself with Some Basic Training

Having a survivor's outlook is essential, but it will carry you only so far if you aren't equipped with any basic survival skills. If it's common sense that those who are prepared for any situation will be able to adapt when things go haywire, why do people consistently lack the foresight to make thorough preparations? *Preparing* for the worst invariably involves making preparations for the unforeseen future ... it's the smart thing to do. If you keep road flares in the trunk of your Firebird, the odds of someone coming to your rescue after your muscle car skids off the bridge increase dramatically. If you know how to properly apply a tourniquet, your rock-climbing partner may not bleed to death after falling off a ledge. So, take the time to prepare yourself for the worst and keep the following keys in mind.

Know That Survival Doesn't Equal Comfort

People who find themselves in scary, unfamiliar surroundings often react by trying to find the most comfortable way to handle the pressure. It's an understandable response and it brings a sense of calm, but it isn't the same thing as making the commitment to survival. Being comfortable means you feel a sense of security, which may be attained without taking steps to ensure safety over the long haul. Planning for your safety encompasses more than finding a momentary resting spot out of harm's way.

Take Care of Your Body, and It Will Take Care of You

Feeling good physically will go a long way toward helping you handle pressure mentally (and vice versa), so ready your body for handling stress. Good health is important for everyday life, but it can be the decisive factor in whether or not you survive.

It's fairly simple: Get in shape. Strength, stamina, and dexterity are important to fending off fatigue, weakness, and pain. In addition, physical fitness can be a major help in building mental toughness, which is why linebackers in the National Football League can go on playing with injuries that would put most of us on injured reserve.

Survival Kit

Include cardiovascular exercise such as aerobics, swimming, or brisk walking in your get-fit program if you plan on embarking on any kind of strenuous activity, especially in the mountains. Novice, out-of-shape backpackers face a severe wake-up call when they start trying to make their way uphill through the thin altitude.

Become Self-Sufficient

You may never end up alone on a deserted island like Tom Hanks in the film *Cast Away,* but it's *theoretically* possible, and you don't want to spend weeks learning how to make a fire, do you? Learn the basics and you will always know you can depend on yourself. You may never need to know how to start a fire without matches, but why risk it? It's also handy to be able to tie knots, procure water, find food, build primitive shelters, provide medical assistance, and establish directions toward safety. It might seem ridiculous to set an organic, man-made trap in your backyard to catch a rabbit, which you then skin and eat, but you could end up being the hero, revered by one and all.

Know Your Terrain

Let's say you're looking to buy a house along the coast of Florida. Wouldn't it make sense to take the time to see how well the area has endured previous hurricanes? How well the community is prepared? What has been done to reinforce the candy store where you work? Where the emergency escape routes are? Where flash flooding is most likely to occur?

Of course it would, because you are making a major investment and you wouldn't overlook these weighty nuggets in a major decision. Still, people often overlook the potentially consequential details regarding the terrain they are entering. Being observant is an important preparation and it can be as simple as locating the nearest emergency exits in your high-rise luxury hotel or as involved as studying the topography, wildlife, and water sources of Africa before venturing into the jungle to take nature photographs. Again, it may seem like busywork, but if you know your terrain and have a good idea where maggots can be found, it may allow you to save a limb or two.

Survival Kit

Rabbits are one the few animals that can be caught and killed by hand, because even though they're quick, they're not too sharp. If you see a rabbit, survey the ground for its tracks and follow them to the bunny hangout. Some rabbits don't travel far from home, so it shouldn't take long to make a rabbit the key ingredient of a tasty stew.

Adventures of a Lifetime

Maggots can be used to chow down on infected body tissue and have been used for treatment during combat. You have to expose the wound to flies for 24 hours and then cover up the affected area. Check regularly to see if maggots have hatched and allow them to eat away until the victim is in more pain and you see vivid red blood. The maggots have done the filthy work and reached live tissue, but you don't want them calling your buddy's leg home, so flush out the wound with purified water and keep checking it every few hours for several days to make sure all the flesh-eating guests are gone.

Practice, Practice, Practice

Think back to when you were a kid and Dad pitched a tent in the backyard to sleep in and practice for the upcoming camping trip. It was a nifty trick because, while you were thinking how much fun it was to catch 40 winks on the whiffle-ball field, Dad was preparing you for your first trip into the forest. In addition to becoming self-reliant, it pays to rehearse calamitous situations with the family. If you live along the San Andreas fault and your family hasn't had an earthquake drill, or if your wife is pregnant and you haven't practiced what to do when her water breaks on the house-boat, well, it could come back to haunt you. Coaches have been known to say that good practices lead to great games, so prepare the family for one of life's curveballs.

Stay Active

One last thing that fosters a survivor's outlook is to constantly stay active, because when it hits the fan, you may be forced to deal with loneliness, isolation, restlessness, boredom, and ultimately helplessness against the cruel forces of the universe. There's a reason the worst prison offenders are placed in *solitary* confinement: Humans are their own worst enemy and your mind can be your downfall. During the time of preparation, keep physically and mentally active; treat a practice situation as if it's the real deal.

It doesn't hurt to envision scenarios you may never encounter, like a hijacking, be-cause a sound game plan will lessen the panic. It sounds silly to visualize the safety steps to take during a hijacking, but what about something more common, like a dog bite, a blizzard, a train derailment, or a giant asteroid hitting Earth? (Okay, so you can skip the asteroid contingency plan; there won't be much any of us can do.)

Survival Kit

The best way to avoid dog bites is to steer clear of stray and/or unfamiliar animals, even if they seem friendly. If a dog approaches you, keep your hands at your side and your feet together. If you happen to be lying down, pull your knees to your chest, tuck your head down, and cover your ears with a fist on each side. Try to be as still and quiet as possible and never look a dog in the eye because making eye contact could be misconstrued as a challenge to fight.

It's impossible to know whether survival skills will ever become a necessity, but it is still worth the time and effort to hope for the best, prepare for the worst, and be ready to stand and loudly say:

I will survive.

During the Great Depression, Americans had to collectively adopt a survivor's outlook to get through their abject poverty and despair.

(Photo courtesy of the Franklin D. Roosevelt Library Digital Archives.)

Survival Kit 101

Now that you are developing a survivor's outlook and preparing to handle life's most challenging situations, let's put together a survival kit that everyone should have.

Each survival scenario will be different, but this is a general kit that should cover all the bases. If nothing else, it will prevent you from falling down the stairs in a pitch-black house, searching for a flashlight while a wicked tornado is bearing down. Obviously, you probably aren't going to bring a generator onto an airplane, but you should still have a kit in the places where you spend the most time.

Whatever container you use for your kit should be durable, waterproof, and able to be locked, like a large tackle box or tool chest. Don't use something too heavy to be easily moved. Make sure that every item is covered in plastic and easy to carry in case an evacuation becomes a reality. Obviously, the size of a traveling survival kit for a single person will be smaller than one for an entire family, but both should be mandatory in your house just the same.

Start by including the following items in your kit:

➤ **Flashlights.** Get a heavy-duty, industrial flashlight, as well as smaller ones for every member of your family.

➤ **Radio.** Get a battery-powered radio to listen to news updates. Consider investing in a NOAA Weather Radio, which features a tone alert that can be left on all the time. (NOAA stands for National Oceanic and Atmospheric Administration.) It has constant updates from the National Weather Service that also includes emergency situations like chemical spills.

➤ **Batteries.** Make sure you get a large supply and replace them every six months or so. Purchase the batteries in bulk to lessen the cost.

➤ **Matches.** Pack plenty of waterproof matches in a waterproof container. You might want to pack a lighter as well, just in case.

➤ **Compass.** Get yourself a metal compass, learn how to read it, and never leave home without it.

➤ **Blankets and/or sleeping bags.** It is vital that these be kept in tight, waterproof bags, because they may be needed for more than a good night's rest. They may have to warm someone who is suffering from shock, hypothermia, or frostbite (we'll tell you more about these in Chapter 7, "It Was a Cold Winter's Night").

➤ **First-aid kit.** We'll look at its contents in a later chapter, but it's worth mentioning twice because it is so important.

➤ **Tools.** Depending on the size of your survival kit, you will want to have a few tools, especially if you are going to be outdoors. A small saw, a fold-up shovel, a sharp pocketknife, a signal flare, a wrench (for turning off leaky pipes), pens and pencils, a hand-held fire extinguisher, and the ever-popular Swiss army knife could all be useful in a crisis.

➤ **Personal hygiene items.** Pack enough soap, eye-care products, shampoo, toilet paper, feminine products, deodorant, toothbrushes and toothpaste, combs, brushes, and so on to last a couple of weeks. Buy a sturdy bucket that can serve as a latrine and get an ample supply of thick plastic garbage bags that can be tightly cinched (for human waste). If it sounds gross, it's better than the alternative, which would be using the basement floor. You can offset the problem by adding water and a little bleach to the bag before it is used as a makeshift toilet. Bury the bags away from your shelter to keep unwanted guests like rats and mice from dropping by.

➤ **Personal effects.** Personal effects are often overlooked, but they may be the most important things in the long run. Start with a healthy supply of cash, which probably shouldn't be kept in a survival kit but also shouldn't be forgotten. Also include personal identification cards for every member of your family, a cell phone, credit cards, copies of insurance policies, extra house and car keys, a list of telephone numbers of close friends and relatives, a detailed list of your family's medical conditions, and an extra supply of prescription medications.

Survival Kit

If you have a serious visual impairment, always pack an extra pair of glasses or contact lenses in your survival kit. If your eyes are suddenly rendered useless, surviving an ordinary day will be a monumental task. Seeing is definitely believing ... and in this case, surviving.

➤ **Clothing.** The amount of clothes to keep in your survival kit is tough to gauge, because they can be bulky and can be washed by hand in a pinch. However, there should be ample changes of socks and underwear, sturdy hiking boots, and thermal underwear for sleeping. Take the elements into account as well and include hats, mittens, ponchos, sunglasses, galoshes, down coats, and ski masks (which are also handy for participation in any terrorist activities that might arise).

➤ **Hodgepodge.** These items aren't vital, but they can sure make life easier. If there's room in your kit, consider duct tape, a whistle, games and books to pass the time, a fishing pole and tackle, a hunting rifle and ammunition, pillows, a cell phone, and a small propane-powered stove.

➤ **Food and water.** We'll look at how to find food and water in later chapters, where we talk about being stranded in the desert, the jungle, and other places. This discussion is just a brief synopsis of what you should pack in your personal

Survival Kit

When an emergency situation erupts, don't forget to clean perishable items out of the fridge. No sense letting food go to waste if it can be eaten in the next few hours.

Tactical Terms

Gorp is a mix of high-energy snacks like raisins, peanuts, dried fruit, nuts, and maybe an M&M or two. Not surprisingly, the word gorp originated in the heady hippie days of 1968, but its derivation is unknown.

survival kit. Normally, you and your family won't have to live off these rations for more than a couple of days, but pack enough for at least a week. These days, water is easy to find; just load up on bottles from the supermarket, but make sure to change them every few months. Figure a gallon a day per person in your fallout shelter (during Armageddon anyway), which includes cooking and cleaning. Make sure nobody guzzles all the water on the first night, and if you use water from an unsure source, always boil it before drinking.

Canned food is the way to go, so don't forget a strong can opener and maybe a few utensils and lightweight dishes. Foods high in calories, carbohydrates, protein, and vitamins are much more beneficial than fatty, salty, sugary snacks. Foods that don't require much preparation or cooking are best, because they will use less water and you won't have to use cooking fuel or propane, which is always a potential danger.

Some good items to include are peanut butter; unsalted crackers; granola or energy bars; *gorp;* canned fruit and vegetables; canned or boxed juices; individually canned meals or soups (or single meals like Cup-O-Noodles, because it's easier to ration, although it needs boiling water); cookies or hard candy (to keep up morale); and anything freeze-dried or prepackaged (it's not the best food in the world, but it will last a long time).

Now that you have a never-say-die survivor's outlook, it's time to go forward, which is the way all people survive the tough times.

The Least You Need to Know

➤ The will to survive is the key to staying alive and overcoming whatever obstacles life throws at you.

➤ Don't underestimate mental toughness. Research has shown that when it comes to emergencies, individual situations matter less than the fortitude of the individuals themselves.

➤ The best outlook to take should be: *Hope for the best, but prepare for the worst.*

➤ A survivor's kit should be prepared well in advance of an emergency situation.

Chapter 2

What It Means to Be a Survivor

In This Chapter

➤ The hunger to survive

➤ Using fire, smoke, and flares to signal for help

➤ Why you should always carry a mirror

➤ Exploiting the X factor

➤ Don't overlook Morse code

Now that you have some idea of what defines a survivor, ask yourself: Am I a survivor?

Most of us would like to think we are, but in reality, how do we know? Is it even possible to know if we have the survival instinct before fate slaps us in the face? Men of equal stature are thrown into battle; some serve valiantly and others faint-heartedly, but is there any way of knowing that beforehand? And, more important, is it better to die with honor or survive with cowardice? Even war hero Douglas MacArthur knew that in the end, even battles of worldly importance come down to a simple principle: Some survive and some don't. He said in his autobiography *Reminiscences,* "That's the way it is in war. You win or lose, live or die—and the difference is just an eyelash."

In that eyelash, a true survivor shines through and stakes his or her claim to stay among the living. After all, survival is the harder line to tow, but all we have in life is our life. No matter what peril we find ourselves in, survivors are ultimately defined by one quality … *they survived.*

The Ultimate Means of Survival

According to an extremely unscientific poll I conducted, *cannibalism* is the number-one interest/concern/fascination/worry/thrill of the average male who wants to learn about surviving anything. (Keep in mind that the poll has an error of margin—my sample consists of three beer-swilling idiots sprawled out on my couch watching the Orange Bowl.) Cannibalism is survival at its most primitive level, the primordial act of eating human flesh to stave off death. Without question, it should only be practiced as a last resort, but it is *the* supreme test to determine if you are a true-blue survivor.

Would you eat another human to ward off starvation? Before you answer, take note of these self-evident, cannibalistic truths:

Tactical Terms

Cannibalism is the eating of human flesh by another human being. The word is derived from the Spanish name for the alleged man-eating Native Caribs who called the West Indies home.

Tactical Terms

Coprolite is fossilized excrement. I told you scientists have ways of finding out.

➤ **Somebody will know.** If you're with a group of 20 passengers on a plane that goes down in the Andes and you return a little bloated with a group of 10, suspicions will be raised. Modern rescue units are so sophisticated that they will be able to find the remains of the day, even if you had no choice and they were already dead. Or, what if nobody ever found out? Could you live with yourself?

It doesn't stop when you're six feet under, either; science may come back to haunt your (and your descendants') good name. Scientists recently discovered that the prehistoric Anasazi residents of the Four Corners (Colorado, Utah, New Mexico, Arizona) practiced cannibalism. How often and whether it was ritualistic or for survival is unknown, but 800 to 1,600 years ago, some of the ancestors of the Pueblo Indians ate human flesh. A *coprolite* was found containing traces of human myoglobin, a protein found in muscle tissues, that will appear only if it was swallowed.

➤ **You'll become infamous.** Cannibals have always fascinated people because it is hard to fathom what it would take to get to the point where dining on another human being becomes a reality. Even in today's forgiving climate, do you want to carry the stigma of being a man-eater? It's a safe bet that in this modern, tabloid, media-saturated, Internet age, the story of your *Homo sapiens* nourishment would be everywhere and you would become a celebrity of sorts. Cannibals aren't as disposable as other television darlings; their legacies last and it might be tough to raise a family, go to college, work at the hospital, or even eat at Sizzler without a lot of whispering, finger-pointing, and questions like, "Do you want a side of waiter with that?"

➤ **You may face Johnny Law.** If you have to eat someone to survive, it might slide, but consider the ramifications if you decide to chow down early on while your companion waits it out. You could be hauled into court and have to face a jury of your peers, all of whom are thinking, "Does the defendant's definition of seasoned jurors include lemon pepper and garlic?" Cannibalism is against the law and it would be a tough pill to swallow if you swallowed the tough Phil and ended up in the clink.

➤ **Is there a cannibal's cookbook?** You may be prepared for just about anything, but it would be impossible to know how to prepare a hearty meal of Frank-and-potatoes. It won't be all that surprising to note that this *really, out of basic human decency, should be an absolute last resort.*

Adventures of a Lifetime

Lewis Keseberg was a member of the Donner Party, a collective group of pioneers who became trapped in the Sierra Nevada Mountains during the winter of 1846 and 1847. Nearly half of the 89 emigrants died as they tried to survive one of the most severe winters on record. Keseberg was finally rescued in April, after the ninth blizzard, after spending roughly seven months stranded in the wilderness. He was the lone survivor, found in his cabin delirious and surrounded by the half-eaten dead. Keseberg told stories of eating human flesh, became a tabloid staple, and was reviled, ostracized, and considered a ghoul for his actions.

If you ever have to resort to cannibalism, consider yourself a true survivor. And remember, one cannibal sitting by the fire said to another, "I really hate my mother-in-law." The other cannibal replied, "Try the mashed potatoes."

On that note, let's move on.

Signaling for Help with Fire, Smoke, and Flares

When it comes to survival, most people want to be rescued or hope to "make it out alive." Imagine a young girl getting lost in the jungle for 30 years and suddenly reappearing with a fistful of bananas and communicating with chimpanzees, having become some sort of half-woman, half-primate creature. The woman didn't fight for her survival per se, but rather *adapted* to a new, hairier way of life that could be turned into a darn fine monkey movie. For our purposes, survival is predicated on getting out of a potentially life-threatening situation to return to civilization, AKA the living room with the big-screen television where *The Primate of Her Life* can be enjoyed on DVD.

Survival Kit

If you're ever trapped in the tropics, look up in the trees and follow the monkeys to their banana hideaway. Once the banana well runs dry, monkeys themselves are a sound food source, and if the movie *Indiana Jones and the Temple of Doom* didn't lie, monkey brains are delectable.

Each survival situation is unique, but most of the time you are going to want to be rescued. Surviving becomes a matter of biding your time until someone shows up in a helicopter, speedboat, or hovercraft to take you home. The first step should be to see if anyone in your group has a cellular phone or a radio, which can be used to send a Mayday message instantaneously and at least alert authorities that you need help.

These won't always apply or be possible, but here are some general ways to signal for help.

Fire Alarms

In Chapter 8, "Yo Ho Ho, It's the Island Life for Me," we'll examine ways to make fire without the benefit of matches, but for now let's pretend you have plenty of long-stemmed matches. At night, fire is the only way you will be spotted from above; on a clear night, a raging inferno can be seen from a good distance. No matter where you are, try to build a fire as soon as possible, because it is a signal for rescue, a source of warmth, and a way to cook food and purify water. Fire is your friend.

Survival Kit

If you are alone, construct a torch out of highly flammable materials so that you can spark the fires the second you hear an aircraft flying into the vicinity.

The international distress signal is a triangle. If it's possible, start three separate fires with enough distance in between them so that they form a large triangle. If you are alone, it may feel like you're stuck in a stale marriage because it's hard to keep all the fires burning, but it's worth a shot. It's better to build three fires in some formation, because unless a rescue team is searching for you, a single blaze may not look like an emergency. Three fires, however, won't be ignored.

Always make sure that the fire you construct is out in the open and readily visible. If you get lost in the forest, you may have to clear out dead trees to create a sufficient area, or try building a fire on a large boulder or a rocky cliff, away from the dense tree line. A general rule of thumb is that if you look up and see plant life of any kind, it's probably not the most advantageous location. Still, any signal fire is better than no signal fire at all.

Try to find a dry spot near your shelter. If stones are available, build a rock wall/pit around the fire to cut down on wind resistance. Make sure it's a large circle though, more akin to a college bonfire than a family camping trip.

Another signaling technique is to burn an entire tree—or bush if you think the ghost of Moses might lead you to the promised land. Collect a pile of dried wood or dead branches and place them around the base of a live tree and in its lower,

SOS

Don't burn a tree unless it is off all by its lonesome. If you happen to start a forest fire, you will probably be found by firefighters, but it will take dental records to confirm your identity. And remember that even if you burn only a few trees, it's a waste of a fuel source.

green limbs. Spark up the incendiary products and after they get to burning, add smaller trees and plants to keep it going, then kick back and watch the entire tree get engulfed in flames. Remember, though, if you are trapped in a place with a limited number of trees, burning one a night will quickly lead to a spot with absolutely no cover from the elements.

Smoking Section

During the daylight hours—which will be numerous if you find yourself lost in the Arctic in the summer—fire is a less effective signal than smoke. The international distress signal should be presented in the same formation for both smoke and fire, so if you are able, send three separate lines of smoke into the sky mirroring the points of a triangle. Build a healthy pile of indigenous vegetation. It can be moss, green leaves, evergreen boughs, cattails, ferns, palms, or whatever you can find. Many materials will burn and give off smoke, but don't forget that you may have to live off these plants, so use the nonedible ones first, like oleander or castor bean. You can also use poison sumac or poison oak for your fire, but don't touch them or breathe in the smoke, and make sure your fire is a good distance away.

Smoke signals are most effective when they are thick and a different shade than the sky. If your car breaks down on a clear day, use the tires or any other piece of rubber to make a charcoal black, smoky fire (and apologize to the atmosphere after you're saved). If it's overcast and cloudy, a near suffocation of the fire in leaves and a bit of water will send a paler smoke wafting through the air.

Survival Kit

It's appropriate at this time to mention that there aren't any detailed listings and pictures of edible (and nonedible) vegetation, fruits, nuts, and trees in this book. If you are going to be traveling in any unfamiliar terrain, I urge you to stop by your local bookstore or outdoor equipment store to pick up a detailed plant/nature guide, of which there are many. I recommend *Identifying Plants by Family and Genus* by Kristin Quinlan (Xlibris Corporation) or the *U.S. Army Survival Manual.*

In the long run, fire is needed for survival, whereas smoke is for getting rescued. Fire is more important, so if you have a limited number of fuel sources, smoke signals should be utilized only under proper circumstances. If planes keep flying overhead, they may or may not be looking for you, but either way it's a good time to take up smoking.

Lastly, smoke signals tend to be most effective on days where you can see for miles and miles. Adverse weather conditions limit their effectiveness, and snow, sleet, wind, and rain dissipate smoke. The chances of being spotted on any day that isn't placid and sunny are a cut above nil, so use your smoke signals wisely.

Flareups

If you happen to have a flare gun, road flares, colored smoke bombs, or a carton of those neon, green light sticks, you are in luck. These devices are great for signaling rescue craft of any kind and they are generally understood in any language as "Help! Help! Help!" The problem is that they are often misused and become worthless. The temptation to use the devices as soon as possible is understandable, but foolish. Maybe if you were on a deserted island, you would save your flare gun to signal a passing helicopter, but what about if your engine peters out in the middle of the night on a lonely highway during a Montana winter? Don't break out the road flare right away. It's better to save them until another person comes across your radar.

Signaling devices like these have a finite life span, some quickly blaze through the sky, while others last much longer on the ground, but they aren't everlasting. Keep them handy, but wait until the opportune moment to use them. While you are waiting, make sure all of these "save me" contraptions are kept dry.

Shiny Happy Signals

Planes, trains, and automobiles (not to mention boats and alien spacecraft) can be signaled by shiny objects reflecting off of the sun. The Fonz of television's *Happy Days* would have been prepared for any survival situation because he never would have hit the highways on his chopper without a travel mirror, which can be a survivor's greatest tool. Mirror signals can be viewed from 50 to 70 miles on a clear day and even farther in the desert. When signaling a plane, try to get to the highest point in your vicinity because you want to stand out from the natural ground terrain and be as visible as possible.

SOS

When it's time to send up the flare, make sure to follow the directions. You don't want to get overexcited and have a flare somehow blow up in your face, causing you to remain stranded, but now with second-degree burns and no nearby hospital.

To use the mirror most effectively, hold it with one hand near your face and extend the other hand out until your palm fills with sunlight. Take your illuminated middle and index fingers, spread them apart into a V-shape and run the sun's reflection through your fingers like the scope on a shotgun and aim at passing airplanes. You will have to adjust the mirror every hour to keep up with the sun, but it is a method of signaling that can be used from dawn to dusk.

Other items you might find yourself possessing that will work for sun signaling include ...

- ➤ Eyeglasses.
- ➤ Metal utensils.
- ➤ Aluminum foil.
- ➤ A tin can.
- ➤ A belt buckle.
- ➤ A wristwatch.
- ➤ A compass.
- ➤ A pocketknife.

X Marks the Spot

After building a fire or three, you should set about crafting visible ground signals, because most search-and-rescue missions are conducted by air. Unlike fire and smoke signals, once a ground signal is made, it's finished and will always be there (unless a heavy snowfall covers it over). Depending on your location, there are a variety of materials that can be used to build a ground signal, just make sure it doesn't blend in

Survival Kit

If possible, make your X red or orange, because those are the universal colors of emergency. Some wilderness travelers carry a small bottle of neon spray paint for this purpose.

with the ground. An X, which officially means "require medical assistance," has become the primary notation for rescue. Other symbols are …

➤ V = Require assistance.

➤ Y = Yes, affirmative.

➤ N = No, negative.

➤ ↑ = Heading in this direction

Unless you have time to kill, it's best to stick with the X, though, because it is the most identifiable and sends the strongest message. You can lay out clothing, towels, blankets, tarps, or tents in an X formation. Anything that's brightly colored works especially well.

If you are in a snow-covered area, stamp out an X and fill it with branches, dirt, rocks or anything darker than the whitewashed horizon. On an island, seaweed and palms offset the sand. In a forest clearing, you can burn an X in a massive fire pit, and in the desert or tundra, aluminum foil could be a lifesaver (although I'm not sure why you would be carrying a roll of foil across the tundra).

The trick is to make sure the X totally contrasts the surrounding area, otherwise it's camouflaged and all your hard work will have been for nothing. Once you are rescued, take down the ground signal so that future explorers don't send out a new rescue team in search of a phantom.

Do That to Me One Morse Time

The specifics of Morse code probably aren't going to be necessary in most survival situations, but you never know. Perhaps you will end up hostage in a POW camp with only a contraband penlight you smuggled in to alert the Green Berets, or you may have to man a yacht's radio in a life-or-death struggle against the ocean, so let's review the classic signal of distress over the radio. It goes—three dots, three dashes, three dots—with a brief pause in between repeated SOS messages. You can use flashes of light or flags, which are held to the left for the dashes and to the right for the dots.

The Least You Need to Know

➤ The ultimate survival situation may require that you resort to cannibalism, but it carries quite a stigma and should be practiced only when all other means of survival have been exhausted.

➤ Fires or smoke signals should be presented in a triangle formation, which is the universal distress signal.

➤ Mirrors, or any other shiny metal, can be used to signal rescue craft.

➤ A giant X built on the ground to contrast with the natural terrain is a great emergency signal.

➤ The Morse code signal for SOS is three dots, three dashes, three dots.

The Road to Survival

There is a lot to be learned from those old-school survival flicks in which the characters are in a plane that's going down; at the top of a burning building; in a foxhole during a lethal firefight; or running from a man-eating werewolf or a killer mummy. One lesson to be learned comes from the all-time great movie cliché in which the hysterical character is told to "pull yourself together." You know the scene I'm talking about, the one where the panicky, rabid, scared-to-death *weak link* in the group is blubbering and screaming that the end of the world is imminent and the *strong leader* has to step forward and firmly slap that sniveling, mollycoddling milksop across the puss.

At which point, everything becomes calm, a concrete plan is developed, put into action, and our hero leads his gang of ragtag survivors to victory over the nefarious circumstances that have beset their ordinary lives.

What should we take from the slap-to-the-face technique?

It works only in the movies. In reality, it stings, it serves no point, it could lead to a bloody bare-knuckle showdown, and quite frankly, it's not very nice. Seriously, has there ever been an intense moment in your life when you thought, "Gee, I could handle this situation a whole lot better if only someone would violently strike their hand across my face … twice, if necessary"?

Maslow's Hierarchy of Needs

Although you may one day find yourself a lone wolf fighting for survival, the chances are much greater that you will be part of a group, be it a few friends or a bunch of strangers. You might be attacked by an alligator while fishing in the Everglades with a couple of buddies, or you may be on a passenger train that derails into the Mississippi River, but either way it's important to have a vague idea of how humans respond to pressure-packed situations. It is impossible to know beforehand how strangers are going to react when faced with the task of fighting on or checking out, but even people you know and love may change under perilous circumstances. After all, the guy/girl who gets slapped could have started out as the life of the party.

For our excursion deep into the human psyche, we will turn to an expert. Abraham Maslow (1908–1970) was born and raised in Brooklyn, New York, and eventually made his way to the University of Wisconsin as a graduate student in psychology, researching dominance and sexuality in primates (it always comes back to monkeys, doesn't it?). Maslow returned to New York and expanded his ideas and investigations into human behavior. He delved into the works of other psychologists, but opened new doors into the mental development of regular folks, not just the sick, abnormal, or insane. Maslow became the trailblazer of a humanistic psychology that studied the whole person and countered adherents to strict *behaviorism*.

Maslow's most famous theory is the "hierarchy of needs," which is a definition of human motivation. If Shakespeare's "to be or not to be" sums up the heightened dilemma of surviving, Maslow's "what a man can be, he must be" explains why people take on heightened roles when it comes down to surviving. Maslow was no pessimist; however, he studied successful people and came up with the hierarchy of needs that must be met before they can reach "self-actualization." Basically, he was saying that there are five basic motivations that have to be fulfilled before the human desire to be what we can be can become the primary motivation.

The five levels of the hierarchy of needs are as follows.

Tactical Terms

Behaviorism is a school of psychology that takes the objective evidence of behavior as the sole consideration of research and bases its theories without reference to conscious experience. Behavior as evidence is taken as measured responses to stimuli.

Level One: Physiological Needs

These are the basic biological needs every human being needs to live, and are strongest when they aren't met. These needs include air, shelter, water, and food, and must be taken care of first because they ensure the continuation of life and preclude humans from reaching any higher levels if they aren't satisfied. In other words, you won't have the strength to build a raft to get off a deserted island if you don't eat and drink anything.

Level Two: Safety Requirements

These needs include protection, security, and a guarding against physical and emotional harm. Let's say you and a partner are lost in the desert, but have a water source and are eating cactus. The problem is, both of you are so afraid of scorpions that paralysis has set in and neither of you is willing to leave the shelter. Well, as actors Tim Robbins and Morgan Freeman both said in the film *The Shawshank Redemption,* "Get busy living, or get busy dying." Inherent in this philosophy is overcoming fear. Once you've killed a couple of scorpions, or gotten stung and dealt with the pain and swelling, fear will subside, safety will kick in, and you and your partner can move forward. It sounds like a contradiction, but it's true: Humans must feel some sense of security before they become fully realized people—people who take control of their lives and live them as they see fit. In our terms, this means people who tell the desert to pound sand and make a commitment to survival.

Humans always feel unsafe during times of stress and emergency, so this need is going to be hard to meet in a survival situation, but it's worth the effort to try and abate your (and everyone else's) fears. Children are particularly susceptible to having this need go unfulfilled, but your calm, reassuring behavior will help the kids believe that everything will be all right.

Survival Kit

Maslow's physiological needs included sex, so just because you are trying to survive doesn't mean you should ignore those natural human yearnings. Plus, if you have to start a new society ....

SOS

Don't forget that security includes overcoming phobias, so ease the worries of the most frightened members of your group. If you are in a plane crash and there are 13 survivors, don't taunt the survivor who suffers from triskaidekaphobia (fear of the number 13) and assumes he's about to die. Assure him that you are all going to make it, prime numbers be damned.

Survival Kit

Use Maslow's theory to your advantage and make others in your survivor group feel safe and an equal part of the team, because they won't give up if they feel like part of a warm, open family. In the classic TV show *Gilligan's Island*, Gilligan may have been the dumbest of the lot, but he always knew the Skipper would never leave his "little buddy" behind.

Level Three: Social Contact

One of the most unfortunate paradoxes to being lost alone in the wilderness is that, while it's technically easier to look out for number one, the isolation and lack of human contact can drive a person mad ... mad, I tell you! This holds true for people in everyday society, so imagine what it would be like deep inside a dark forest when the first snow falls. Maybe nobody cares when the plane is going down, but as soon as the survivors get their first three needs met, it's inevitable. Humans crave affection, a sense of belonging, acceptance, companionship, and the chance to give and receive love with another from their species (and possibly others, but that's a topic we'll be avoiding).

Simply put, your significant other is more likely to forge on through a blizzard if he or she knows that you care about his or her survival as much as you care about your own. People want to be part of a collective. Loneliness is the cruelest killer (with the Abominable Snowman a close second).

Even Texas cowboys need to be loved to survive.

(Photo courtesy of the Library of Congress.)

Level Four: Ego Support

This is closely related to the social category, but has more to do with self-worth than love from others. Everyone wants to feel useful and valuable on some level and have self-respect and the respect of the group. Ego usually doesn't kick in until one is satisfactorily situated in a comfortable environment. Ironically, it is easier for people to become autonomous knowing they have the recognition of others. For our intents and purposes, it is essential to know that everyone wants to be a part of the survival machine. Nobody ever wants to feel inferior, so stroke the egos of your fellow survivors.

Suppose you are one of a group of 10 diplomats taken hostage in an unstable country in the middle of a coup. Everyone gets thrown in a POW camp and nine members of the group take charge performing useful functions like catching grasshoppers for protein. What about the last timid guy who does nothing but whistle Frank Sinatra tunes? Take time to thank New Blue Eyes during the daily dose of gruel for keeping everyone's morale up with serviceable reproductions of *Summer Wind* and *The Way You Look Tonight.*

Ego becomes important if you are trapped for a long time and have to create a mini-society, which could be a utopia if none of its citizens feel worthless. Consider that helping others feel loved will help keep the family whole, including those who have no marketable skills, and feeding the ego of others will help the machine run smoothly. Levels three and four in Maslow's hierarchy of needs are psychological needs, but knowing this ahead of time will give you a heads-up when it comes to starting a colony from scratch.

Level Five: Self-Actualization Needs

In the world according to Maslow, self-actualization is the highest level a human can achieve. Very few folks reach this summit, when men or women become what they are capable of being, a fulfilled self. It is the Maslow prophecy consummated: "A musician must make music, an artist must paint, a poet must write, if he is to be ultimately at peace with himself." It boils down to those people we all envy, the ones who don't consider *living life to its fullest.* Maslow felt that those who climb their way to self-actualization have a fuller existence because they have more *peak experiences* throughout their days.

This psychology tutorial has been well and good, but how does self-actualization relate to surviving anything?

Tactical Terms

Peak experiences are penetrating moments of happiness, love, clarity, and euphoria when people are totally alive and independent but understand that they are part of the world at large and are aware of truth, justice, and the global way.

It is the very definition of surviving anything, because once you are placed in a life-or-death situation, your "calling," AKA your "self-actualization," is to become a "survivor" in the total sense of the world. You don't want to be a person who slowly withers away on a deserted island because you can't figure out how to catch fish and have to live off coconuts. Technically, you are surviving, but you haven't become a full-fledged survivor, which is presumably what anyone who purchased this book wants to be. Maslow's theories helped therapists develop ideas that people possess the inner resources for growth, regeneration, healing, and the will to overcome obstacles and climb to higher levels.

A self-actualized person is a true survivor, getting the most out of life on his or her own terms, and there is no more fulfilling endeavor than overcoming the worst situations that life has to offer. Ebeneezer Scrooge didn't become self-actualized until he saw the awful reality of his life and the horror that it could become. And what did he say before he became a true survivor? "I want to live ... I want to live."

I will survive.

Adventures of a Lifetime

Maslow published the hierarchy of needs in 1943, and it has held up relatively well to scrutiny and changes in science over the last six decades. Researchers have noted that Maslow's hierarchy mirrors the human cycle of life. To a newborn infant, physiological needs are of primary importance, but as the baby grows it needs to feel safe and loved. As babies become young children and break from their parents, they want to belong to a group, and their need for belonging increases throughout adolescence, when socialization and esteem are of utmost importance. Adults want to be recognized for their work and to feel like they've made it. Ideally, the development of their lives will lead to golden years of self-actualization.

The levels on the hierarchy are not mutually exclusive and they are constantly shifting. After all, a survivor may start a peaceful colony beyond our capacity to understand at this moment in time, but she still has to wolf down a cheeseburger and fries to fend off starvation.

I Am Superman (or Superwoman)

Having a general idea of what makes humans tick will go a long way if you are ever forced to oversee group dynamics in an emergency situation. It will make you a better leader in a situation that calls for leadership above all else. Don't you want to be a hero? Don't you want to be Superman in the eyes of your fellow survivors (and I mean that in a unisex Woman/Man of Steel kind of way). In addition, becoming self-actualized, a true survivor, will give you the street smarts, AKA the ability to read people, to get through anything.

The self-actualized are better than you and I (well, me anyway) and are equipped to survive anything because ...

➤ They are spontaneous and creative and see what isn't there ... yet.

➤ They attract disciples, and people heed their words of wisdom.

➤ They don't take life for granted, but they also don't take themselves too seriously.

➤ They realize that personal growth often times must supersede safety and they are willing to take risks.

➤ They try to tell the truth and accept things as they come.

➤ They have an understanding of reality and they trust their place in the world.

➤ They have integrity and don't fall under the influence of the foolish dictums of others; they let people be who they want to be.

➤ They have a sense of purpose and dedicate themselves to accomplishing whatever makes them whole—in our case, survival.

These are some of the qualities of the true survivor, and you can probably come up with a few more (knowing how to disarm a bank robber never hurts). If, however, you think there is no person like this on Earth and that this sounds like a character out of a fairy tale, you're right, but only to a degree. People who reach the self-actualization level don't necessarily have all these qualities and they certainly can't adhere to their best instincts

SOS

Never assume that any members of the animal kingdom adhere to Maslow's principles. They pretty much stick to physiology and safety, which means they will have no problem attacking or eating you for violating their space (except for maybe dolphins).

Survival Kit

The Maslow saga may seem like a bunch of psychological mumbo jumbo, but the higher the level, the more active the person. A passive outlook can thwart survival efforts long before not knowing how to kill a warthog with a bamboo spear.

all the time; but when push comes to shove and you are about to give birth in the back of a city bus that's on fire during a riot, you want the assistance of the self-actualized.

A strong, positive mental outlook makes the reality of surviving anything much greater, and it was Abraham Maslow who said, "Human nature is not nearly as bad as it has been thought to be."

You may be curious as to why we don't discuss understanding human behavior before we talk about sending out distress signals (See Chapter 2, "What It Means to Be a Survivor"). Isn't deducing who a true survivor is the most important detail in making it back to civilization in one piece? Well … no. Get your signal going right away, because it would really stink if you were explaining the function of ego to your companions in the Arctic and missed the biplane flying overhead. Surviving anything encompasses many layers, but mainly it encompasses getting back home safe and sound—so take care of the signals pronto.

The Union needed a few self-actualized men to win the Civil War. Think any of these soldiers qualified?

(Photo courtesy of the Library of Congress.)

Everyday People

If your SUV crashes through ice, personality traits won't matter one whit, but they will always matter in the unknown span of time that follows an emergency. Even if you never stand up in front of the group of survivors and announce, "Quiet down, everyone … okay, let's begin by breaking down possible courses of human interaction based upon Maslow's hierarchy of needs," subconsciously the properties will be a strong determining factor in the ultimate outcome.

Tucking away the details of Maslow's hierarchy of needs somewhere in the recesses of your brain can be beneficial because it will make dealing with difficult personalities less of a burden. If you have a basic understanding of what people want, you might understand why they're acting like such pains in the behind. Being a true survivor entails helping others survive, even if you would never sit down for a grilled-cheese and chocolate-milk lunch back in the real world. Put another way, you normally wouldn't give a loudmouth narcissist the time of day, but that person may know how to construct a waterproof hut, so try to understand why he or she is acting like a jerk.

Adventures of a Lifetime

One trick to keep the mind sharp and to keep from going stir-crazy while under duress is to continually recall lists, lyrics, dates, names, and so on. Why not recite the great Dylan Thomas poem *Do Not Go Gentle into That Good Night*, a survivor's treatise if there ever was one. Thomas wrote it for his dying father, but it's adaptable to any emergency where the will to live is vital. The first two stanzas are:

> *Do not go gentle into that good night,*
> *Old age should burn and rave at close of day;*
> *Rage, rage against the dying of the light.*
>
> *Though wise men at their end know dark is right,*
> *Because their words had forked no lightning they*
> *Do not go gentle into that good night.*

Here are a few unpleasant personalities you may encounter:

➤ **Whiners.** Usually, in a life-and-death situation, whining will take a backseat to surviving, but just try to ignore these types. If that doesn't work, give them whatever slow-going busywork you can find and set them up where they can't be heard.

➤ **Know-it-alls.** Invariably, people who know very little will claim to know everything. Let them run their mouths, gently explain why their ideas are flawed, and then complete tasks the right way.

SOS

Don't consider the back-stabbing, two-faced, crude, uncaring, looking-out-for-number-one personalities from TV's *Survivor 1* and *Survivor 2* to be a boilerplate for how your companions will act. Nothing brings out the worst in people like a shot at winning a million bucks.

➤ **Do-nothings.** One would hope that when it comes down to raging against the dying of the light, those who tend not to be of any help whatsoever would suck it up and do whatever is necessary to follow the magic words of the Bee Gees to keep *Stayin' Alive*. Do-nothings are probably the most frustrating, but they have the ability to do *something*, so sternly let them know that everyone has to pitch in or everyone suffers (and then add that they'll be the first ones eaten, if it comes to that).

➤ **Giver-uppers.** These types are willing and able to help up to a point, but then they decide that this is it and life is coming to an end. Try to point out all the things that are working and offer encouraging words, but whatever you do, don't let their outlook soil the outlook of the group. If monster movies have taught us anything, a good, hard slap might be necessary (angry mobs traditionally never take the time to listen).

➤ **Crazy ones.** Sadly, trying to survive intense situations for a long period of time will push some people over the edge (think of Christopher Walken in the film *The Deer Hunter*). It's imperative that you don't let people's animal instincts infect the group's will to live or you could have a violent outbreak, à la *Lord of the Flies,* and nobody wants another dead piggy.

The Least You Need to Know

➤ According to Abraham Maslow, humans have a hierarchy of needs and in a survival situation the physiological and safety needs must be met right away.

➤ Ego becomes important if you are trapped for a great length of time and have to create a mini-society.

➤ No matter what the situation, people want to feel as if they are part of a team—ideally a team of self-actualized members, living life to the fullest.

➤ Being a true survivor entails helping others survive, even if you don't like them.

➤ Sadly, trying to survive intense situations for a long period of time will push some people over the edge.

SPLINTERS, SPLINTERS...

Chapter 4

Lifesaving Skills 101

In This Chapter

➤ Medical housekeeping: What to do before you leave on a trip

➤ Performing CPR and the Heimlich maneuver

➤ Common-sense rules for avoiding water hazards

➤ Don't burn, baby, burn

➤ Treating small cuts and lacerations

In a letter to Thomas Mann Rudolph Jr. dated July 6, 1787, Thomas Jefferson wrote: "With your talents and industry, with science, and that steadfast honesty which eternally pursues right, regardless of consequences, you may promise yourself everything—but health, without which there is no happiness. An attention to health then should take place of every other object."

All men may be created equal, but the shells they are delivered in don't hold up to the same standards, and at some point survival is going to come down to whether or not you know how to perform basic life-saving techniques.

So, let's get started.

What You Won't Learn on *ER*

You may have the eye of the tiger, the soul of a warrior, the heart of a champion, and the drive of souped-up monster truck, but sometimes the mind is willing while the

Survival Kit

In a survival situation, keeping your body and clothes clean will help ward off disease and infection. Try to keep soap on hand, but if that isn't possible, ash or sand can wash away the germs. Airing out your dirty laundry (the kind you wear, not pent-up hostility toward your lover) and brushing your choppers with a twig will keep bacteria and parasites at bay.

SOS

Even though Tom Hanks sported a manly mane in *Cast Away*, it's actually beneficial to shave and keep it close on top if feasible. Lice, mites, and fleas love to nestle in human hair and they often come bearing gifts like typhus or plague.

body is weak. The chances of facing a medical emergency increase substantially in survival situations and knowing how to handle them immediately and thoroughly are all that stands between you and the unpleasant task of digging a grave for the burial of a companion.

Before setting out on your journey, do a little medical housekeeping:

➤ **Get your immunizations up-to-date.** Make sure you and your family are up-to-date on all immunizations, and check with your doctor regarding what shots you may need when traveling to out-of-the-way places like the jungle.

➤ **Bring a supply of medications.** Make sure you have an ample supply of your family's medications before a long trip, a dangerous weather system, or any event that will place you far from the closest hospital.

➤ **Attend emergency medical classes.** Although this chapter outlines the basic steps of certain rescue procedures, you should take emergency medical classes taught by professionals so that you can learn the best techniques firsthand. It's also a good idea to practice what you learn with other members of your group before setting off to explore the planet. If you aren't sure where to sign up for classes, try the local clinic, hospital, or the medical center at a college in your area. Another great resource is your local Red Cross office, which offers a variety of first-aid classes and can arrange to bring instructors to an office, school, or community center.

➤ **Look into herbs.** Alternative medicine is very hot these days, but the funny thing is that the alternative is simply a return to our roots ... and herbs and plants. Versing yourself in the healing powers of vegetation could be a godsend in unfamiliar terrain, and earthly products are still used as medicines in many parts of the world, so trust the natives. Studying a book on plant life might open your eyes to the fact that boiling the thick root of the water lily will create a fluid that eases diarrhea and/or sore throats (don't question it, accept the mysterious properties of nature).

Give Me a "C," a "P," an "R" ... What's That Spell?

The human heart is a well-oiled machine, but sometimes the pressure just gets to be too much, especially when a tornado is bearing down on your residence and your homeowners insurance isn't up to date. If you see the following signs, cardiac arrest may have set in on a member of your party:

➤ Distressful pressure, pain, or clutching in the center of the chest for longer than a minute

➤ Discomfort throughout the chest coupled with dizziness, loss of consciousness, sweating, vomiting, or shortness of breath

➤ Uncommon heart palpitations and/or weakness and fatigue throughout the body

➤ Radiating pain spreading from the chest region to the neck, shoulders, arms, and fingers or chest pressure

If a victim isn't breathing and there is no heartbeat, it's time to administer cardiopulmonary resuscitation, known to you and me as CPR. Here's how to do it:

1. Lay the victim down flat on his or her back on a solid, dry surface. Quickly find out if the victim is showing any signs of responsiveness by shaking him or her at the shoulders and loudly asking, "Are you okay?" or "Can you hear me?"

2. If the victim is unresponsive, kneel by his or her side and place one hand on the forehead and your other hand under the chin. Tilt the head back and lift the chin (unless you suspect neck or spinal injury).

3. Get down close to the victim's nose and mouth to listen to see if he or she is breathing and then examine and feel the chest to check for breathing.

4. If the victim isn't breathing, pinch the nose tightly and give two slow (2 to 3 seconds) full breaths into the mouth. You'll know the breath is reaching the lungs if the victim's chest shows movement. If the first breath doesn't go in, reposition the head and give another breath.

Survival Kit

If you have a phone at your disposal, always dial 911 the second your victim is unresponsive and then return to the victim to administer treatment.

37

Tactical Terms

The **carotid** refers to either of two arteries, one on each side of the neck, that carry blood from the aorta to the head.

5. Check for the *carotid* pulse by placing your fingertips on the side of the victim's neck for 5 to 10 seconds. If there is a pulse but the victim still hasn't started breathing, give breaths at the rate of about 12 per minute.

6. If the victim still isn't breathing, start chest compressions. Place the heel of your hand against the center of the chest below the breast line, place your other hand on top of it, and press down with a quick push. Repeat 15 compressions for every two breaths and continually check the pulse. After each set of 15 compressions, give two breaths.

Know the Heimlich Maneuver

Everyone should know how to administer the Heimlich maneuver to prevent someone from choking to death on a piece of food or other object stuck in the windpipe. Use a finger sweep to clear the mouth of any foreign objects, dentures, broken teeth, food, twigs, and so on. Ask the victim if he or she is okay and can speak.

Survival Kit

You can perform the Heimlich maneuver on yourself if you are all alone and start choking. Find the closest, sturdy, waist-high object like a branch, back of a chair, boulder, or sawhorse and thrust your body weight upon said object. The pressure inside your chest is hastily increased and the object will be forced up and out of the air passage.

If the victim is still choking, grab the victim from behind with your fist, thumb side in, placed in the abdomen above the navel with the other hand placed firmly over the fist. Then thrust your fist upward, firmly and quickly, into the top of the stomach in order to force the object up the windpipe. Repeat the process until the air passage is cleared or the person becomes unconscious, then implement CPR. Don't quit!

You may end up in a survival situation with an unconscious infant (under the age of one) and there is no bigger hero then the one who saves a baby. Infants usually choke on foreign objects and you will be able to recognize it if an infant has trouble breathing or crying, makes uncommon high-pitched noises, tries to cough and fails, and/or the face starts to turn blue or purple. Follow these steps:

1. Make absolutely sure the infant is choking before administering first aid because the treatment is rough on the child's developing body.

38

2. Using your thigh or lap for support, lay the infant face down along your forearm with the youngster's chest in your hand and the jaw between your thumb and index finger. Keep the infant's head lower than his or her body throughout.

3. Give five strong, rapid smacks between the infant's shoulder blades with the palm of your other hand.

4. Roll the child over so he or she is facing up on your opposite arm and quickly check to see if the infant has started breathing again.

5. Repeat until the object is dislodged, but stop immediately if the infant loses consciousness. Check an infant's pulse at the brachial artery, which is on the inner arm above the elbow where the arm bends.

SOS

Never begin CPR on an infant until the air passage is cleared, and never try and retrieve the object stuck in the throat with your hands. There is a good chance that you will lodge it further down and it isn't a chance worth taking.

These steps for performing CPR and the Heimlich maneuver are meant strictly as a guide. It really would behoove you to take a CPR course at the local Red Cross or look it up at the webmd.com site, and to learn the Heimlich maneuver from the same professionals. Imagine you and a companion are lost in the Arctic and what would happen if you didn't know how to perform CPR. It's awfully tough to build an igloo and trap seals on your own.

Adventures of a Lifetime

One common outdoor activity, deer hunting, may be as dangerous to Elmer Fudd as it is to Bambi. A Michigan study of hunters with an average age of 55 found that the heart rates of hunters skyrocketed, even doubled in some cases, when they spotted a buck deer, even if they were as still as wax figures. Shooting a deer sent heart rates soaring as well. The combination of adrenaline-infusing thrills, physical exertion over rough terrain, and a high-beer, high-fat, high-tobacco diet can be deadly, which is bad for everyone (except the deer, that is).

Whenever someone stops breathing, time, time, time is not on your side ... *no it isn't.* It is imperative that you get air into the victim's lungs right away because irreversible brain damage can happen in a few minutes. Having prior knowledge of how to handle emergency medical situations will allow you to take charge and show authority, which will calm the others while you try to save the life of a fellow human being.

In many ways, mental toughness is the most important factor in saving others or yourself. The scene is going to be crazy and chaotic, so a cool head that can compartmentalize a list of how to administer first aid and life-saving techniques, could literally be the last stand against the Grim Reaper. Picture doctors in war, or doctors in war on television, like Hawkeye from *M*A*S*H.* And maybe, just maybe, you'll be able to stabilize someone long enough until the victim can be evacuated to a hospital and a smile returns to the face of a healthy human, thanks to you.

During World War II, a nurse wheels a soldier to his bed in the orthopedics ward of an Army hospital (1943).

(Photo courtesy of the Franklin D. Roosevelt Digital Archives.)

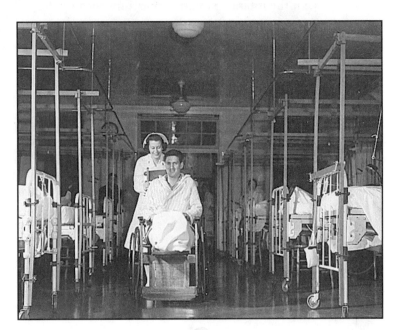

Water Hazards

It doesn't matter if you find yourself basking in the liquid splendor of a cool little spring in the jungle, a mammoth lake in the mountains, a sailboat on the ocean, or a backyard pool, there are basic common-sense rules that will prevent unnecessary water emergencies:

➤ Don't hit the water under the influence of drugs or alcohol, which are hard to come by in most survival situations. Nonetheless, your perceptions will be skewed and it's an easy way to get in trouble like, say, getting swept up in the current of a river.

➤ Don't dive or jump into a water source without checking it first. Go in one foot at a time; looks can be deceiving and you never know how deep it is. The water also may not be of a suitable temperature, so give your body time to adjust.

➤ Don't try to swim your way to survival if you aren't an expert. Swimming is hard and if you aren't properly trained (and dog-paddling from the deep end to the mai-tai station doesn't count), it could be your ultimate downfall.

Survival Kit

If you're on a plane that goes into the ocean and find yourself in the water *wearing* a lifejacket, use the dog paddle because it's easy and takes little energy. If you're *without* a lifejacket in calm waters, keep your head above water by floating on your back with your arms at your sides. In rough waters, or if you have to travel a long way, you should try to use the breaststroke because it's the best combination of speed and power.

If you have to cross a river or stream, which is likely anywhere outside of the desert, swim with the current while keeping your body horizontal to the water. In quick, shallow rapids go on your back, feet first and up, to navigate the rocks. Keep your arms and legs in so that you will become more buoyant and less likely to jam your fingers on a stone. If you have to make your way across sluggish, deep, darker, slower waters, do the opposite: Go headfirst on your stomach and swim in a diagonal pattern toward the opposite shore. In both cases, keep an eye out for currents meeting because they can create strong swirls that can pull you under.

An Amazing Tale of Survival and Watery Death

Here's one of the most tragic, unbelievable survival stories you'll ever hear. In 1841, an American ship the *William Brown* left England for Philadelphia with a load of cargo, 65 passengers, and 17 crewmen. Two hundred and fifty miles off the coast of Newfoundland, the *William Brown* rammed into an iceberg and began a rapid descent into the icy waters of the Atlantic. There were two lifeboats; the captain and most of the crew took the small boat, and some of the passengers climbed aboard the larger boat with first mate Francis Rhodes and seaman Alexander Holmes. (Thirty-one passengers went down with the *William Brown* because there wasn't enough space on the larger lifeboat.) The boats stayed together through the night, but the captain decided there was a better chance of being rescued if they split up. Rhodes told the captain that his boat was overcrowded and that they would have too lighten the load in order not to capsize.

SOS

Don't be afraid to take a dip in your birthday suit and tennis shoes if you're in an emergency situation such as having to cross a river to reach civilization. Clothes tend to get caught, rip, and add drag to the lower half of your body, so get naked except for your feet and jump into the water. Make sure you fasten your clothes to your knapsack if you're carrying one, so that if it gets swept away you only have to retrieve one soggy lump.

The conditions worsened, and the boat was taking on too much water from the rain and the waves. Rhodes decided that their only chance of survival was to throw some passengers overboard. It was reported that Holmes and the other crewmen threw 14 single men into the freezing water and two women who were sisters to one of the men and volunteered to die in solidarity with their kin. The next day, the lifeboat was spotted and the survivors were rescued. The saga of the *William Brown* spread throughout Philadelphia and caused a fair amount of public outrage. The U.S. District Attorney charged Rhodes and Holmes with manslaughter, which is a lesser charge than murder because it is defined as killing without malice. Rhodes disappeared for good, so Holmes stood trial alone.

Holmes's lawyers argued that it was an act of self-preservation and that he didn't have to wait until the absolute last possible moment because then the boat would have sunk and they all would have drowned. The judge instructed the jury that there are exceptions to self-preservation, one of which is when a person accepts the responsibility that implies putting his or her life at risk before taking the lives of others, a duty accepted by seamen.

The jury deliberated for 16 hours before they reluctantly found Holmes guilty, which was accompanied by a plea of mercy. Holmes was sentenced to six months in prison and fined $20. The case established that self-preservation was not always a justifiable defense if the accused was, in effect, the caretaker of the deceased.

What to Do When Someone Is *En Fuego* (on Fire)

Unless you get trapped in a four-alarm melee, burns tend to be minor and you are much more likely to be affected by a bug bite, a sprained ankle, or stomach flu. Still, it's possible that you'll drop a pot of boiling water on your forearm or "accidentally" stick your toes in a hot spring, so it's important to know how to ease the pain of a burn, prevent a burn in the first place, and snuff out a flame:

➤ **Stop, drop, and roll.** You learned the jingle when you were five and it's embedded on your brain for a reason. Follow it!

➤ **Douse 'em with water.** Again, pretty obvious, but water puts out fire. If you have a limited water supply, try using sand, dirt, ashes, or soil.

➤ **Get out of the sun or at least wear sunscreen.** Okay, so you probably won't go up like a string of firecrackers in the blazing sun, but sunburn is much more prevalent and troublesome. If you can't stay out of the sun altogether, wear sunscreen!

➤ **Don't grease up.** Grease, jelly, fat, and other oily substances of this type will impede the healing of a burn and can lead to bigger medical problems. Use ice (or ice packs) or towels dipped in cold water, and apply rags soaked in a solution made by boiling inner-tree bark of hardwood trees to ward off infection.

➤ **Keep burns exposed to the air.** Keeping cold, wet cloths over the burns is fine, but don't bandage them until they are cooled and dried in the air. If they start to blister, don't touch them because a popped blister is much more likely to become infected. Leave them alone!

SOS

Burns are often the product of overzealous fire starters. The chances of injury lessen with the size of the flames. Use restraint: A single candle will warm a small shelter like an igloo, and a bit of gasoline from the tank of your overturned snowmobile will spark a fire.

(Don't) Let It Bleed

Here are the basics for small cuts and lacerations. Be sure that any external bleeding isn't severe, because the loss of a single quart of blood can induce the beginning symptoms of shock. The first step in curbing bleeding is to apply direct pressure to the affected area with a shirt, bandage, towel, or, if necessary, leaves. Elevate any bleeding limbs and use your fingers to apply pressure strong enough to stop the bleeding and to dam up the surface. The old trick of applying pressure and checking the progress, applying pressure and checking the progress is not recommended. It's better to apply direct pressure for 20 to 30 minutes, which should be enough time; otherwise it is much more problematic.

Tie a bandage around the wound, preferably over a thick, sturdy gauze or dressing, and leave it be, even if the bleeding hasn't totally subsided. The bandage should be tighter than a standard, day-to-day compression, but not so tight that circulation is cut off (good rule of thumb is that two fingers should fit under the wrap). If the skin starts to turn blue and/or numbness, tingling, or pain sets in throughout the limb and extremities, the bandage is too tight and should be rewrapped.

The Least You Need to Know

➤ Be aware that no matter how horrific the survival scenario, keeping your body and clothes clean will go a long way to warding off disease and infection.

➤ If a victim isn't breathing and there is no heartbeat, it's time to administer CPR.

➤ Knowing how to administer the Heimlich maneuver can save someone's life.

➤ Don't dive or jump into a water source without checking the depth and temperature first.

➤ Be sure that any external bleeding isn't severe, because the loss of a single quart can induce the beginning symptoms of shock.

Part 2
Wilderness Survival

Even city dwellers are bound to come face to face with a wilderness challenge now and again. Granted, it might be nothing more than finding yourself lost in a winter ice storm, but as simple as that sounds, it can also be the most deadly terrain you've ever encountered.

In this part you'll learn basic steps for survival in almost any climate at any time. Learn what to do when the heat is really on if you find yourself lost in a desert. Face down jungle fever and win. You'll also learn what to do when you are lost in a winter ice storm and how to make yourself safe in your car or on foot. Find out what to do when trapped on a desert island, how to deal with snakebites and hippo attacks, and even where to find food on a mountain.

Chapter 5

I'll Have Desert

In This Chapter

➤ An explanation of desert terrains

➤ Strategies for beating the heat

➤ Recognizing and treating heat cramps, exhaustion, and stroke

➤ What to do if you're caught in a sandstorm

➤ Tracking down water in the desert

➤ It's a mirage ... or is it?

There may come a day when you find yourself in the desert on a horse with no name or staggering around in the brutal frying-pan level heat with only your imaginary friend Ducky, a feisty rainbow-colored minotaur, at your side.

Your car may break down in Arizona or you could get caught in an Iranian sandstorm, but whatever the circumstances, you will have to deal with the overpowering entity known as the sun. The question is, will you be able to make your way back home?

A Course in Desert Terrains

Those of us who grew up watching cartoons know one thing is certain: The desert is no place for the weak. Whether it's the constant mirages of Hollywood swimming pools, the mouthfuls of sand, or the burning red sun that's close enough to touch, the desert can be a cruel place that leaves weary travelers melting in the sand. So how can you avoid the fate of so many of our animated heroes? For starters, you can prepare for the wide range of elements found in the desert.

There are three main types of deserts:

1. **Remote interior basins.** These are typically what you think of when you stop to think about deserts (you do stop to think about deserts, don't you?). The Sahara Desert in North Africa and the Gobi Desert in East Asia are examples of areas that are simply too far from any sources of moisture, so storm systems, in turn, have lost all of their moisture by the time they reach the baking land mass. In other words, they never get any rain.

2. **Rain shadow.** Rain shadow deserts are created when a storm system pushes its way across a continent via strong global air currents. When the moist currents run smack dab into the side of a mountain, they go up the range, cool down, condense and often fall back to Earth as rain. As the air reaches the other side of the mountain it has often lost its moisture and the land on the other side of the mountain is a desert. The rain shadow is prevalent in North America and influences all U.S. deserts. You may not even realize you are in desert territory on the side of a mountain, but don't count on any precipitation.

3. **Coastal.** Just so you realize all deserts don't look alike, coastal deserts are found near the western edge of continents in both hemispheres near the Tropic of Cancer and the Tropic of Capricorn. Oceanic currents with a source in the poles tend to keep oceans in these regions cold, which impedes evaporation and thus the formation of rain clouds. There are also persistent high pressure systems, which block incoming storms. A familiar desert of this type is the Baja in Mexico.

Adventures of a Lifetime

Anyone who has driven through Nevada probably thinks deserts must cover a huge portion of the United States, but that isn't the case. The U.S. has about 500,000 square miles of desert, which isn't a lot compared to the whopping 3.3 million square miles, give or take a few, of the mammoth Sahara Desert.

Deserts are not just made from the sands of the hourglass, these are the terrains of our lives:

➤ **Mountains.** Deserts aren't solely low-lying areas. And mountain deserts, called high deserts, are characterized by a smattering of ranges broken up by dry, flat glens and open spaces. Oftentimes the region is hilly, but it can reach levels thousands of feet above sea level. The air in the high desert can be very thin and there is generally not a lot of vegetation.

➤ **Salt marshes.** Salt marshes are relatively barren areas that have patches of grass but little else in terms of vegetation. Rainfall collects in dry regions, evaporates and leaves deposits of alkali salts or water (as in the Great Salt Lake).

➤ **Wadi.** Wadi is dissected terrain in arid regions that is formed by rain that erodes sand and creates small canyons or depressions. Wadi can become as large as several hundred meters wide and deep and have sharply defined twists and turns.

➤ **Rocky deserts.** These deserts are marked by both solid and jagged rocks on or around the surface of rocky plateaus. The rocks often offer natural reservoirs that fill with rainwater, which could be a godsend if you are facing dehydration.

➤ **Sand dunes.** These are the sprawling areas covered in sand, gravel, and dunes. Sand dunes are ridges of sand piled up by the wind. There have been dunes that are over 1,000 feet high and 10 miles long.

SOS

Salt marsh water is too salty to drink and there is usually a hard, thick crust cover. Don't even consider taking a big swig of the saltwater because it could make you sick as a salty dog.

Tactical Terms

Warm deserts cover about one-fifth of the Earth's surface and temperatures can reach above 55°C. There are also so-called **cold** deserts, which cover about one-sixth of the Earth's surface and are marked by extremely chilly temperatures and can be covered in a sea of never-ending snow and ice.

These five terrains bleed into one another, creating one of the most amazing, and dangerous, wonders of nature, in both *warm* and *cold* deserts.

In this chapter, we'll stick to the warm deserts (winter wonderlands are covered in Chapter 7, "It Was a Cold Winter's Night").

The Heat of the Moment

Heat casualties occur when the human body is pushed beyond its limits. The body has an internal thermometer and cools itself through perspiration that evaporates. It needs a certain amount of water for activity at a given temperature and the warmer the body gets, the more you perspire. Sweating causes the body to lose most of its water, which has to be replaced right away.

The lack of water is what defines a desert. To be called a desert, an area must get less than 10 inches of rain a year, and the annual evaporation rate must exceed 10 inches. This should lead to one simple conclusion: Always have water readily available when spending any length of time whatsoever in the desert.

There are simple ways to battle the heat, even in the hottest of deserts:

➤ Drink lots and lots of water throughout the day. Thirst is not an accurate barometer of what your body's needs, and you won't get enough liquid if you wait until you're thirsty. Set a regular schedule to imbibe H_2O, because constant sipping cools your body temperature and reduces sweating.

➤ Get out of the sun if possible—shade is your friend. If there is no shade, lay a heat buffer like a sleeping bag, blanket, clothes, or even a newspaper between you and the ground.

➤ Conserve your energy by keeping movements to a minimum; do as little as possible in the blazing afternoon sun. Try not to speak, because breathing through the nose takes less energy and keeps dust out of the throat.

➤ Save that sweat—it's human gold. Cover up as best you can to keep sun rays from directly hitting you. Wear light-colored outerwear and keep sweat-soaked clothes on your body to help lower its inner temperature. Wrap that beautiful mug of yours in a scarf, and wear a wide-brimmed hat as well.

➤ If you have a limited amount of water, don't sit down to a four-course French dinner. Digesting requires water, so eat nothing and use whatever liquid you have for internal cooling.

Survival Kit

If you are in extreme heat, whether it's the desert or farm country in August, don't drink anything with alcohol or caffeine in it because they cause dehydration and will only worsen the situation. In the Mojave, it's rarely Miller time.

Not Feeling So Hot: Heat Cramps, Exhaustion, and Stroke

There are three primary types of heat-related complications: cramps, exhaustion, and stroke. Left untreated, one condition can quickly escalate to another. Here's a look at each category and how to treat it if you get caught in the desert and no medical attention is available.

➤ **Heat cramps.** Heat cramps are muscle aches and pains, spasms due primarily to a loss of salt because of heavy sweating. Heat cramps may start out as mild discomfort and are the least troubling of the three conditions, but they are also a red flag that your body is starting to malfunction. The symptoms are cramps in the abdomen, arms, or legs. The cure is simple: Get in the shade, lightly stretch out the affected area, and sip some cool water every few minutes. The important thing to remember here is that if conditions are ignored and you continue to perform physical activity, you are in for much greater danger.

➤ **Heat exhaustion.** This is caused by the loss of a large amount of water and salt. If you are in the desert, it's probably not a good idea to do your daily Tae-Bo routine, because heat exhaustion is the result of heavy physical exertion. Symptoms include excessive sweating; dizziness; flushed, pale, clammy skin; goose bumps; mental confusion; nausea or vomiting; strong headaches; and severe cramps. People suffering from heat exhaustion go into a form of mild shock because blood flow to the skin increases and vital organs get the short shrift. This is dangerous because the person's temperature is rising and the person could face heat stroke. Get the person out of the heat immediately.

Once the person is out of the heat, loosen tight clothes and have the victim lie down, preferably on a stretcher or at least 1½ feet off the ground. Apply wet cloths, towels, or blankets, or sprinkle water on the person, fan the person and, if the person is conscious, make sure he or she drinks water. Ice packs applied at the neck, groin, and armpits are recommended. Keep the person from talking and moving and help him or her get some nice, cool rest.

➤ **Heat stroke.** This is a life-threatening injury in which the person's temperature control has stopped working and the body is no longer cooling itself. In the most severe cases, the body temperature can skyrocket and result in brain damage or death. The symptoms include; the person going in and out of, or losing, consciousness; having hot, burned, skin; not sweating; having a weak, but rapid, pulse; intensely vomiting; and rapid, shallow breathing. If you have a thermometer, try to take the person's temperature because he or she may not be damp, which might make you think the person isn't burning up inside.

SOS

Although it's possible for the application of ice to send a heat exhaustion victim into shock, cooling the person down is still the top priority. The person must be cooled as quickly as possible from fevers that can run up to 107°F. To avoid death or brain damage, use ice as a cooling mechanism, but pay close attention to the victim's response.

Survival Kit

It's not the most pleasant self-inventory in the world, but the color of your urine will tell you whether you're drinking enough water. If it's light and clear you are probably drinking enough water, if it's dark and yellow, start gulping.

The same steps as heat exhaustion will work, but it is imperative that the person is cooled down. Splash or pour water on the body, even if the water is polluted or undrinkable; fan the victim's body to cool it by evaporation. You can also try wrapping the person in wet blankets from head to toe. Massage the victim's arms, legs, and torso, but don't let the person drink anything until he or she stops vomiting and becomes semi-coherent, otherwise the person may choke. Heat stroke is very serious and your actions may be all that stand between life and death.

Cactus in the Mojave Desert.

(Photo courtesy of the National Park Service.)

Do Dunes Spell Doom?

Now that you know the sun can kill you, let's talk about why you might find yourself in the desert in the first place and what you can do to prepare yourself for an experience that can quickly become too hot to handle.

Driving in the Desert

Even if you are driving a short distance through the desert, an overheated engine is always a possibility. Let someone know of your travel plans beforehand, so someone will be aware if you haven't reached your destination in a reasonable amount of time. Before setting out, call the National Park Service, local highway patrol, or county officials to learn about the desert and its hazards. Make sure your car has plenty of gas, and take detailed maps of the area. Bring as many jugs of water as you can, both to cool an overheated car and, more importantly, to drink in case you're stranded for any length of time.

Don't Forget the Sun Block

One vital element to remember is that deserts often have extreme temperature changes over the course of a day. In a high desert, the temperature can range from 120°F during the day and cool down to 40°F at night. Pack warm clothes and blankets in the trunk of your car in case you're stuck there at night. Be sure to bring the following items if you plan on driving and/or hiking through the desert:

➤ **Basics:** waterproof matches, sturdy, broken-in hiking boots, a daily gallon of water per person, food that won't rot or melt in the sun, a rain poncho, and a snakebite kit.

➤ **Sun protectors:** sunscreen, sun block, a long-sleeved shirt or a light jacket, sunglasses, and a face scarf or a wide-brimmed hat.

➤ **Emergency tools:** road flares, a neon ground covering (plastic tarp or lightweight blanket), a knife, a rope, easily repaired auto parts (fan belt, spark plugs, oil, fluids), a front windshield cover, and—I can't emphasize this enough—extra gallons of water kept in the trunk, just in case.

Mr. Sandman You're Not

If your car breaks down in the desert, don't leave it unless you are 100 percent sure of reaching a nearby destination that's no more than a mile away. Drape the tarp on your car to make it as visible as possible during the afternoon hours. Take shelter out of the sun to save moisture. If you must go for help, travel early in the morning and late in the evening, resting in the shade the rest of the day, when the temperature is hottest. Leave a note at the car telling where you went. Don't leave children alone, either, even if you think your adolescents are mature. Deserts tend to appeal to outlaws and drifters and there have been tragic stories of well-meaning parents going for help, only to return to find ... you get the picture.

Survival Kit

Moonlit desert nights are normally calm and crystal clear with excellent visibility. Save your flares for these early nighttime hours because other motorists will see them for miles. On the flip side, if there is no moonlight it is virtually impossible to see anything and moving around is asking for trouble. You could get lost, twist your ankle in a hole, or fall into a ravine. Stay put.

A Stroll Across the Desert

If you are driving through Joshua Tree National Park (which I wholeheartedly recommend) and you think, "Boy, I'd like to get out and walk around, but after reading *The Complete Idiot's Guide to Surviving Anything*, I'm scared to death of the desert." Don't be afraid; a stroll through the desert is one of the truly unsung joys to be had. Just take plenty of bottled water and use good judgment:

➤ Enter the desert heat gradually, walking through the hot sun for brief periods at a time, which will give your body the chance to adapt. If you have a walking pal, monitor your partner's water intake (and vice versa) and let each other know if you want to go off to a scenic view, use nature's facilities, or be on your own for some other reason.

➤ Keep close watch on your walking partner for signs of a heat-related problem. If your partner wants to sit and rest, don't push your pal to go on. Take a load off in the shade, but don't lie directly on the ground because it's hotter down there, and don't let your walking pal take off his or her shirt and fry. By all means, relax and enjoy your desert saunter, but don't overexert yourself physically.

Adventures of a Lifetime

The Joshua Tree National Forest features majestic trees named by Mormon settlers for the biblical figure Joshua, because the trees' raised limbs resemble praying and the lifting of arms to the heavens. If you are a plant lover, Joshua trees grow best at elevations between 2,000 to 6,000 feet and can grow to be over 30 feet tall. Mature Joshua trees produce stunning white flowers, and the beautiful bloom is one of the highlights of desert hiking.

Joshua trees.

(Photo courtesy of the National Park Service.)

Dust in the Wind

Temperatures of desert sand and rock are often 30 degrees higher than the air, but that isn't the only potential hazard. Sandstorms are also a threat, and sand-laden winds are a near-constant in many deserts. The "Seistan" wind in Iran, for example, can blow nonstop for over three months. If you are traveling through a remote interior basin desert, it is essential to follow a few guidelines:

➤ Carry goggles and a thick cloth to cover your eyes, nose, and mouth when the swirling sands hit. Goggles also cut down on eyestrain due to the glare off the sand.

➤ If it's impossible to make your way through a sandstorm, lie down and try to ride it out, but make sure the sand doesn't cover you over.

➤ If you use a radio, cell phone, or walkie-talkie, have a backup signaling device as well, such as flares, because dust and sand can clog transmissions.

➤ Be wary of drinking any water you come across. The water source may be contaminated, and you could get dysentery from drinking it. If you can, boil any water you find before drinking it.

➤ Take sunburn seriously. Cover your body right down to wearing a pair of gloves. Cover any visible parts of skin with a strong sunscreen. Blisters, burns, and sun poisoning can all lead to dehydration and a further loss of water. Don't forget that the risk of sunburn is the same on cloudy days, and the higher the altitude, the stronger the rays. Never rest in the sun, because if you happen to doze off there's a chance you will never wake up after an acute case of heat stroke. Catching some rays in the desert is never a good idea.

Water, Water Everywhere

Let's suppose for a moment that you're stranded in the desert for a long period of time and you run out of food and water. Unfortunately, many deserts have little vegetation and survival is best suited to animals that can go without water for long stretches of time, such as camels. But even if there are no lakes or streams, you can find water in other sources.

Cactus, Anyone?

Many desert cactus can be good sources of nourishment. Try these delicacies at your next desert dinner party:

➤ **Prickly pear cactus.** These cactus are flat and look like an oven mitt with numerous furry circles that have sharp points. They are found throughout the

SOS

According to more than one outdoor expert, cactus as water sources are overrated. If you are not used to ingesting them, they can cause severe vomiting, diarrhea, or allergic reactions. Still, some physical discomfort is better than dying slowly of dehydration.

Survival Kit

Be careful when picking plants, because insects are a great concern in the desert. Scorpions, spiders, ants, bees, lice, mites, and wasps all call the desert home, so never reach into something without first inspecting it. Many insects like to hide in ruins, abandoned buildings, and caves. Also, leave the cologne and perfume at home because they attract insects, and shake out your clothes before wearing them.

Americas. All of the plant is edible, although you want to make sure all the hairs are plucked. Crush them up and they are also a good source of water. The pulp is also a good antidote for open wounds.

> ➤ **Desert gourds.** This member of the melon family grows on a long vine on the ground. The gourds are grapefruit-sized and yellow when ripe. They are found in certain areas of all deserts and will grow no matter how hot it is. The flowers are tasty, but avoid the pulp because it'll make you sick. The stems offer water when chewed.

Other Water Sources

Aside from plants, water can be found other ways. Find the highest vista in the area and take a wide look around, which can not only help you find water, but can help you get your bearings and possibly figure a way back to civilization. You won't be able to rely on rainfall, but if you spy seed-eating birds circling in early morning or late evening in a straight flight path, follow them. You can also search for animal tracks, which will be going both ways on trails, to and from water. The easy way to find the way toward water is to see how the trails converge. If the direction you are walking has side trails converging, you are headed for water. If trails are branching off, you are leaving water.

Here are some other tips for finding water:

> ➤ Look for any vegetation, because the greener the shrubbery, or the more groups of trees, the more likely water is on the scene.

> ➤ In a sand dune belt, water may be found under the original floor along the edge of the dunes. Whenever you find damp sand on the surface, dig deeper and you may find liquid gold, particularly along pronounced twists in a dry streambed. Dig on the concave side of a sharp bend.

➤ Valleys, low-lying areas, at the foot of cliffs, and/or depressions or holes in rocks may yield water. Just make sure to dig a deep well in the ground, so that runoff water can seep down inside, and keep a plastic tube handy to siphon water out of porous rocks.

Is That a Mirage I See?

A mirage is an optical illusion caused by the refraction of light through hot, rising air from a stony, gravely, or sandy ground. It makes it tricky to identify objects off in the distance and it gives the surface a blurred image that looks like you are surrounded by water. Natural points of reference become harder to identify and gauging distances becomes a monumental task.

The best thing to do is realize that mirages do exist and don't trust your senses whole-heartedly. The overheated air doesn't waft above the height of the standard basketball hoop, so try to get at least 10 feet above the desert floor to get hold of reality once again.

The Least You Need to Know

➤ Deserts often have extreme temperature changes over the course of a day, so if you must travel, do so during early morning and late at night, when it's coolest.

➤ Although there are different types of deserts, the lack of water is what defines them and the standard is an area that gets less than 10 inches of rain a year, and whose annual evaporation rate exceeds 10 inches.

➤ To avoid heat illnesses, carry sun block, stay in the shade, and, most importantly, drink plenty of water.

➤ Carry goggles and a thick cloth to cover your eyes, nose, and mouth when the swirling sands hit, and if you can't move, lie face down but don't allow too much sand to pile on top of you.

➤ Water can often be found by following seed-eating birds in a straight flight path to a source.

➤ A mirage is an optical illusion caused by the refraction of light through hot, rising air from stony, gravely, or sandy ground.

Chapter 6

It's a Jungle Out There

In This Chapter

➤ The jungle—you'll know it when you see it

➤ The importance of being prepared

➤ Making your way through the jungle

➤ Dealing with insects: You mite want to pack plenty of insect repellent

➤ Tracking down water and food

It may be a jungle out there, but it's warm and safe in here. Here being the cozy confines of your favorite hammock, hung in the grassy jungle of your backyard where you struggle to find nourishing liquid because the last beer in the cooler is buried deep in a sea of melting ice. Foraging for food is also a life-or-death proposition because that hammock is really comfortable and the cold cuts and potato salad are *all the way inside the kitchen.*

On the other hand, if you are actually planning a trip into the Congo, this chapter is for you.

Welcome to the Jungle

Unlike the dry, sandy desert, the *jungle* is alive and kicking—and biting and raining and slithering and creeping and crawling and swimming and growing …. Everything thrives in the jungle; it's like a giant petri dish with millions of life forms co-existing in relative peace … that is, until you show up.

Tactical Terms

The term **jungle** is not a strict ecological definition, but rather a general description applied to any type of tangled, impenetrable mass of vegetation or growth of thicket.

Survival Kit

If you plan on even flying over jungle see your doctor about getting some shots—vaccinations are a necessity.

Jungles are found in the tropics, the areas between 23½ degrees north and 23½ degrees south of the equator. Jungles come in a variety of forms, and varying tropical areas have varying properties. Tropical regions are often thought of in terms of their dense jungles that can't be penetrated without a powerful machete. Tropical regions, however, are cultivated and the jungles make up only a small portion of the terrain, which can include steep mountains, hills, and farmlands. Let's look at the types of jungles you may encounter:

➤ **Rain forests.** Almost all tropical rain forests are on the equator and have an average rainfall of about 100 inches throughout the year. The climate doesn't change a whole lot; it's hot at night and hotter during the day. Naturally, vegetation flourishes, with five layers ranging from trees that are 150 to 300 feet high to an undergrowth that includes shrubs, seedlings and woody climbers. In between are woody plants, vines, lianas, and bamboo, which are enormous grasses that can shoot up to 75 feet high.

Rain forests are breathtaking, but they also receive little light because the big, leathery leaves of the large trees combine with the smaller trees, vines, ferns, and herbaceous plants to form a wall of vegetation topped by a green canopy. If you get lost in the rain forest, it is going to be very hard for a rescue helicopter to spot you from above.

➤ **Secondary jungles.** These jungles are very similar to rain forests, but they grow along river banks or where man has leveled rain forests that previously called the region home. Tropical growth can easily take over abandoned or fringe areas.

➤ **Savannas.** Savannas are found in the tropical regions of South America and Africa and they look like a meadow. Clumps of tall grass with trees scattered about and red soil in between the clumps. The high-grass savannas surround the rain forests and feature thick grass that can reach 15 feet, whereas the bunchgrass savannas consist of grasses closer to 3 to 5 feet.

➤ **Thorn forests and tropical scrub.** For those of you who vacation south of the border, you will find thorn forests and tropical scrubs along the Western coast of Mexico (and in other places such as Venezuela, Brazil, Angola, and Zimbabwe). These forests have a dry season and the trees are leafless during that time. Grass is rare, most of the plants are thorny, and fire is always a hazard. During the dry season, food is hard to come by in the thorn forests and tropical scrub.

➤ **Swampland.** Saltwater swamps are frequently found near coasts and are created by flooding; freshwater swamps are found inland in low areas. Swamps are popular spots in the jungle—animals and insects flock to them.

SOS

If you find yourself trapped near a swamp (or any other tropical waters), keep your eyes peeled for crocodiles and alligators. They usually float like driftwood with their eyes poking out of the water, and may slowly get out of the water before you spy them. Don't thrash around drawing unnecessary attention to yourself. If you are chased by an alligator or crocodile, run diagonally in an exaggerated zigzag pattern. If it gets close, try to cover its eyes with whatever is handy; if you end up in the jaws of the beast, sock it squarely on the end of the snout.

Now that you know what you will be facing, let's discuss what you should bring to the party.

Jungleland

The main concern in surviving the jungle is the ability to move, because rescue may not be possible. Unlike being lost in the desert or on the tundra, you will be hard to spot amidst the dense vegetation, and if you aren't mobile, you aren't going home. With that in mind, make sure you pack the following:

➤ A sharpened *machete,* which will become your best friend as it hacks through vines and trees, cuts down mangoes from above, lops the noggin off a king cobra, strips trees to build shelter, and slices the wild pig that it killed for dinner. Stroke upward with the machete to reduce noise and, to preserve your strength, chop only where necessary.

Tactical Terms

In case you weren't brought up on slasher flicks, a **machete** is a big, hefty knife that can remove underbrush and also works as a deadly weapon.

➤ Sturdy, waterproof hiking boots are a necessity. Protecting your feet is vital because there are billions of insects waiting to nibble on your toes. Comfortable walking may also be the key to saving yourself.

➤ A sheet of mosquito netting will make your nighttime sleep that much more peaceful. If you go down in a plane crash, try using a parachute as netting or as some kind of tent-like covering.

➤ A hammock that can quickly be strung up between trees makes a good temporary shelter and keeps some of the ground-dwelling mites and ants at bay.

➤ A compass is important not only for figuring out your present location, but also to help maintain a consistent direction in which to travel to get help or find safety.

➤ Don't forget to pack plenty of the strongest insect repellent known to man, and grab some garlic pills to keep the bugs (and vampires) from sucking your blood. The smell of garlic supposedly discourages some insects.

Adventures of a Lifetime

Military trackers in the jungle often rely on their sense of smell to hunt down the enemy. If the winds are favorable to smokers, the earthy aroma of Camel unfiltereds can be picked up from a quarter mile away. The scent of cooking food can drift many yards beyond your campsite. Cologne or scented soap kept British ambushes from having any effect against guerrillas in Malaya. If the smell isn't indigenous, be aware that it is likely to draw insects or predators.

Navigating the Jungle

Making your way through the jungle can be quite a challenge, and you will need to pay attention to your surroundings at all times. In the following sections I'll tell you what to consider when moving through the jungle.

Getting Underway

The easiest route to safety is also the safest route and this is the one for you. This starts with the proper attire. No matter how hot it is, cover your arms and legs to avoid scratches and bug bites. It might be uncomfortable in the heat, but it beats infections or illness.

Before starting off, use your machete to chop off a big branch and whittle it into a solid walking staff. Besides easing your journey, a good walking stick can be shoved into spots you can't see to check for snakes. It can also be used to spread vegetation open and thereby lessen the impact on the insects living on the vine you want to dislodge.

As you're walking through the jungle, learn to look past the green kaleidoscope of foliage in front of your face and focus on open, lighted areas. Its important to train yourself to have a vision that extends beyond the dense jungle; otherwise, you may end up going around in circles. Take your time while making your way through the jungle and look for any sorts of landmarks, from massive trees to unusual ferns. The more you look and learn, even in a brief span of time, the more likely you are to figure out where the jungle ends and civilization begins.

> **Survival Kit**
>
> Move smoothly through the jungle by doing the "jungle boogie." Wiggle, duck, slide, twist your body, turn sideways, bend, squeeze, and change your strides to avoid cuts and abrasions from the undergrowth.

Following the Road Most Traveled

Find paths that have been used before by man or beast. Tracking the trail of an animal makes sense because it may lead right to your dinner. The trail may lead to a stream or river, giving you a clear marker to follow that will deliver a larger body of water that you can navigate by raft. It can be tough to get through the foliage, but you will be on a course toward a definite destination. There is also water readily available and animals will frequently flock there for a drink, which, coupled with the edible plants, offers a veritable jungle buffet. Human tracks are very reliable and often lead to man-made or natural wells or runoffs, as well as villages or settlements where you might get help.

In jungles of developed nations, phone and/or electrical lines might be the roadmap you seek. Look up, and look down at the ground to find established trails. Keep checking your bearings using your handy compass to make sure you're headed in the right direction, which is whatever direction common sense tells you to head. Normally, this would be in the direction of the natural flow of the stream or trail, but

SOS

Be wary of trails that have man-made accouterments like standard ropes, loops of braided vines, wires, nets, and poles, because there is a good chance they are camouflaged animal traps. Be careful not to touch any of these, lest you end up getting bonked on the head by a rock or swinging upside-down from a tree.

don't be afraid of your instinct either. Panic and fear are your worst enemies in the jungle, so take a deep breath and survey the situation. Your confidence will grow as you make your way through the jungle, and calm, cool, collected explorers are much more likely to get home safely.

Setting Up Camp

If you have to set up camp, do so while there is still plenty of daylight, because darkness falls quickly in tropical areas. Clear away a good portion of the underbrush and build a fire. Make sure the fire is constructed in a clearing or along a stream, so any rescue teams will be able to locate you in the night while you sleep. Don't get too close to water if it's the heavy rain season, because flash floods are common. Inland, avoid camping near water sources because there will be a parade of animal visitors throughout the night. If it doesn't look safe, find somewhere else to camp for the evening.

Sand by Your Man: Dealing with Quicksand

A friend of mine recently noted that the "quicksand epidemic" seems to have passed. On TV, everyone from *Charlie's Angels* to the *Six Million Dollar Man* used to fall in quicksand.

Survival Kit

If you have to move across quicksand, lie flat facedown, spread your arms like you're making a snow angel and slowly slide your way to safety. Make sure the walking staff or branch is in front of you in case you start to sink.

Television may have grown weary of quicksand as a plot device, but the jungle hasn't. Quicksand is a bed of soft sand soaked with water that is usually deep, but gives under weight and leaves a vacuum behind. Quicksand is a danger on flat shores near rivers heavy in sediment, or near the mouths of bigger rivers. To check if a sandy region features quicksand, throw in a stone or piece of driftwood and see if it sinks. If you get caught in quicksand and start to get sucked under, take your trusty walking stick or a tree branch and lay it flat across the trouble spot. Flatten your body across the stick as best you can until you stop sinking and tighten up your muscles to become more buoyant.

Moving Through Mangroves

In saltwater swamps lie the mangrove trees, which can reach heights of over 10 meters and have masses of sprawling, dense roots. If you come upon a swamp filled with mangrove trees on the inland side, wait for low tide and carefully go forward through the narrow clusters of trees toward the mass of water.

Jungle Fever: Protecting Yourself Against Insects

Snakes, man-eating lions, and cannibals might be the most glamorous fears of the jungle, but insects should be your greatest fear in the moist tropical atmosphere. Mosquitoes may carry malaria, which is marked by chills, vomiting, and fever, severe in the worst cases. Mosquitoes may also carry dengue (also called "breakbone fever"), which is marked by rashes, soreness, joint pain, and headaches. Flies spread a wide range of infectious diseases, including dysentery. They also can cause acute cases of diarrhea, which will sap all of your energy and strength. Ant bites can lead to incredible discomfort, red mites in the Far East carry a form of typhus fever, and fleas are still known to set up shop in rats and carry the Old Middle Ages favorite, the bubonic plague. If you don't believe that insects are a threat, take a second to think of the uncomfortable scene in *The African Queen* when Bogie fights off those weird-looking, bat-like bugs.

Protect yourself against insects by constantly reapplying insect repellent and always covering yourself in as many clothes as possible. Tuck your gloves into your sleeves, your pants into your boots, button up your collar, and if possible, sport a mosquito net over your face. You can cut a swatch of netting and glue it to the front of your hat to protect your face. If you can't cover your skin with repellent or clothing, try nature's makeup—mud.

At the end of every night, it's important to thoroughly check your body for any bug bites, particularly ticks. If a tick is burrowing into your skin, suffocate it with tree sap, Carmex (or any lubricant), or thick clay. Using tweezers or your fingers, remove the entire tick, being careful to lift the tick where its mouth has grasped onto the skin. Avoid squeezing the tick's body.

Surviving the jungle is tough enough without the mild irritants or serious diseases brought to you, compliments of jungle insects. Do whatever you can to keep from getting nibbled upon.

SOS

Never walk anywhere in the jungle barefoot. Is exposing yourself to the potential danger and illness brought by insects worth running the sand through your toes, no matter how good it feels?

Finding Water and Food in the Jungle

Finding water in the jungle isn't as easy as locating the monkeys passing out bottles of Poland Spring, but it isn't the ultimate survival test either. Water is readily available, but not all of it is safe to drink. Dig a hole in the sand about 10 feet off the bank of a river, lake, or stream, wait for water to fill up, and there you have it. Water procured in this fashion must be boiled, especially if it comes from a muddy, still source.

Following animals that graze for their meals can work, but don't trust the carnivores because they often get all their necessary liquid through the prey they devour. Insects can also be reliable, and don't be afraid to trust the bees and ants (trust them, just don't come in contact with them). Bees don't travel far from home and there is normally a water source within range; and an army of ants marching down a tree may be heading to their private stash of H_2O.

Survival Kit

If you get lost in the northeast section of South America, be careful when entering, fishing, or drinking from the indigenous rivers. They are infested with piranhas that attack in schools and will make mincemeat of your flesh in a matter of minutes.

There are also tropical vines that can provide water. Look for the ones with rough bark. Cut a hunk of vine above your head and let the liquid drip into a container or directly into your mouth. Many vines will irritate the skin, but the clear fluid is safe. *Do not drink* of a vine that is acrid, sticky, milky, or sappy, because it may be poisonous. Plants with pulpy hearts have water within as well, which can be accessed by smashing the pulpy innards. Bamboo stalks also have water in their interiors. Just slice a hole in the bottom and drain it.

If you can dig up a plant's roots from the ground, there is water for the taking. Slice up the roots in bits and pieces and suck them dry. If you are trapped in a rain forest for any length of time, it's possible to use a plant's condensation by tying a plastic bag around the branches of a leafy green or putting pieces of vegetation in said bag. Condensation will leave enough water in the bag to survive on, but its probably not going to be enough to wash down a freshly cooked anteater.

Once you've found water, it's time to take care of your food needs. Vegetation reigns, so there is always plenty to eat, but it might be hard to obtain in the rain forest. Nuts, berries, and fruit are probably too high up to grab, and climbing trees can sap your energy and/or lead to a potentially fatal fall. If you are a Tarzan at heart, by all means, start scaling trees for bananas, wild grapes, bael fruit, almonds, or cashews (edible when roasted).

By the way, before leaving for your trip, it pays to pick up a tropical field guide and familiarize yourself with the pictures of edible plants. While the jungle is ripe with all sorts of plants you can safely devour, it is also ripe with poisonous plants. Make sure you know the difference—it could save your life.

Adventures of a Lifetime

You probably never even considered another danger of the jungles of Vietnam—Bigfoot. According to a Vietnamese professor, a "wildman" with a footprint 28 by 16 centimeters is roaming the "three borders" (the meeting point of Laos, Cambodia and Vietnam) region of Asia. There have been numerous reports of the wildman, and reports vary on his size and color of body hair, but there is consistency in the description of a man/ape type of creature. Is it a new species of mammal? A descendent of early man? Bigfoot? A myth? Maybe you'll be the lucky one who discovers the truth.

Use your machete to take out one of the ground-dwelling or tree-living animals and prepare a fire for your feast. Hedgehogs, porcupines, mice, monkeys, anteaters, deer, and (if you are some kind of super hunter) lions all have meat that can be thrown onto the fire, and will give you the protein that's essential for keeping up your strength.

The Least You Need to Know

➤ The term jungle is not a strict ecological definition, but rather a general description that is usually applied to any type of tangled, impenetrable mass of vegetation or growth of thicket.

➤ A sharpened machete will become your best friend in the jungle; stroke upward to reduce noise and, to preserve your strength, chop only where necessary.

➤ As you're walking through the jungle, learn to look past the green kaleidoscope of foliage in front of your face and focus on the open, lighted areas.

➤ Protect yourself against insects by constantly reapplying insect repellent and always covering yourself in as many clothes as possible.

➤ Water and food are readily available in the jungle if you know where to look.

Chapter 7

IT'S NOT THAT BAD.

It Was a Cold Winter's Night

In This Chapter

➤ The chilly truth about wind chill and other storm components

➤ Your best protection against the cold: layer, layer, layer

➤ Building a snow shelter: snow domes, tree pits, and igloos

➤ Awwwwaaaaalllllllanche!

➤ Finding frozen food

Sleigh bells may be ringing, and there may be some snow in the lane that is in fact, glistening. It is quite possible there's a beautiful sight; you certainly have the right to be happy tonight and by all means enjoy walking through your winter wonderland.

Just be ready for whiteout conditions, a wind chill of –30°, no visibility, frostbite creeping through your extremities, and hypothermia attempting to take over your body as you go *mano a mano* with Jack Frost while wandering across the tundra searching for a morsel of food. Now how wonderful is that winter wonderland again?

Anatomy of a Winter Storm

The most dire of winter storms come in all shapes and sizes and are usually accompanied by brutally cold temperatures. Cold weather is a hellcat, because if it reaches a certain point, there is little that can be done to find relief. Unlike the blazing hot sun, from which you can find relief in the shade, it's hard to find adequate shelter in subzero temperatures. It is also harder to find bread and water and if you aren't dressed properly … ladies and gentlemen, presenting the human Popsicle. Before you reach that icy state, let's look at the basics of a winter storm:

➤ **Cold air.** Anyone who has spent a winter in Alaska, the Yukon, or even Chicago knows what it's like when the air is so cold you can hardly draw a breath. Once the thermometer drops below 15° F, human flesh can freeze within a few minutes—and that's on a person who is properly dressed and without factoring in the wind chill. Shivering will let you know when your body is starting to get cold. It's an internal mechanism that produces heat. Cold air basically begins to be considered dangerous when it drops below the freezing point, and in arctic regions this is most of the year.

➤ **Wind chill.** Wind chill is Old Man Winter's way of slapping you across the face for not respecting his impressive displays. As wind increases, heat leaves the human body at an accelerated rate, decreasing the body temperature. Theoretically, the wind chill factor is the effect of freezing winds and temperature on exposed skin. The higher the wind speed, the lower the wind chill temperature. For instance, at 15° F, a wind of 24 to 28 knots has wind chill factor of –25° F, at which point flesh can freeze within a minute. At –40° F, a wind of 24 to 48 knots has a *wind chill factor* of –100° F, at which point human flesh can freeze within 30 seconds.

Tactical Terms

Many members of the scientific community feel the **wind chill factor** is a rough estimate at best. The standard index doesn't account for heat loss in the shade as opposed to in the sun, and it's based on tests that measure the temperature at which water freezes, which is different for human flesh. Weather people report outrageous wind chill numbers that are overestimated, but that doesn't change the fact that it doesn't take long to freeze in an arctic winter.

➤ **Snow.** Snow is precipitation in the form of solid white ice crystals by the sublimation of water vapor at temperatures below 32° F. Snow acts as an insulator against the ground, but it also cools the overlaying atmosphere. Temperature changes in cold environments can happen rapidly, so a snowstorm can break out suddenly and can make traveling nearly impossible. The glare of ultraviolet rays shining on snow—snow blindness—is also a concern. Snow blindness causes headaches, dizziness, and irritated, painful, watering eyes. Continued exposure to snow blindness can cause severe permanent damage.

Survival Kit

Sunglasses are the easiest solution to snow blindness, but you can also fashion eye protection by cutting slits in a piece of cardboard, bark, plastic, or other material. Natural eye black like mud or soot will do in a pinch—just smear some under your eyes to cut down on glare and you'll look like a major league star.

➤ **Ice.** Sleet forms when raindrops freeze into little ice balls and pelt the ground. Sleet bounces off most surfaces, but if it piles up it can make driving impossible. Freezing rain falls below 32° F and can freeze on objects, particularly roads, in a glassy sheet. Ice storms occur when rain freezes as soon as it touches down on cars, power lines, highways, and so on, making it virtually impossible to travel by foot or in a car.

➤ **Blizzards.** Some warm-weather denizens might assume blizzards are strictly treats at the Dairy Queen, but they are actually intense winter storms. Blizzards feature strong winds of 35 mph or more, chilly temperatures of 20° F or lower, and driving snow. They occur most often in the northern Great Plains states like the Dakotas, but have wreaked havoc from coast to coast. The worst storm in American history was the Blizzard of 1888, which hit the East Coast between March 11 and March 14, dumping up to 5 feet of snow in some areas, killing 400 people, and leaving in its wake $20 million in damage.

Cold-Weather Coping Strategies

Winter health dangers are a reality. Dressing for the elements is the first rule of battling the winter elements, and it starts at the top:

➤ Cover your head, face, and neck because you can lose over half your body heat if these areas aren't protected from the cold.

➤ Dress in loose layers instead of one big bulky coat or sweater. Tight clothes cut off blood circulation and cut down on the warm, insulating air between each layer. Layering also makes it easier to take clothes off and put them back on to handle the changes in temperature.

➤ Mittens are more effective than gloves because fingers stay warmer when they rub up against one another.

➤ Don't get too warm because overheating leads to sweating, which cools the body while dampening clothes and weakening their powers of insulation.

➤ Stay dry at all costs. Inner layers are going to become wet from sweat to some degree, so it is imperative you wear water-repellent outerwear because soaked clothes keep heat away from the body. If your clothes do become wet, change them and dry the wet items by the fire, in the sunlight, or as a last resort, put them under your sleeping bag before morning to keep them from freezing.

➤ Remember the old outdoor adage—cotton kills. Instead of your favorite T-shirt, wear polypropylene, wool, or fleece. These materials will keep you warm even if they get damp.

➤ Dirt, mud, and grease diminish the insulating properties of clothes. Clean clothes also lower the chances of developing a rash or infection that will be hard to treat and very uncomfortable.

SOS

Don't leave your mouth uncovered in subzero temperatures because you will be breathing in extremely cold air. Take short breaths through your nose and keep talking to a minimum.

If you are the victim of a winter weather injury, you better know how to treat it right away because there aren't too many hospitals across the frozen tundra.

Hypothermia

Hypothermia takes hold when the temperature of the human body drops to between 95° F and 77° F. If the victim isn't attended to immediately, allowing the body temperature to drop below 77° will almost inevitably result in death. Hypothermia is a common killer of people who get lost in the mountains, so be aware of the symptoms: drowsiness, uncontrollable shivering, lack of coordination, slow or slurred speech, memory lapses, sluggishness, exhaustion, and confusion.

To treat hypothermia, remove wet clothing, move the victim to a horizontal position, and make sure he or she is wearing a hat—even wrap a sleeping bag around the victim's head—to prevent further heat loss. Slowly warm the person's torso first. Start by transferring your own body heat with a bear hug; then, if possible, place the victim's torso in warm water, around 100° F. Don't place the victim's entire body in a hot bath because cardiac arrest and/or shock can result. Warm the person's extremities last because stimulating the limbs first can send cold blood racing to the victim's heart. If there is no bath available, try giving the victim warm water enemas or get naked together in a sleeping bag. Your body heat will transfer quickly to the victim. If you can, put bottles of warm water at the bottom of the sleeping bag and at the victim's neck and groin. Work slowly and make sure the victim isn't subjected to warming or cooling overload. Handle the person gently in severe cases to avoid shock. Rewarming and/or removing the victim from the hot bath into the bitter cold can result in fatal circulatory problems.

And speaking of cardiac arrest, many fatal heart attacks occur when average Joes who aren't regulars at the gym decide to go out into the winter weather and shovel acres of snow. Treat shoveling snow like a workout—stretch, do warm-up exercises, and don't overexert yourself. Better to shovel a third of the walks in the morning, a third in the afternoon and a third at night. Better yet, get your teenage son or some kid from the neighborhood to do it.

Survival Kit

If the hypothermia victim is conscious, give him or her a hot-sweet beverage like warm water with honey. Never give alcohol or caffeine to anyone with hypothermia or frostbite, because alcohol can slow the heart and gum up the blood flow, and caffeine can speed up the heart and overwork the ticker.

Frostbite

Frostbite occurs when tissues start to freeze, a reaction to extended exposure to bitter cold. A loss of feeling in your toes, face, fingers, nose, or ear lobes, or a dull, white skin tone are signs of frostbite. Surface frostbite isn't hard to treat, but deep frostbite can cause excruciating pain and permanent damage. The best preventative medicine against frostbite is to monitor your walking pal to see if his or her complexion changes color. If you are alone, try to cover your face every couple of minutes and keep trying to wiggle your fingers and toes.

If you are lightly frostbitten, rewarm the affected areas in the same manner as you would for hypothermia. If you are deeply frostbitten, don't totally thaw out the affected area unless you are safe and sound in a heated home or plan on seeking the company of trained medical professionals very soon. Weigh the costs of rewarming to prevent serious injury against the possibility of thawing during the evacuation process, because a deep frostbite injury that is thawed and then refrozen can lead to severe damage. Make sure your children understand the symptoms of hypothermia and frostbite and tell them to come inside at the first signs of trouble.

Dehydration

The layers you are wearing in the cold might keep you from realizing how much body moisture you're losing. The body needs water in the cold just as much as it does in the heat. You may also be afflicted with cold diuresis, which is an increased release of urine (that is, you'll urinate more frequently) due to exposure to freezing weather. Cold diuresis depletes bodily fluids, which must be replaced as soon as possible. On that note, if you are winter camping, drink a lot of water during the day, but hold off before going to bed because every time you get up to use nature's restroom, you lose the valuable heat you've built up inside the cozy sleeping bag.

Water in the arctic regions is generally cleaner than it is in other parts of the world, but it's always best to purify water by boiling it before drinking. However, running water from streams, springs, or rivers is probably safe and refreshing. Melted ice is better than melted snow because ice contains more water than snow—just be sure you melt the ice or snow before putting it in your mouth. Place the ice or snow in a bag and melt it by hanging it near a fire or under your sleeping bag.

Survival Kit

One bonus to being trapped in the cold is that you can feel free to abandon your diet. The body uses the first 2,000 calories—your normal daily ration—just to keep itself warm, and you need many more calories if you're exerting yourself. Skimping on food is a good way to get hypothermia, so indulge in that extra Snickers bar.

SOS

Don't start a fire or burn a kerosene lamp or stove in the snow dome. There isn't going to be enough ventilation to ensure that the carbon monoxide fumes escape, and you don't want to asphyxiate yourself in your new home, right?

Trench Foot

Keeping your feet dry is essential because you may develop trench foot, which makes it tough on travelers. If your feet get wet at freezing temperatures and you proceed to march on them all day long, the nerves and muscles will suffer and in extreme cases, amputation is the only answer. Do yourself a favor, wear dry socks, change them every day, and make sure your boots aren't too tight.

A Home in the Snow

Igloos have provided adequate shelter for Eskimos for many centuries, but igloos are tough and time-consuming for the novice to build. Snow domes and tree pits are easier and quicker to construct, and offer some protection against the cold and wind. Keep in mind that building an effective snow shelter works only if the temperature is below 25° F; otherwise, the snow is prone to melting.

Snow Dome

A snow dome can be constructed in just a few hours. Start by making a pile of snow roughly 6-feet high with a diameter twice that size. Poke $1^1/_2$-foot sticks into the dome from various spots along the upper part of the perimeter of the snow pile, angling them toward the middle of the dome. Let the snow dome sit for a few hours, then shovel out a 2-foot tall entrance and hollow out the inside of your new abode. It is imperative that you carry a small shovel, axe, or saw of some kind when roaming through snowy regions. Once you've shoveled out enough snow to see the bottom of your sticks, it's time to move in. Poke a couple of holes in the roof for ventilation and you'll be snug all night long.

Tree Pit

If nightfall is rapidly bearing down on a weary winter camper, a tree pit is quick and easy to construct and will provide ample protection from the wind. First, locate an evergreen tree with large, full branches that will provide cover. Second, dig out the snow that surrounds the trunk until it is low enough for you to rest comfortably or, obviously, if you hit the ground. You should be comfortable, but the pit shouldn't be so wide that the opening can't be covered with branches. Pack the snow in tight in your inner circle and around the edge of the top. Cut off long, fresh, evergreen boughs and lay them flat over your tree pit residence so that you look up at the greens.

Igloo

If you're going to reside in Alaska over the course of an entire winter, an igloo is just the ticket. It's cheaper than a condo and you don't have to hassle with the landlord in your apartment complex. It might take a few attempts to get it right, but if you have the time, it'll be worth it. Start by checking the snow. It should offer solid resistance up to three feet and should be a large enough area of thick snow from which to take the igloo "bricks." The snow should be tightly compacted, which makes it easy to carve out large chunks.

Take your snow saw and cut 40 to 50 bricks at about 6 inches by 36 inches each. If you don't have a snow saw, you can use any basic sharp-edged tool, or a large stick whittled to a sharp point. The first few bricks probably won't come out cleanly, because you have to get into the trench to cut them out uniformly. Try to keep the digging area square, so that each brick is the right shape and size. It is going to take a little while for you to get the hang of it, so you may want to build a tree pit (see the previous discussion) for the nights while your igloo home is under construction.

Once the bricks are ready to go, draw a circle 12 feet in diameter about 8 feet up from where you dug out the blocks. Pat down the snow around the circle, start placing snow bricks around the circle, and then anchor them by patting down snow around the base. Once the circle is complete, remove a couple of the bricks for an entrance. Start hauling bricks into the shell and construct the igloo from the inside, making sure to lean the bricks inward so they are solidly in place. Replace the entrance and cut two 5-foot slopes in the first tier of blocks. Lock each brick and slant them along the slope, so that the higher up you go the bricks almost lay flat. Ideally, each brick will fit snugly along the corner of the one below it, but don't be afraid to shape each one to fit. Use snow to fill in any gaps in the igloo's frame.

Once the last brick is in place above your head, take your saw and start digging out the igloo. You should also dig a trench that runs from the base of the igloo to the area where you dug out the snow bricks in the first place. The trench should be about 3 to 4 feet long and it can be covered with extra bricks or branches. Once inside, cover the entrance with a brick or a plastic tarp. If the igloo's well built, the temperature inside will be tolerable at around 30° F, and the colder air will sink into the trench. You can store equipment in the tunnel and lay your sleeping bag safely inside the igloo. In the area surrounding the igloo, you can build a little kitchen with tables and your gas stove, a fire pit, and chairs to relax and enjoy an arctic winter's two hours of daylight.

Adventures of a Lifetime

Here are a few American temperature records to send a chill through your bones:

➤ *Lowest temperature:* Endicott Mountains of Northern Alaska, Jan. 23, 1971, −79° F.

➤ *Lowest temperature in the lower 48:* Rogers Pass, Montana, Jan. 20, 1954, −69° F.

➤ *Greatest temperature drop in 24 hours:* Browning, Montana, Jan. 23–24, 1916, 100-degree drop from 44° F to −56° F.

➤ *Greatest temperature drop in 27 minutes:* Spearfish, South Dakota, Jan. 22, 1943, 58° drop from 54° F to −4° F.

Look Out Below!

Avalanches are rapidly descending masses of snow and ice adhering to the laws of gravity. They are natural forms of erosion, but can be killers to people caught in their paths. They are triggered by people, earthquakes, sun, wind, or rainfall on slopes of a high grade. Avalanches swallow everything in their path, and they are hard to escape.

If you are trapped in an avalanche, try to swim your way out of the moving snow. Pretend it's a giant, white, sliding swimming pool and use freestyle technique or the crawl to keep on top of the avalanche. If you get buried, it will be tough to get out because the snow is wet and packed—you're in the belly of a giant snowman. Hopefully someone saw you, but if not try to poke a hole in the snow with your ski pole, walking stick, or foot.

The best way to combat an avalanche is to avoid it altogether. Here are some rules to follow to keep from becoming a casualty:

➤ Avoid fresh snow or snow warming in the sun, which is much more likely to cause an avalanche than settled drifts or snow that has frozen overnight.

➤ Test the snow with an ax or ski pole. If it's tough and tight all the way through, the risk of avalanche lessens. Look for distinct changes in the layers—hard crust atop wet spongy snow—and stay away from areas where you find it.

➤ Don't go hiking, skiing, snowmobiling, or camping by yourself in areas that are prone to avalanches.

➤ Carry an avalanche beeper to alert others to your location electronically. Another potentially lifesaving device is a long, neon avalanche cord that will float to the top of the pile if you're trapped.

Survival Kit

If you've been buried by an avalanche and are lucky enough to have room to maneuver, dig a small hole for a breathing space and spit into it. Watch which way your saliva slides. If it flows downhill, you'll know you're facing up, and that's the direction that you'll will want to dig to get yourself out.

➤ Avoid the sides of mountains away from the wind, and mountains with slopes around 45 degree, where avalanches tend to occur.

➤ If you must ski down a mountain in avalanche country, ski down one person at a time so everyone else can serve as a lookout. If you have a rope, link up with your buddies if the chance of a snow slide looks good, and cross slopes as high up as possible.

➤ Look for signs warning of avalanches; rangers post them daily.

➤ Snowmobiles frequently trigger avalanches, so don't take them high up into mountainous territory.

➤ If you can't find a companion after an avalanche, start by looking at the trees that were in the wake. Anything still standing might have stopped your companion's downhill progression.

➤ If you see someone get caught up in an avalanche, try to pinpoint where he or she went down and listen for sounds from below the surface.

Mt. Rainier in the state of Washington received 789 inches of snow in the winter of 1916–17.

(Photo courtesy of the National Oceanic and Atmospheric Administration [NOAA].)

Food Sources

Finding food in the arctic outback isn't impossible, even though you may not get your recommended dose of daily greens. The tundra is treeless, but there are berries galore and a few other plants. A great book to pick up before any sojourn into the great white open is *A Naturalist's Guide to the Arctic* by E.C. Pielou (University of Chicago Press). Also consult a plant guide to familiarize yourself with the following cold-weather delicacies:

➤ Cranberry

➤ Crowberry

➤ Woolly lousewort

➤ Spadderdock

➤ Dandelion

➤ Bearberry

➤ Fireweed

➤ Arctic willow

Caribou, musk oxen, porcupines, foxes, moose, mountain sheep and goats, rabbits, seals, walruses, an ocean of fish, and the occasional yeti are usually found wandering the tundra. If you have a high-powered rifle or a strong animal trap, you're in business. Make sure to skin and cook the game while it is still warm and cut the meat into pieces, which can be frozen for later use. Take the meat back to your shelter and store the extra pieces in nature's freezer (that is, your unending snow-filled backyard). Leave the fat on the frozen, uncooked meat and it should keep throughout the winter.

Seal meat is a feast fit for a king, and seals are not hard to catch and kill. Never go after polar bears, though, because they are the most dangerous of all bears and extraordinary hunters. If you do kill a seal, keep your eyes open for any polar bears, because they will want to take your kill away from you.

The Least You Need to Know

➤ The wind chill factor is the effect of freezing winds and temperature on exposed skin; the higher the wind speed, the lower the wind chill temperature.

➤ For maximum protection against the cold, dress in loose layers instead of one big bulky coat or sweater, and avoid cotton.

➤ Hypothermia takes hold when the temperature of the human body drops to between 95° F and 77° F.

➤ Handmade shelters such as snow domes, tree pits, and igloos provide protection against the elements.

➤ If you are trapped in an avalanche, try to swim your way out of the moving snow using the freestyle technique or the crawl to keep on top of the avalanche.

➤ Food sources are available; look for berries, small mammals, and fish and remember that meat will keep throughout the winter in nature's freezer.

Chapter 8

Yo Ho, Ho, It's the Island Life for Me

In This Chapter

➤ Tsunami: the dreaded harbor wave

➤ Come on baby, light my fire

➤ Learning how to drink water all over again

➤ The marvelous, versatile, life-saving coconut, and other food sources

➤ Some island wisdom from two experts

If pop culture has taught us anything, it is how to survive on a deserted (or sparsely populated) island. One need only follow the examples presented to the masses on TV shows like *Survivor* or *Gilligan's Island* and movies like *Swiss Family Robinson* or *Cast Away* to experience a smooth, successful lifestyle on a tropical island in the middle of nowhere.

You never know when a three-hour tour is going to turn into much longer, or a slow boat to China is going to capsize, leaving you and your mates desperately searching for the first available land mass, which may be a deserted island. Most conversations about life on a deserted island revolve around questions like, "What 10 albums would you bring if you were stranded?" Be advised that after making an emergency water landing or abandoning a sinking sailboat and swimming for your life until you drift upon a lonely beach, your favorite Beatles album isn't going to do you a lick of good. Keep reading for advice on how to survive the solitary life on a tropical isle.

A Boy Named Tsunami

One of the first natural calamities you should be aware of is the *tsunami,* often referred to as a tidal wave. Tsunamis hit the Pacific coastlines (and occasionally an Atlantic coastline like the infamous 1929 tsunami that pounded Newfoundland).

The majority of tsunamis are generated from the Ring of Fire, a 24,000-mile-long zone of volcanoes and seismic activity and are caused by underwater earthquakes. But they can also come about from landslides, volcanoes, or the impact of a meteor. A set of concentric waves, similar to those caused by throwing a rock in a lake, is created when the ocean floor is disturbed, and the waves speed off in all directions.

Tactical Terms

Tsunami is a Japanese term that translates to "harbor wave" in English. Many people refer to tsunamis as tidal waves.

A tsunami can have wavelengths of 60 to 120 miles and the time interval between wave crests can range from 5 to 90 minutes. The wave speed averages about 450 mph as it travels hundreds of miles across the ocean floor. When tsunamis reach the low-level coastal areas, the waves, which may have been only a few feet tall out on the ocean, decrease in speed and increase in height. Tsunamis have tremendous power when they strike coastal regions, with waves that can reach as high as 100 feet. The mix of intense energy and large amounts of water can wipe out coastal settlements.

A tsunami crashes down on Hilo, Hawaii, in April 1946.

(Photo courtesy of National Oceanic and Atmospheric Administration [NOAA].)

Like all other natural disasters, the physical, financial, and psychological impact of a tsunami can be mitigated with advance planning:

➤ **Learn the properties of a tsunami.** If you're on an island and the ground starts trembling, an earthquake is coming and there's a good chance a tsunami will follow. A rapid change in the rise and fall of water along the coast is another red alert.

➤ **Go up!** If you have a radio and hear a tsunami warning, or if you see a giant wave coming your way, head to the highest ground possible. Run from low-lying areas and climb to the summit of the island, be it a large rock or a tree, as far away from the shore as you can get. Depending on the size of your island, remember that if you can see a tsunami, you're probably too close.

➤ **Remember that waves come in waves.** Much like the ritual at college football games, the waves will keep coming long after you tire of them. A tsunami is actually a series of waves, and even if you can safely enjoy the magnificence of a 50-foot crescendo from on high, don't run down to the beach assuming it's finished … it's not. In fact, the initial waves are often not the most powerful.

➤ **Don't take them lightly.** Tsunamis have been known to lift rocks, boats, or dune buggies weighing tons from the beach to a few hundred feet inland. Tsunamis can hit any time day or night, so don't figure there's a safety zone, either.

➤ **Cut your losses.** The odds are good that whatever grassy hut or bamboo shack you constructed for your home sweet beach home will be destroyed, so accept it and move on up. Water from a tsunami is usually polluted and may be toxic, so don't eat any fish or other sea creatures you find strewn on shore. It would be a shame if you survived a massive tsunami only to get acute stomach flu.

Adventures of a Lifetime

The Hawaiian Islands have been hit by roughly 40 tsunamis since the early nineteenth century. One of the most powerful tsunamis hit Hilo, Hawaii, in 1946. Eight waves, some reaching 30-foot crests, crashed down, flooding the downtown area and killing over 150 people.

SOS

If you're stranded on a tropical island with rivers and streams that flow into the ocean, stay away from them. Tsunamis can travel up the waterways and crash deep in the heart of your home in paradise.

Let's Get the Fire Started Right

Obviously, if you are stranded on an island, you will be surrounded by water, but that doesn't mean you can safely drink it. Over 75 percent of your body is water and you will lose plenty of it sweating in the hot sun of your island home. So how can you purify saltwater for human consumption? For starters, light a fire and boil the water,

Adventures of a Lifetime

The Japanese may have coined the word tsunami, but it's safe to say they probably never again want to feel the wrath of a tsunami like the one that hit in 1897. An underwater earthquake about 93 miles offshore resulted in a tsunami that killed 27,000 people on the Sanriku coast of Northern Honshu Island.

Survival Kit

If you happen to have an aerosol can of insect repellent, try spraying your tinder and kindling *before you light the fire.* The insect repellent will make it more flammable and keep away insects as a bonus. Just stand back when you toss the match.

but be aware from the outset that it's never a good idea to drink saltwater. Unless you have quite a still built to catch evaporated water you'll just end up with a pile of salt.

The first item you need to get a roaring fire going is tinder, dry material that will ignite with a simple spark. Look around the island for feathers, the rotted portion of logs or trees, wood shavings, or bark. Take a handful of the tinder you gathered and arrange it in the shape of a nest with a small piece of kindling (combustible material such as a piece of bark, dried leaf, or twig) inside the nest, and you're ready to start your fire.

Once you've got a small fire going, add more kindling to raise the temperature of the fire and get it hot enough to burn living trees, animal fats, moss, bones, coal, or just about anything else. Island kindling can also include pencil-thin pieces of wood or small logs.

If you happen to have a candle, light the wick and use it to light your fire; the wick will burn longer than a match so you won't be wasting extra matches trying to get the fire going. But what if you have no matches or lighters? You can still build a fire. Try these surefire techniques for building a fire using materials that you may have on hand:

➤ **Lens.** If it's a bright, sunny day (likely) and you have plenty of time on your hands (very likely), use the convex lens from your binoculars, telescope, camera, eyeglasses, or a magnifying glass, which might be a part of your compass. Angle the lens so that the rays of the sun are focused on the tinder and hold the lens above the same spot until it starts to smolder. Once the smoldering starts, lightly blow on the tinder until a flame is sparked.

➤ **Metal.** If you have a pocketknife or any other metal object, you can generate sparks and ignite the tinder. Find a solid stone or a piece of flint (hard quartz) and hold it above the tinder. Strike down on the flint with the piece of steel so that the sparks hit the middle of the pile of tinder. Or you can take one piece of metal and scrape another piece (or the blade of your knife) against it in a whittling motion; ideally, sparks will find their way into the tinder and kindling.

➤ **Wood, method 1.** This is the way they always do it in the movies, but it should be your absolute last resort because it's time-consuming, frustrating, and hard to accomplish. First you need to make a bow. Find a piece of wood a couple of feet long and an inch in diameter and string a cord of some kind (possibly a shoelace) for the bowstring. Take another piece of wood, $1/2$ foot in length and $1/2$ inch in diameter, and attach to it a handle made of strong wood or stone. This is the screwdriver. Take a piece of flat, softer wood and place it on the ground. Make a dent in the soft wood and place the screwdriver in the dent. Then press the screwdriver into the soft wood to anchor it. Surround the screwdriver with a tinder nest, and wrap the bowstring so that it loops around the middle of the screwdriver and pull it tight. Hold the handle of the screwdriver on top with one hand and rapidly spin the bow with your other hand, applying pressure through the handle. Done correctly, the friction between the soft wood and the screwdriver will ignite the tinder.

➤ **Wood, method 2.** If you have no other choice, rubbing two sticks against each other is a possibility. Cut notches into a piece of wood (use bamboo if possible) and fill them with tinder. Secure the wood to the ground with your foot or a heavy rock, or brace it with a Y-shaped stick. Take a stronger piece of wood and vigorously stroke it along the piece of wood on the ground until, theoretically, friction will spark up the tinder. This system works a whole lot better in cartoons and in the innocent psyches of eager Cub Scouts, but you might get lucky.

Survival Kit

To keep your fire burning throughout the night, set large, dry logs on top of the fire. The interior of the logs should burn slower through the middle. If that doesn't work, try placing a bed of rocks in your fire early in the morning and covering them with dry earth before you go to sleep. They should still be smoldering when you wake and tinder can be sparked up for that day's fire.

The Old Watering Hole

Once you have a system for boiling water, head down to the beach for a day in the sun, searching for H_2O. Water can be collected from the ground, so start digging a deep hole and wait for the rain to fill it up. Water will fill up the hole, which can then be scooped up in your metal pail, helmet, pot, conch, or any other container that can be hung over the fire to boil.

If you don't get rain, heat rocks in your fire and drop them in the hole. Cover the hole with a cloth or the leaf of palm tree, which should absorb some of the steam that will arise from the damp ground. Wring out the cloth or lick the leaf clean to get enough water to survive another day while waiting for that ship to save you.

Other sources of water include ...

➤ **Dew.** Island natives have been known to tie rags or thick absorbing fibers around their ankles and wander to and fro through the dew-soaked grasses before sunrise in order to collect moisture for the day.

➤ **Insects.** Follow the ants, bees, centipedes, or wasps into their holes in the trees and bring along a dipping cloth or a drinking straw. And, don't forget, swallowing a few insects is extra protein (although for obvious reasons it's best to avoid ingesting live bees and wasps).

➤ **Banana trees.** Plantain or banana trees are a liquid gold mine. Simply chop off the tree, leaving a foot-high stump, which should be hollowed out, because the roots are going to fill the empty stump with water. At first, the water may be bitter, but it will get better and can last for a few days. Just make sure to find a suitable stump covering.

Survival Kit

Milk from unripe (green) coconuts is good, but milk from ripe coconuts acts as a natural laxative, which could be bad because you will probably be using leaves as toilet paper.

➤ **Other plants.** Many plants, including bamboo, contain liquid. Bamboo should be hacked off at the base of a joint to hit pay dirt. Young, green bamboo thickets are filled with clear fresh water. It can be obtained overnight by cutting off the top of the thicket and tying it so that the new hole drips down into your trusty water container. Roots are also a good source of water. Liquid can be sucked out after they are dug up and cut into little pieces.

➤ **Birds.** A group of birds or piles of bird droppings around a crack in a rock, crevice, or hole in a tree is a good indication of a water source.

Surf and Turf: Island Fare

Rule number one: Learn how to procure coconuts, because they can be found on just about any island. Start by taking your knife, a sharp shell, or the claw of a coconut crab and cut footholds in the coconut tree about 3 feet apart, forming a makeshift ladder. Put the soles of your bare feet flat on opposite sides of the trunk and grip the tree with one hand on the back and one hand in front of your chest.

Notches make it easier to move upward, but if you have no tools, apply pressure to both sides of the tree while driving your body by extending your legs and then bringing your feet back into position (think of the way a frog hops). Done correctly, your feet will support your body weight, allowing for rest intervals. Try to make it all the way to the top of the tree by pulling yourself up from the second or third level of palm leaves. You can stand on the levels of palm leaves near the top of the tree and twist the coconuts until their stems break and they fall. If the palm leaves aren't too thick, it's much easier to knock down a whole mess of coconuts by bracing yourself than supporting your weight. Be careful on the way down, don't let gravity do all the work unless you want broken limbs or scrapes and abrasions. Keep a tight grip on the tree while moving your feet down the sides of the trunk.

Other edible plants and fruits include mangoes, cashews, sea grapes, bananas, plantains, sugar palm, water fern, and sea purslane, which is a juicy, green plant that grows close to the ground and will cover rocks and sand; it tastes good raw or cooked and is loaded with essential minerals.

Survival Kit

Coconuts are a staple of island living and are actually quite versatile. Smoldering coconut husks keep mosquitoes at bay, and the juice of unripe, green coconuts battles liver, kidney, and heart disorders as well as gonorrhea (which may not be a problem where you are).

The coconut crab has claws that are strong enough to open coconuts, and are edible by humans (Palmyra Island, Line Islands, Kiribati).

(Photo courtesy of Dr. James P. McVey/National Oceanic and Atmospheric Administration [NOAA] Sea Grant Program.)

You probably won't encounter too many cows on your deserted isle, so if you don't care for seafood, you're out of luck. Shrimp, lobster, crabs, and mollusks can be scooped up by hand or with a simple net fashioned from coconut palms or cloth from a T-shirt. Although they can be eaten raw, it's best to boil or steam the shellfish, especially if they are not covered by water at high tide.

Fish will also be floating by in schools a bit farther out in the ocean and they can be speared for a filling feast. Take a straight stick, sapling, or (preferably) a length of bamboo, and either shave it down to a sharp point or fasten a blade, whittled bone, or jagged piece of metal to it. Wade out to a rock or a fish run and patiently wait for the fish. Use as movement as possible, and if it's night, carry a torch. Gently place the spear in the water until fish become accustomed to it and you can get as close to your aquatic friends as possible. After driving the spear into the fish, hold it along the bottom until you can reach down and lift your dinner out of the water.

The Down-and-Dirty Advice of Two Island Experts

You may be thinking, "Doesn't this author live in New York City? How could he know about being on a deserted island? I bet he's in the library right now!" Well cynical reader, I've brought in a couple of ringers. My brother Brian Sauer and his friend Callen Taylor spent two years teaching in Micronesia. Granted, it's not deserted, but they also visited islands that were inhabited by no more than a few natives. Either way, they picked up plenty of island-living tidbits along the way, which they are more than happy to share:

➤ **Lobster.** Does a beautiful full moon rising over the peaceful ocean horizon mean romance is in the air? Nope, that's the time to hunt for crustaceans. The brightness of the full moon tempts the lobsters out of their hiding places and makes it easier to find and catch the succulent spiny creatures. (Melted butter on the side isn't quite as easy to procure.)

➤ **Octopus.** Just because you are hundreds of miles from a fine restaurant—or any restaurant for that matter—doesn't mean you can't enjoy a little delicacy. When searching for octopus, look for clusters of rocks. These eight-legged creatures spend most of their time hiding out under these rocks. Using a sharpened stick, poke it under the rock until the octopus leaves its hiding place. Once the octopus has been caught, it will wrap its arms around the closest object, you. To kill the beast, bite it as hard as you can between the eyes.

➤ **Sea cucumbers.** These long black creatures can be found all over the sandy floor of the shallow ocean. Sea cucumbers are easy to catch and can be cooked or eaten raw.

➤ **Dental floss.** After an oceanic feast, nothing is worse than spending hours picking bones out of your teeth. Using a palm frond taken off a coconut tree, tear off the spine or the hard part that runs down the middle of the leaf. Peeling away the layers will provide a tough, stringy dental floss.

➤ **Exfoliation.** After a long hot day of searching for food, you'll need a good bath. Jump into the clear blue ocean, grab a handful of white sand, and start scrubbing. The sand will scour away the dirt on your body.

➤ **Body lotion/hair conditioner.** Just because you're stuck on an island doesn't mean you can't have shiny lustrous hair and baby-soft skin. Look for an old coconut with a dark brown color. Using a rock, hit the coconut to crack it into two halves. Scrap out the hard coconut meat. Once you clean out the coconut meat you can put it in your palm and use your thumb to squeeze out the milk to use for conditioner and body lotion, which will prevent sunburn and ease itching.

SOS

The reef poses many obvious dangers, but you also need to watch out for the hidden ones. Fire coral looks like most coral—like tiny cacti lining the bottom of the ocean floor. Although most coral will cut up your feet, fire coral adds a little insult to injury. A cut from this coral creates a strong burning sensation.

➤ **Natural plastic wrap.** Ran out of aluminum foil? Walk through the jungle and cut a large green banana leaf right from the tree. Hold it over the steam of boiling water for about five seconds. Repeat on the other side. Voila! The steam from the water will toughen the leaf, providing you with a wrapping for your food to keep away pesky flies.

➤ **A tropical bed.** After a full day of climbing coconut trees and hunting lobster, you'll want to rest under the gentle sway of the coconut trees. Cut down a group of coconut fronds and lay them down in the sand away from any trees to avoid taking a nut on the noggin. Pile them on top of each other for a comfortable sleep under the stars.

➤ **A day at the races.** One thing you won't run out of on a deserted island is time, and lots of it. Would you sell your soul for an hour of ESPN? Not so fast! Hermit crabs can provide hours of entertainment. They can usually be found along the beach or underneath bushes. Break them up into teams, create leagues, keep stats, wager lobster tails. A 10-foot-long hermit crab race will provide hours of entertainment … literally.

The Least You Need to Know

➤ Tsunamis are sea waves primarily generated by underwater earthquakes, but they can also come about from landslides, volcano eruptions, or the impact of a meteor.

➤ The first item you need for starting a roaring fire is tinder, dry material that will ignite with a simple spark.

➤ There are lots of places to find water—bamboo and banana trees, the morning dew, the milk from unripe coconuts, and even insects.

➤ After coconuts, seafood is the primary option for sustenance, so fashion a pole out of a stick, make a sharp point on it, and patiently learn the art of spearfishing.

➤ The brightness of the full moon tempts the lobsters out of their hiding places and makes it easier to find and catch those succulent spiny creatures.

Chapter 9

Climb Every Mountain

In This Chapter

➤ What to do if you're attacked by a bear

➤ How to avoid being bitten by a snake—and what to do if you are

➤ Squirrel stew, anyone?

➤ Something's fishy: catching fish without a rod and reel

➤ Navigating by the stars

The mountain man, the rugged frontiersman fighting the elements to build a new life in the wilderness, has always been held in high esteem in American mythology. The story that isn't so often told is that of the frontier traveler who enters the pristine wilderness and is never heard from again. It starts with the main character getting lost, and ends with the traveler slowly dying to the echo of his own voice in a rocky valley, or an endless search for a way out of a maze of evergreen forests.

It isn't a pretty story, so keep reading to learn how you can survive in the wilderness, like a modern day mountain man or woman—a king of the wild frontier.

There's a Bar! Whar? Over Thar!

Let's begin our look at wilderness survival with the question that flies out of the mouths of big-city dwellers when given the chance to do a little harmless camping:

"What should I do if I get attacked by a bear?"

First and foremost: *The chances are very slim that a bear will attack you.* Beyond that important point, there are steps you can take to lessen the chance of you and a bear going mammalo-a-mammalo. The stories of bears running amok and gnawing on human jerky are greatly exaggerated. With the exception of polar bears, bears are generally not carnivorous. It isn't natural for bears to bother humans; however, a bear will attack if provoked or to protect her nearby cubs. Often their aggression is a learned behavior driven mainly by the easy access to food that humans too frequently offer. If you take proper care of your edibles and follow some basic common-sense steps, you should never have to cancel your trip for fear of bears.

If you are entering a national park, stop at the ranger station and ask if there have been any recent bear sightings. A little forewarning goes a long way, and if a sow and her cubs have been hanging out in your prospective camping space, go elsewhere.

A grizzly bear sow and her cubs roam Yellowstone National Park.

(Photo courtesy of the National Park Service.)

Here are the "bear" necessities to keep in mind:

➤ Hike in a group and make a lot of noise with whistles, bells, singing, yelling, busting a rhyme, and so on, especially in thick forests with limited visibility. Some people recommend carrying pepper spray.

➤ Leave the dog at home or in the RV. A dog will often antagonize a bear into a fight, and the dog—or you—will lose.

➤ Never move closer to bears for a photo "op" because they can run as fast as horses and cover a lot of distance in a hurry.

➤ A mother bear defending her cubs is the most dangerous, because her natural instinct is to attack when her babies are threatened. *Stay away from the cubs!*

➤ Never make eye contact with a bear. To a bear, this is like saying, "You want a piece of me?" He just might take it.

➤ If you happen upon a bear, especially a sow and cubs, back away quietly and try to stay upwind, because bears generally avoid humans when they smell them ahead of time.

➤ Don't climb a tree to escape unless it is an absolute last resort because black bears will come up after you and grizzlies will violently knock and shake the tree.

➤ In most situations, making like a statue and staying put is the most effective tool against bear attacks. Don't provoke the animal by doing something stupid like flinging a rock at its head—bears are easily angered.

➤ If you are attacked by a bear, lie as still and silent as you can, because attacks often cease if humans don't fight back. If you play dead, hopefully the bear will get bored with you and wander away. However, if the attack continues, use whatever means available to strike back. Aim for eyes and snout; it's a bear's weak spot (but that term is used very loosely).

If you plan on camping in areas with bears, find out if the sites provide bearproof wires to hang your food. These cables are strung about 20 feet above the ground, but you'll need to carry your own rope or cord to tie up your food, so figure on bringing 40 to 50 feet. Also bring two nylon, cloth, burlap, or (in a pinch) plastic garbage bag "stuffsacks" so you can divide your food in half to balance the load. Tie a rock to one end of the rope and a stuffsack with half of your food to the other end. Throw the rock over the wire and pull the attached stuffsack up in the air. Then tie the other stuffsack to the end with the rock and push that sack up until both sacks are balanced at least 15 feet off the ground. Make sure that all food is packed up, including that half-eaten Clark bar in little Howie's pocket and even canned food, because bears can sniff out *anything*.

Survival Kit

You should also place your smelly or scented items inside a stuffsack. Whatever has a scent can attract, so if you are in bear country, hang up colognes, soaps, sprays, diapers, the clothes you cooked in ... even toothpaste.

If there are no bearproof wires provided, try to find a nearby cliff ledge and hang your stuffsacks over it. A 15-foot tall ledge says *no* to bears with a capital *N* because bears cannot climb rock faces. You can also hoist the stuffsacks up a single tall tree branch, but it isn't always easy to retrieve the bags if they get caught in the thickets. The other thing to keep in mind is that throughout many parts of America it won't do any good, because black bears can climb trees.

Grizzly bears, on the other hand, can't—which is handy to remember if your summer backpacking trip includes the backcountry of Glacier or Yellowstone national parks. Although Alaska and parts of Canada are still home to many grizzlies, there are only an estimated 1,000 left below the Great White North in Yellowstone and Glacier (and even that paltry number came about only through the federal Endangered Species List). Grizzlies in the national parks have become more domesticated and accustomed to feeding on human garbage, so it is imperative to string up the stuffsacks.

Snake Eyes

Once the bear question has been resolved, the next question is invariably, "Well, what about rattlesnakes?" A fair and relevant query, to be sure, but don't let our slithery friends keep you from enjoying the fruits of any woodsy Garden of Eden.

Many poisonous snakes live in forests, but the odds that you will come across one outside of the local reptile house isn't all that high. Still, any time you're venturing into potential snake country, it would be smart to bring along a snakebite kit. There are primarily two groups of snakes that are dangerous to man: *proteroglypha* and *solenoglypha*.

Tactical Terms

Proteroglypha have permanent "fixed" fangs in front of their teeth, while the **solenoglypha** have erectile "folded" fangs that are lifted into position. The proteroglypha feature venom that works its way into the nervous system, making it impossible for the victim to breathe. The venom of solenoglypha attacks the circulatory system and leads to internal hemorrhaging. The really bad news is that most snakes have both venoms but only one is dominant, so choose your poison.

Unfortunately, there are no overriding characteristics for the untrained eye to instantly differentiate between a poisonous snake and a cuddly snake. The best defense against a snake is a good offense, by taking advance measures and using common sense to avoid snakes. Start by talking to wildlife officials or other people in the area who are familiar with the terrain. Other snake-avoidance tips include ...

➤ When entering snake country, wear sturdy boots, thick socks, and long pants.

➤ *Keep your eyes open*—most snakebites happen by accident when a hiker steps on a napping serpent. Keep your wits about you and use your walking stick to poke around in bushy, woodsy areas before entering them. Snakes are cold-blooded and like to warm their scales by taking five on a rock in the sun; watch for the reptilian sunbathers.

➤ Like adolescents, snakes are sensitive and don't like to be teased. Leave them be! Don't prod, touch, wake, or rouse a serpent that's minding its own business.

➤ Snakes coil before the attack and can cover a few feet in the blink of an eye. If you come upon a viper, slowly back away and give it plenty of respect. If you're trapped near a coiled snake that looks ready to strike, and you fear there is no way out, carefully grab your hat and whip it as far as you can, away from both your body and the snake. Ideally, the snake will strike the hat while you hightail it out of there.

Snakes can be hard to tell apart, so carrying a reptile guide with color pictures is a good idea. It will put your mind at ease if you are able to identify the attacker as a harmless garter snake. Also, knowing the kind of snake it is will help local medical personnel identify the seriousness of the situation. Some poisonous snakes that make their home in the mountain wilderness include the American copperhead, bushmaster, cottonmouth, eastern diamondback rattlesnake, jumping pit viper, tropical rattlesnake, western diamondback rattlesnake, and the tri-colored coral snake.

Snakebitten

If you or someone else is bitten by a snake, try to remain calm: It's rarely a death sentence. In fact, only a quarter of snakebite victims will have serious internal problems, but it's still a frightening experience. Keeping your cool is more than a platitude, though, because hysteria and panic ratchets up the circulation, so the toxins spread more quickly through your body. The first thing to do is to check the bite to see if it was from a poisonous snake. You'll be able to tell this if the bite has fang marks, starts to swell, goes numb, or if the person starts to feel weak or even paralyzed after a couple of hours.

If you're carrying an antivenom with you, use it only if the victim is 100 percent sure he or she isn't allergic to it (everyone should check with their doctors prior to a romp in the wilderness). Otherwise, start by washing the bite with soap and water. This is important even if the bite is from a nonpoisonous snake because allergic reactions and/or infection can result, both of which will hinder a return to civilization and proper medical attention. Follow that up by ...

1. Laying the victim down flat and keeping him or her as still as possible, because movement increases blood flow. Keeping the bitten area lower than the heart will decelerate the spread of venom.

2. Tying a 2- to 3-inch wide bandage (loose enough to place a couple of fingers underneath) above the bite to slow the venom, but don't make it tight, which could cut off the blood flow and destroy an extremity or limb. The old remedy

SOS

Do not suck out venom with your mouth. The vessels under your tongue will instantly begin taking the poison to your heart.

of applying a tourniquet and making a deep cut across the bite is no longer recommended because it can lead to severe infection, massive bleeding, and gangrene.

3. If you have a mechanical suction device (as part of a first-aid or snakebite kit), covering the bite mark with the suction cup and removing the venom, or simply squeezing the affected area, but try to avoid making an incision.

4. Giving the victim small amounts of water and continuing to clean the bite. Don't apply ice or anything cold to it because it will entrench the venom.

Soup's On

All that rugged mountain climbing can really make you hungry, but what if your grub was swiped by a smarter-than-the-average bear? Fear not: Trapping, killing, and cooking dinner is no problem in the mountains.

Snake Steaks

With all this talk of poisonous snakes, it's time for a little payback, because all snakes, even the poisonous ones, are edible. It can be a dangerous proposition, so go after venomous snakes only if you're desperate for food. Early morning is the best time to hunt for a reptilian breakfast. The easiest way to kill a snake is to hit it on the head with a rock, club, or log. You can also pin a snake down by its head with a V-shaped stick and then pick it up with your index finger on the back of its head and clench behind its jaws with your thumb and middle finger. Don't let your finger slide off the snake's head or it could turn around and chomp down on your hand.

Survival Kit

Make sure the snake is dead when you proceed to cut off its head. Even separated from its body, a snake's natural reflex will occasionally cause it to bite down and send venom coursing through your veins.

Capturing a snake can be beneficial in more ways than one. Once the snake's head is removed, slit open the belly and remove the guts. The innards can always be used to bait a trap for a larger animal, but otherwise properly disposed of or bury them. Peel the skin back like a reptilian banana and cook the meat over a fire. The skin can be dried and used for a tie, belt, handle, or overpriced pair of Fifth Avenue shoes.

Squirrel Kabobs

Squirrels are cute and cuddly when they are fed popcorn on Boston Common, but you'll get over that after a couple of hungry days in the mountain wilderness. Squirrels aren't that hard to catch. First find a tree populated by squirrels, and then make a trap out of a large stick and some wire, fishing line, or possibly wild reeds. Wrap the wire around the stick, with four to five sets of three or four nooses small enough for a squirrel's body spaced a couple of feet apart. The nooses should hang off the sides and the bottom of the stick when it's leaned up against the trunk of a tree where it extends into branches.

In a short time, a squirrel should get caught in the snare wire noose and your supper will be acquired via a hanging. If this doesn't work, you can also throw a net over the nearest squirrel and club it on the head, but they are fast critters.

As you should do with all animals upon their capture, cut the throat of the squirrel to bleed it. Take it to the closest stream or river to clean and cool it. Cut the fur along the top and stretch it back to either end to expose the meat. Remove as many of the innards as possible and be aware that it's much harder to cut out the meat from a squirrel than it is from a bigger animal. Remove the skin by running a knife between the hide and the flesh. You can easily roast the squirrel over a fire by sticking a sharpened stick through its mouth. It isn't a huge meal, but if you're just trying to stay alive and don't know how to bring down a deer, it will suffice.

You can use the same noose system to capture other forest dwellers like the marmot, groundhog, mole, or porcupine. Just watch where they make their home and adjust the noose to fit in the entrance to their lair. Fashion a noose out of the snare wire and fasten it to stakes on the opposite side of the hole where the animal comes and goes. If this is too complicated, most small animals—including beavers or muskrats—can be flushed out of their homes with a forked stick, a belt, or a rope that is dropped in and out; or if there's nothing else available, by a human foot circling their terrain.

Survival Kit

Animals up in the mountains aren't used to human behavior, and simple calls can sometimes bring them out of their habitats. Loud whistling may bring marmots, squirrels, and/or woodchucks out into the open. A low hissing or whistle can make a rabbit stop to investigate, and a loud duck call may bring a flock of gourmet fowl to your dinner table.

A River Runs Through It

In Norman Maclean's family, there may have been no clear line between religion and fly-fishing, but you need to make the distinction and pray that someone finds you while fishing to survive. Without a modern rod and reel, fishing is much harder than trapping small animals; but if you're hiding out in the mountains for any length of time, you may want to try a change of pace.

For our catch, we're going to use a large net, which will take some time to build, but can pay huge dividends. Use whatever you have available to make the body of the net: a towel, sleeping bag, sheet, or tent, for example. You can also use your extra clothes if the weather's warm enough to go without them; just tie the clothes together so there's a large target area in which you can catch the fish.

If you have a length of rope or wire that will stretch across a stream, tie it between two strong branches that are hammered into the ground on each side of the stream and attach your net to the center of the rope. The net should sit at a 45-degree angle so that the current flows into it. If you have two people, get on either side of the stream and walk towards one another to grab the fish when they bump up against the net. If you're by yourself, it will take a lot more time but you should be able to catch at least a few fish.

Starlight, Star Bright, Help Me to Get Home Tonight

On a clear night in the mountains, so many stars will be visible it will feel like you can grab the Milky Way and put it in your stuffsack for later. Use the stars to your advantage: Your future could literally be written in that giant Lite-Brite in the sky. The North Star will lead you directly northward. Since most of you who get lost in the woods will be everyday hikers and backpackers and not falling from the sky like D.B. Cooper, you will probably have some idea of the lay of the land. If you know from which direction you entered the forest, you can use the North Star as a guide to civilization and the closest Holiday Inn.

The North Star isn't the brightest star in the sky, but if you locate the constellation Ursa Major, known to you and me as the Big Dipper, you'll be in business.

To find the North Star, follow a straight line upward from the two stars at the right end of the bowl of the Big Dipper. The line points directly to the North Star at roughly five times the distance between the two stars themselves. The North Star is also known as Polaris, because it is the star nearest the north celestial pole (known to you and me as Santa's home, the North Pole). For those of you who are constellation buffs, Polaris can be also found in the extreme end of the handle of the Little Dipper.

Adventures of a Lifetime

The Big Dipper is the common name of a part of a prominent constellation in the northern celestial hemisphere, near the North Pole. Fittingly for this chapter, it was known to the Romans as Ursa Major (the Great Bear). A section of the constellation features seven bright stars that construct the identifiable outline of a "dipper," which could also be described as a long-handled cup. In the Hindu tradition, the constellation marks the seven rishis (holy ancient sages).

In the Southern hemisphere, the constellation Southern Cross can help you figure out which way is south. Tilted to one side, you should be able to find four bright stars in the general shape of a cross. Two of the stars will have a larger space between them, just like on the stem of a regular cross. (If you think about a cross that's nailed into the ground, it's akin to the vertical wooden plank.) Using these two stars, draw an invisible straight line five times its own length from the star at the base of the Southern Cross. Follow the invisible line until it reaches the middle of the sky and look straight down upon a landmark on the horizon. You are now facing southward and can start your long journey back home.

Both of these tricks work anywhere, except for deep in the heart of a smog-choked city; but in that case you can simply ask a convenience store clerk for directions. Of course, you can always follow the sunset to the west or the sunrise to the east, but I wanted to give you a veritable buffet of direction markers.

Indigo Lake at Sawtooth Mountain in Willamette (Oregon) National Forest.

(Photo by Chris Jensen, courtesy of the United States Forest Service.)

The Least You Need to Know

➤ If you are entering a national park, stop at the ranger station closest to your destination and ask if there have been any recent bear sightings. A little fore-warning goes a long way.

➤ Most snakebites happen by accident when a hiker steps on a napping serpent. There are very few fatal attacks every year.

➤ Animals up in the mountains aren't used to human behavior, and simple calls may bring them out of their habitats.

➤ You can catch fish by stretching a makeshift barricade across a stream and scooping up the fish in your homemade net.

➤ To find the North Star, follow a straight line upward from the two stars at the right end of the bowl of the Big Dipper. The line points directly to the North Star.

Chapter 10

AHH... HOME SWEET HOME.

Whales, Tigers, and Scorpions ... Oh, My!

In This Chapter

➤ Why fast food is dangerous for animals

➤ Why you should never leapfrog a whale

➤ How to handle a shark attack

➤ Outfoxing the river horse

➤ Masking your identity from a tiger

➤ Treating a scorpion bite

The stories that have been passed down since the days of the grunting oracle have always portrayed animals as creatures to be feared. Be it the serpent in the Garden of Eden serving up forbidden snacks to the naked innocents, or the Great White off the coast of a peaceful New England beach munching on unsuspecting swimmers, "beasts" have always been cast in dark shadows. Man has been trained in its collective conscience to fear the animals that can kill, which has often become a mandate to destroy.

Do the animals deserve this fate? Certainly not; like the rest of us, they just want to be left alone. Still, man and animal are going to come in contact with one another. Whether you have an encounter with a coyote or a killer whale, the rules of escape generally remain the same.

I Want to Walk with the Animals

Rule number one when dealing with the animal kingdom—don't assume all creatures act like they do in the movies. Take sharks, for example. If one were to take biology lessons from the *Jaws* movies, it would be safe to assume that all sharks are man-eating predators that need to be eliminated. The reality is that there are roughly 350 species of shark and 80 percent are incapable of harming humans. Most prefer fish, immobile invertebrates, or other marine mammals; a few eat plankton, and the majority of sharks never encounter humans.

Here are the a few things to consider to avoid animal attacks:

➤ **Animals and man don't have to be enemies.** In reality, people are their own worst enemies and worst enemies to just about every other creature, and we don't live by the same biological laws as the rest of the animal kingdom. Humans have the ability to think and reason, so we are the ones creating 99.99 percent of the encounters. Animals have an innate fear of humans, aren't stirring up trouble, and often end up being killed anyway.

➤ **Animals love fast food as much as we do.** Animals spend a good deal of their time foraging for food, so if they find an easy source—namely, easily accessible piles of human food—they are going to keep returning to eat. Eventually, it will become as routine as our trips to the McDonald's drive-thru, and just think of how angry you would be if all the sudden the supply of Big Macs dried up. It could be tigers dwelling near homes on the outskirts of jungles, coyotes in the Hollywood Hills, or alligators near golf courses, so make sure your community doesn't make it easy for animals to chow down and become more aggressive.

➤ **Safety in numbers.** If you were in the jungle, would you rather happen upon one lion or a pride of lions? Animals feel the same way—they'd rather encounter one of us instead of many. There is strength and safety in numbers, so always travel with at least one other companion in untamed areas. It is always safer to have a partner if a serious situation unfolds.

➤ **If you poke, it will provoke; if you frighten, it will be bitin'.** Animal attacks are almost always the result of human provocation, even if the provocation isn't deliberate. If you startle a rattlesnake by inadvertently stepping on it, the snake will naturally react aggressively. It may be impossible to prevent an accidental spooking of an animal, but keeping your wits about you will reduce the chances. What can be avoided is foolish and potentially deadly behavior, like throwing rocks at a pit bull or teasing a wolf by dangling a chicken over a balcony. Animals don't have the ability to reason—and if you engage in this kind of behavior, apparently neither do you.

A wolf darts through the snow in Yellowstone National Park.

(Photo courtesy of the National Park Service.)

➤ **Don't partake in the free-for-sprawl.** Wildlife officials in the West have noted an increase in animal attacks in the past two decades. One major reason is the ongoing encroachment by humans on wildlife habitats. In an ever-increasing race to build the most secluded summer home, people are constructing dwellings in areas that had been previously left to the animals. This has a threefold negative outcome: It leads to more development, which in turn makes the area "overcrowded," sending folks farther into the wilderness to find "peace and quiet"; it leads to desensitized, aggressive animals who don't fear humans; and the basic ecosystem is permanently altered.

Adventures of a Lifetime

The debate over development versus a natural ecosystem is always lively. Consider Long Island, parts of which exploded with construction and are now overrun with basically tame, human-dependent deer. Some environmentalists say it is because their natural predators were chased out (although there are still plenty of eastern coyotes, albeit also more domesticated). Others believe it is simply a case of deer easily attaining human food, because the deer population is rumored to be higher than in colonial times. Regardless, many of the deer are sick and malnourished, and something will have to be done because they are eating the bulk of certain plant life.

➤ **Use common sense.** It is never a good idea to get within 10 feet of a bison in Yellowstone National Park to get a picture to send to your brother stuck in a cubicle in New York City. Bison can weigh upwards of a ton and charge at 20 mph, goring or trampling whomever is in their path. Common stupidity leads to many attacks and the animal ends up paying for it. Other than house pets, animals aren't man's best friend, so no matter where you are, don't assume they're harmless. This warning is especially timely because the number of visitors to national parks has skyrocketed in recent years.

➤ **Mind your children.** Anyone familiar with the infamous baby-stealing dingo doesn't need to be told that it is best to watch your children whenever they are likely to interact with animals. Children are particularly susceptible to animal attacks because their smaller size resembles standard prey. In addition, their bodies aren't developed so they won't be able to fight back or prevent internal damage. Make sure they understand that taunting animals is asking for trouble and that barricades are there for a reason. Tragic developments have unfolded at zoos, circuses, marine shows, rodeos, and other places, so be extra careful with kiddies.

Adventures of a Lifetime

Killer whales are not the biggest whales, but they are the largest predators of mammals known to man. Males (bulls) average roughly 20 to 21 feet long and weigh 4 to 6 tons, but the largest ever recorded was 32 feet long and weighed 11 tons. Females (cows) average around 17 to 18 feet long and weigh 1½ to 4 tons; but even though they are smaller than males, female whales are higher on the social scale because killer whales are a female-dominant society.

A Whale of a Tale

Now that we have covered the overall picture of the animal kingdom, let's look at a few individual creatures and how to behave in their presence. We'll start big.

Killer whales (also called orcas) may be the most amazing predators on Earth, majestic kings of the sea who have been held in awe since ancient times. Cave drawings in Norway, thousands of years old, have been found with pictures of the killer whale. They have long been viewed as an amazingly predatory animal; Navy manuals just a few decades old claimed that this whale's *modus operandi* was to attack humans whenever possible.

If you fall into the Bering Sea, be glad that you'll probably die of hypothermia because there is little you can do to prevent a killer whale from swallowing you whole. What you can do, however, is follow a few guidelines for whale watching from your yacht or charter boat:

➤ It is illegal to hunt, chase, move, or break up pods of killer whales. Beyond the illegality, however, diving or swimming in their vicinity is an invitation to nearby orcas to come say hello—a really bad idea.

➤ Don't approach killer whales from the front or back; slowly approach their sides and avoid rapid shifts in speed, movement, or direction. If they give chase, stay in the same direction while fleeing and never try to go around or leapfrog the sea giants.

➤ Never come any closer than roughly 300 yards and don't make any loud noises. Cut the engines, silence the air raid horns, and turn off the CD player, or a killer whale may come to see what's shaking (which will be your boat as it gets knocked over in the freezing ocean).

➤ Don't trap an orca between your boat and the shoreline, and let sleeping killer whale pods (usually numbering five to 50) get a good night's rest.

A killer whale "spy-hops" (suspends vertically with its head above the surface) and surveys the icy terrain.

(Photo courtesy of the National Oceanic and Atmospheric Administration [NOAA].)

Swimming with Sharks

Thanks to Peter Benchley, who wrote *Jaws*, and Steven Spielberg, who directed the blockbuster movie of the same name, sharks are one of the most feared creatures, even though you have a much better chance of drowning in your backyard pool than dying as a result of a shark attack. Still, attacks do happen, so here are some tips:

➤ Don't go into the ocean if you're bleeding, either with an open wound or when you're menstruating. Sharks have an acute sense of smell and are attracted by the scent of blood in the water.

➤ Never swim or dive near areas where any kind of sewage, waste, or bait is dumped into the ocean. Refrain from leaving your own waste as well in shark-infested waters.

➤ Don't swim where you can't see; don't swim while wearing shiny or glistening jewelry (sharks will mistake your jewelry for fish); don't go diving at dusk or late at night without an experienced guide; don't lie on the surface in scuba gear like a floating seal; and don't swim around deep slopes or drops where sharks tend to find their prey.

➤ If you see a shark, remain calm, because most will take a look and keep on going. But if it arches its back and/or pectoral fin, it may be go time, so get ready to protect yourself.

➤ If a shark isn't in attack mode, try to make yourself look bigger by bringing your arms and legs in and swimming away with short, strong strokes, but don't take your eyes off of the predator.

➤ If a shark attacks, fight back. Hit the shark with everything you've got, preferably in the eyes or gills, not the nose as per the standard advice. Like the schoolyard punk, sharks tend not to fight if they don't think they have the advantage.

➤ If you or a companion are bitten by a shark (the shark swims away after the initial attack, or you're able to drive it off), begin trying to control the bleeding in the water, but get ashore as quickly as possible. Lay the victim on the beach sloping the head down toward the water to increase blood flow to the brain. Give the victim sips of fresh water, cover him or her in a warm blanket, and go for help, but never move the victim because shock can increase and shock is a prime cause of fatalities.

Adventures of a Lifetime

The bull shark has a specialized osmoregulatory system, which means it can live in both fresh and salt water and has the ability to travel back and forth between oceans and the rivers that lead into them.

If you're concerned about whether there are sharks in the area, watch the fish. They fear sharks too, and for much better reasons. Keep in mind, though, that fatalities from shark attacks are extremely rare, but 600,000 to 700,000 tons of sharks are caught and slaughtered every year, according to some estimates.

Hungry, Hungry Hippos

Hippopotamuses appear docile and relaxed as they cool off in the jungle mud or munch on the abundant plant life. After a day of wallowing, herds come ashore and travel up to five miles inland to graze on short grasses. An adult hippo will put away roughly 100 pounds of grass each night, mowing the lawn with its strong lips, not its teeth. Sounds like a cushy life, doesn't it? How rough and tough could a herbivore be?

Even though the river horse (that's what hippopotamus means in Greek) spends most of the day chilling in water, the hippopotamus is one of the more ill-tempered mammals in the wild. By some accounts, hippos kill more humans than any other wild animal—lions, tigers, and gorillas included. Hippos have been cast in an ugly light as a danger to man and as murderous monsters, but their reputation has been greatly exaggerated through myths passed down by explorers.

Make no mistake, hippos are fiercely territorial and defend their territory and young without hesitation, but many biologists feel that hippos aren't innately malicious. Hippos have been known to attack boats that infiltrate large herds and fisherman who work along the banks, and frequently lay waste to inland farms, fields, crops, and cattle while roaming the land at night (to stay out of the sun, by the way). Hippos are dangerous in the sense that they are enormous, 12 to 15 feet long, five feet high, and weighing up to 8,000 pounds; fast, they can reach land speeds of 20 mph; and have big, strong choppers, canine teeth that can be as long as 20 inches. Hippopotamuses can literally bite crocodiles in half, so it doesn't take an active imagination to think of what they can do to the soft, fleshy human body.

If you go diving in jungle rivers or lakes, make sure there are no hippos in the region, because they have webbed feet, are fantastic swimmers, and can easily catch divers. They can also stay underwater for five to six minutes and can walk along the bottom of rivers or lakes. If you encounter a hippo, go ashore as quickly as possible, because it's much clumsier on land. Angry hippos are hard to fend off when they charge, but whatever you do, stay out of their mouths. You may not be able to outrun a hippo, but if you can outmaneuver the river horse and scream for help, hopefully African locals will come to your rescue. If you end up in a hippo's mouth ... let's not think about it.

> **Adventures of a Lifetime**
>
> A hippo has a thick gray or brown hairless hide and its skin contains glands that ooze a protective oily liquid whose red color has led to the oft-repeated myth that hippos sweat blood. The oil helps keep the skin moist and possibly helps heal wounds and combat germs.

A Tiger in the Woods (and the Jungle)

Tigers are one of the most breathtaking species on the planet: grand, elegant, and potentially lethal kitty cats of the highest order. Unfortunately, they have long been a favorite of poachers, loggers, farmers, and hunters, so the large number of tigers that once walked the Asian (note: they don't call Africa home) countryside has been reduced considerably, and several subspecies are gone forever. Tigers are strong and fast and, in the wild, they stalk their prey, go on an eating binge, and then don't snack for several days thereafter. Tigers cover a wide territory of 10 to 20 square miles, depending on the amount of food available. Siberian tigers may cover as many as 120 square miles.

107

Tigers like large prey such as antelopes, buffalo, wild pigs, deer, and the occasional human. They will patiently stalk their prey and can leap 30 feet to bring down their victim. Tigers hold down their prey and kill it by biting the neck; then they drag their meal to a secluded spot near a source of water and commence feasting. Adult tigers tend to survive on their own, and will guard their meal as they eat, nap, stretch, eat, nap ... sort of like Thanksgiving Day for you and me, minus the football games. Tigers don't attack humans often, but there are about 50 fatalities every year. One of the most troublesome spots on the planet is the Sunderbans, a large, forested, river delta area in India and Bangladesh that is the home of 250 tigers that have gotten used to snacking on humans.

If you plan on journeying to the Sunderbans, remember these tips:

➤ Old, wounded, or sick tigers are most likely to attack humans because they are incapable of catching their usual prey.

➤ If you're planning on building a home alongside the jungle, consider buying a human dummy and hooking it up to a car battery or some electrical source. Believe it or not, tigers will get shocked when they chomp down and ideally their taste for human flesh will diminish.

➤ As you're walking, check behind you often, because tigers usually attack from behind. You can also buy a rubber mask or make your own and wear it on the back of your head to fool the tigers into thinking you are facing them.

➤ Surviving an attack is basically up to the tiger, but keep in mind that it often goes for the throat of its prey.

Adventures of a Lifetime

Siberian tigers aren't white and don't camouflage themselves in the snow. White tigers are Bengal tigers found in India, and they aren't albinos either. They have white fur with chocolate stripes and blue eyes, and all white tigers in captivity are descended from a northern Indian male tiger named Mohan.

The Sting of the Scorpion

Scorpions are found throughout the United States, and although they are commonly thought to inhabit the desert, they can also be found in forests, tropical areas, grasslands, suburbs, and caves. There are an estimated 1,300 species of scorpions, 90 of which are found in the United States, almost all west of the Mississippi River. They have a skinny, elongated body and a segmented tail with a venomous stinger. Scorpions come out at night to feed primarily on other insects; their sting can occasionally be fatal to humans.

In reality, only 20 species of scorpions (one in the United States) have venom toxic enough to be dangerous to people, and even a sting from one of those scorpions isn't invariably a trip to death row. Antivenom is available for the worst cases and hospitals throughout the Southwest, Arizona in particular, know how to handle scorpion bites. To avoid scorpions, don't put your hands underneath rocks, under loose bark of dead trees, or in any dark corner where the nocturnal creatures might hide. In the morning, thoroughly shake out your clothes and boots before putting them on, because scorpions like to take cover in shoes, socks, and clothes left on the ground at night.

If you are stung by a scorpion, remain calm and see if the pain subsides within the hour. Wash the affected area with soap and water and raise it to heart level. If you are a tobacco user, this is your shining moment, because a wad of snuff or any chewed-upon tobacco can be placed over the bite to ease the pain.

Survival Kit

Scorpion stings can be fatal to children and the elderly, so take their bites very seriously. There is often no distinct swelling or discoloration, so don't trust your naked eye.

Scorpion stings may cause temporary pain and/or swelling, numbness, convulsions, difficulty breathing, and even frothing at the mouth. If these symptoms persist, try to get the victim to a hospital, because most fatalities are the result of respiratory and/or heart failure hours after the scorpion attack.

So, there you have it, a variety of ways to handle a variety of animal attacks. Remember, fatal animal attacks are rare, especially among healthy adults, but it pays to keep these precautions in mind. Still, if a Gila monster in a Southwestern desert bites you and holds on to you with its incredible grip, driving its teeth and poison into your skin, try holding its head under water or apply a flame under its jaw. Gila monsters hate that ... oh, wash out the bite with water while allowing it to bleed and go see a doctor.

The Least You Need to Know

➤ Animals almost universally have an innate fear of humans and most will not attack unless provoked.

➤ You may never be in a boat that comes across a killer whale, but if you are, don't approach the whale from the front or back, and avoid rapid shifts in speed, movement, or direction.

➤ If you or a companion are bitten by a shark, begin trying to control the bleeding in the water, but get the victim ashore as quickly as possible.

➤ If you encounter a hippo, go ashore as quickly as possible, because it is much clumsier on land than in the water.

➤ Tigers usually attack from behind, so buy a rubber mask or make your own and wear it on the back of your head to fool the tigers into thinking you are facing them.

➤ Scorpion stings aren't necessarily fatal, but victims should still go to a hospital, especially children or the elderly.

Part 3
High-Tech Survival

Since the dawn of time, it seems that man has been fighting the elements. From the ice age to the greenhouse effect, we have gradually been learning more about our environment and how to survive its toughest attacks. But what about when man's inventions grow minds of their own—the apocalyptic nightmare of technology run amok? What should you do if your car hits thin ice or flames suddenly erupt in your peaceful 25th-floor office?

The chapters in this part will teach you the intricacies of surviving our own creations. You'll learn what to do if your small plane to Barbados suddenly takes a plunge, and how to survive a train derailment. You'll also learn safety for that most trusted vehicle, the family car.

Chapter 11

My Little
Deuce Coupe

In This Chapter

➤ Where to enjoy the nuclear winter

➤ Slip-sliding away: how to handle driving on ice

➤ Escaping a frozen lake

➤ Handling a carjacking

➤ What to do if your car catches on fire

As the old commercial noted, there is nothing more American than baseball, apple pie, and Chevrolet, but in reality there are a whole lot more people in this country who forego dessert and ignore the World Series than live without cars. Hopping into an automobile and hitting the highway has become the ubiquitous metaphor for the freedoms of the United States. From Jack Kerouac to *Easy Rider*, "getting your kicks on Route 66," to "having fun, fun, fun till your daddy takes the T-Bird away," the role of the car in America can't be understated.

The dark side of the car culture is that automobiles need drivers, and human beings are prone to mistakes, which can prove fatal. Going down with the ship may be romantic and heroic, but croaking for a Toyota Camry doesn't have quite the same noble ring to it. This chapter will help you, the driver (or passenger), learn how to survive an auto emergency.

Cruising Through the Nuclear Winter

If you are out for a leisurely spin and word comes over the radio that a nuclear war is going to break out by the end of the day, here is a list of places to avoid and head towards. The primary targets, in order, of the Cold War were (still are?) reportedly: Washington D.C.; Central Montana (Minuteman missile silos); a 75-mile radius of Minot, North Dakota (more Minuteman silos); 80 miles north, west, or south of Grand Forks, North Carolina (even more silos); and 100 miles north or east of Rapid City, South Dakota (those darn silos again).

SOS

If the nuclear bombs start raining down, don't forget to bring lots of long books like *War and Peace, The Rise and Fall of the Roman Empire,* and *Infinite Jest.* Fallout shelter time is slow time.

If you're on the road, this is where you should point the compass as the mushroom cloud grows: the Pacific coast from San Francisco to Canada; the Channel Islands southwest of Los Angeles; the southwest corner of Utah; the Durango area of southwest Colorado; northwest New Mexico; and the Big Bend region of Texas. Although now that the Communist superpower is a thing of the past and smaller terrorists, some homegrown, are more of a threat, maybe it doesn't matter. Happy motoring!

Ice-Capades

If the car you're in falls through the ice, it's possible to survive, but you have to know exactly what course of action to follow and react quickly.

There is no such thing as ice that is completely safe. If you're driving onto the ice to go ice fishing or for some other reason, always follow the these precautions:

➤ Ice should be at least 9 inches thick for a small car, but a 12-inch thickness is preferable. Be careful, though, because a foot-thick spot isn't the standard for the entire body of water.

➤ New ice is safer than old ice, ice near the shore isn't as strong as ice at the middle, and the worst time to test your luck is late fall or early spring ... stick to winter.

➤ River ice is more dangerous than ice on lakes, especially at the mouth of the river, and be wary of fresh snow on ice because it weighs the ice down.

➤ Move your car to a different spot every so often and don't drive close to another car because automobiles cause waves, which can crack the ice if they slam into one another.

➤ If you must drive across ice with cracks in it, traverse at a right angle and don't park near the fractured ice.

Falling Through the Cracks

If your car drops through the ice—or skids off a bridge and plunges into any body of water, for that matter—your best chance of survival comes in the early moments before the car fills up like a human fish tank. Here's what to do:

➤ **Immediately roll down the car windows.** It's best to keep the windows open when driving on ice because if you go into the drink with the windows closed, you aren't coming back. In the seconds between sliding off a bridge and hitting the water, try to roll down the windows. A car will float momentarily, but once the window level goes under, it is virtually impossible to open the windows or doors against the water pressure. If the windows are partially open, the inside and outside pressures will equalize, allowing you to get out.

➤ **Open the car door.** For the same reason, leave your car door slightly open while traveling on ice and don't drive with the doors locked or seat belts fastened. Again, if you can remember in the harrowing moments, open the door before going into the drink.

➤ **Carry a beacon.** Keep a waterproof flashlight in the car in case you escape quickly but get trapped under the ice. It can help you find a hole in the ice or alert rescuers to your location.

➤ **Try to break the glass.** You might start sinking and find that the power windows have gone south or the window handle has already called it quits, in which case you need to try to shatter the glass. Try kicking the window with your feet or striking it with a heavy object like a hammer, pick, crow bar, or anti-theft steering-wheel lock (known to you and me as the Club).

➤ **Swim for your life.** If you don't escape the car before it goes under, know that the pressure will eventually equalize once the car has settled and you will get a shot to open the door and swim for your life. Reaching the surface under these deadly circumstances may seem unimaginable, but we are talking about *surviving anything,* don't forget.

Cars falling through ice and sinking are not as common as hot-doggers on snowmobiles meeting a watery fate. If you drive your snowmobile at a

Survival Kit

The hardness of ice is based on numerous factors, including the amount of traffic on the ice paths (people, cars, and animals); depth of the water; size of the body of water; chemical makeup of the water; temperature of the water; and atmospheric fluctuations. Some of these factors are not apparent to the naked eye, so always use extreme caution if you venture onto ice.

high speed on ice, you may not be able to stop in time to avoid a big hole even if you spot it in your headlight ahead of time. Nobody should need to be told this, but motoring across ice like it's a NASCAR event is a stupid and potentially deadly way to chase thrills.

Adventures of a Lifetime

The number of deaths attributed to cars falling through ice has increased sharply in the last few decades as more and more anglers take their vehicles across ice-covered waters looking for the perfect spot. Reportedly, a new scientific phenomenon known as the deep freeze has arisen as well. There are survivors of frigid waters who should have drowned but didn't because they were saved by a protective freeze and suffered no severe brain impairment. There have been numerous cases of people who are essentially suspended in a frozen sleep and although scientists aren't exactly sure why it happens, it is an acknowledged phenomenon.

Survival Kit

Whenever you intend to walk or drive on ice, it's a good idea to carry an "ice claw" of some sort (like a small pick or large nails) to make it easier to grip the ice from the water. In your car, you can fasten a claw to a length of rope, which can be pulled by someone on strong ice while you scratch your way to the surface.

Out of the Car, into the Water

Once you plunge into the water, try to remain calm and keep your wits about you (easier said than done, I know). Head back in the direction from where you fell through the ice. Assuming you don't have a pick handy, use your hands and arms to try to get level on the solid surface of the ice, while kicking your feet up onto the surface.

There's a good chance the ice will continue cracking, but don't give up. Keep working yourself onto the surface. You will feel clumsy and helpless, but continue to wiggle forward. Once your body is out of the water and on the surface, gently roll away from the hole or crack until you reach a thick patch of ice.

Hit the Road, Carjack, and Don't You Come Back No More

Although crime dropped precipitously in the late 1990s, carjacking still remains a favorite of gun-wielding thugs. Carjacking tends to take place after dark, between 10:00 at night and 2:00 in the morning, frequently at unpopulated stopping points such as fast-food joints, parking lots, stop signs, empty downtown streets, freeway ramps, red lights, parking garages, alleys, and gas stations. Surviving a carjacking isn't normally a matter of life or death, although we have all seen the occasional grisly footage on the 11 o'clock news.

Here's how to avoid becoming a victim of a carjacking:

➤ Always keep your car doors locked and windows rolled up while driving, particularly at night. Many carjackers simply open the car door while the driver is stopped at a red light or stop sign.

➤ When leaving your car to go inside to pay for gas, buy a newspaper, or use the restroom, always lock the doors and roll up the windows. Carjackers can slip into an unlocked car or unlock a car through an open window. And of course, never leave your car running while you go inside to take care of something, even if you'll be only a moment, because your car may not be there when you come back.

➤ Find a "driving friend" for nighttime excursions. Single drivers, women in particular, are the main targets.

> **Survival Kit**
>
> One of the classic con games is for two people to rear-end a car, and when the driver gets out to inspect it, one flashes a gun and the other one steals the car. If you are rear-ended and are suspicious about the other driver, don't get out of the car. Instead, motion the other driver to follow you and drive to the nearest police station. Try to get the other car's license plate number if you can.

➤ Park in well-lit areas. If you see someone lurking about, ask a security guard or a store employee to escort you to your car.

➤ Drive (and idle) in the center lane if possible and don't be afraid to peel out on a red light or out of a parking lot if you suspect danger is in the air.

➤ Don't forget, you have a 2-ton weapon at your disposal. More often than not, carjackers want the car (not you), but don't hand it over if you can drive away without peril. Say a brainless carjacker stands in front of the vehicle ... gun it and watch the punk dive to the pavement.

117

➤ A car can be replaced, you can't. If the carjacker has the advantage (in the form of a gun or a knife pressed to your throat), surrender the car without a fight. *Surviving* a carjacking means you make it out alive, nothing more, nothing less. (Besides, you were getting tired of driving that Cadillac anyway, weren't you?)

Days of Fire

Igniting or exploding cars may make for great visuals on TV shows and in movies, but most of us aren't equipped to handle a car fire and they are frightening when they occur. The key to avoiding a car fire is to take care of your automobile and know when it's time for a dead soldier to be buried. Here are some other tips:

➤ Older cars are more susceptible to car fires, so have a mechanic check it out for holes, drips, loose hoses and wires, and corroded parts.

➤ Gas does not belong in the cooling system, carburetor, crankshaft, or any other part of the car besides the gas tank. Gasoline spilling on a hot engine is the cause of many a service-station bonfire.

➤ Lots of interior fires are sparked by cigarettes, so smoke 'em if you got 'em, but don't let 'em fall through the dashboard or under the seat unless you want a *really* smokin' ride.

Adventures of a Lifetime

Did you know that two thirds of vehicle fires are due to mechanical or electrical failure? Over 200,000 car fires that occurred between the years 1991 to 1995 were the result of mechanical mishaps. In fact, it's been estimated that 20 percent of *all* fires in the United States originate under the hood.

If your car does start on fire, here's what to do:

➤ **Pull over immediately and get out of the car.** Drivers tend to be wary of cars with smoke rings billowing from under the hood and will most likely get out of your way. Get to the shoulder, curb, or off ramp and get out, putting a good distance between you and your burning Bronco. Studies in my head have shown that people who try to drive a car that's on fire aren't very bright and have nobody to blame but themselves for the smell of charred flesh.

➤ **Use a fire extinguisher, if you have one.** Using a fire extinguisher comes with this warning: *If you don't know how to use it, forget it.* If the fire is small and you feel comfortable putting it out, go ahead, but it isn't worth getting up close and personal with a gas tank that is about to spew like the Fourth of July.

➤ **Move well away from the fire.** While waiting for the fire department to arrive, don't stand in or near any fluids that are leaking from the car. They're most likely poison and/or flammable. Stand clear of the entire car because there are numerous parts that can explode.

➤ **Stand upwind of the fire.** You may survive the fire only to breathe in a bunch of toxic fumes if you don't get upwind of the flaming wreckage. Newer cars burn quicker and the plastics will emit toxins you don't want in your system.

➤ **Keep an eye on traffic.** Your family might be in panic mode, so it's up to you to adopt the survivor's mentality and take charge of the scene. After everyone is safe, keep onlookers away and make sure that your fellow passengers don't forget that becoming mesmerized by a flaming Firebird might get them pancaked by an 18-wheeler.

Most deaths by car fire occur in collisions and rollovers because passengers weren't wearing their seatbelts, and get knocked loopy or sustain an injury that keeps from fleeing the car. Being burned alive or getting killed by smoke inhalation is a foolish price to pay for cruising around without a seatbelt.

SOS

Never open the hood of a burning car. Doing so will give the fire more oxygen to burn and spread the flames.

Survival Kit

If your have the "simple" problem of a car breakdown, stay by your car. Use your road flares judiciously so that they will last for more than a night. Truckers often roll through the dark hours and will often call for help if they see the flares, but you don't want to run the risk of expending the supply. During the day, set up orange or red warning flags or reflective triangles to alert other drivers.

The Least You Need to Know

➤ In the event of a nuclear war, the safest places to head for are the Pacific coast from San Francisco to Canada, the Channel Islands southwest of Los Angeles, the southwest corner of Utah, the Durango area of southwest Colorado, northwest New Mexico, and the Big Bend region of Texas.

➤ There is no such thing as ice that is completely safe.

➤ Always leave your car windows open when traversing ice because if your car goes under, this will equalize the inside and outside pressure, enabling you to escape.

➤ Carjackers tend to prey after hours in deserted locales on folks who leave their windows open and doors unlocked, sit too long at traffic lights, or don't pay attention while gassing up.

➤ If your car starts on fire, pull over immediately, get out, and move well away from the fire.

Chapter 12

It's a Bird, It's a Plane ...

In This Chapter

➤ Relaxation techniques for calmer air travel

➤ Splashing down doesn't have to mean a watery grave

➤ How to safely shake, rattle, and roll

➤ Keep that blood flowing: preventing deep vein thrombosis

➤ A crash course in landing an airplane

➤ Dealing with your friendly neighborhood hijacker

There's an old flying axiom that says a *good landing* is one where all the passengers walk off the plane at their destination, and a *great landing* is one where the plane can be used again.

But seriously folks ... what's the deal with airline food?

If you're not quite comfortable flying the friendly skies, you are not alone. Fear of flying is one of the most common phobias, ranking up there after public speaking, violent death, and in-laws. The information in this chapter will ease your apprehensions, because it provides the details for happy-go-lucky air travel, even if you have to land the big bird yourself.

Stress-Free Flying

Before we delve into combating a variety of airline catastrophes, let's talk about the simple act of surviving a routine flight, which is anathema to many of you who are

Survival Kit

Prior to the 1970s, most people who were scared of flying had never been on an airplane, but now almost everyone who suffers from "flight fright" has been on a successful jaunt from one landing strip to another.

SOS

If you're afraid of flying, don't drink alcohol before the flight. The atmosphere in a cabin is pressurized to about the same altitude as a Denver Broncos game, so any booze you drink will have a stronger effect than at sea level and may dull your senses. Alcohol can also cause some passengers to lose control, which sends rippling anxiety throughout the cabin.

forced to fly because of work. If you're not comfortable flying, airline travel can be stressful. Here are some things you can do to lessen the anxiety:

➤ **Arrive at the airport at least an hour before your flight (two hours if it's an international flight).** Get your ticket and check your bags before the line forms at the ticket counter. Then you can take a deep breath, relax, and maybe have a snack or a cup of coffee while peacefully waiting for your row to be called. No matter how scared you are of flying, your body will respond better to the trip if it's calm. Arriving early also gives you a better chance of getting a seat on another flight if your flight ends up getting delayed or canceled.

➤ **Eat a well-balanced diet.** We all know that a healthy body equals a healthy mind, but did you know a sound diet will actually make flying easier? Don't board a plane without eating shortly beforehand because, if you're hungry, adrenaline will be released to compensate for a lack of blood sugar which, in turn, will send your anxieties to the moon. Eat a well-balanced meal, avoid the refined carbohydrates and sugars, and the trip will be snap. Caffeine acts as a stimulant, so overloading on soda, coffee, or chocolate won't help.

➤ **Use your common sense.** Take a deep breath, close your eyes, and repeat after me, "It's okay to be afraid, but it doesn't mean something horrible is bound to happen." Try to calm yourself enough to quit envisioning doomsday prophecies. Fear is natural and in many ways healthy, but use your common sense: Fear doesn't equal tragedy. To turn it around, when you are joyous, do you rush out to buy lottery tickets because there is no way you can lose?

➤ **Get help.** Some people with full-blown phobias just don't respond to rational thinking. But you don't have to let your fear of flying get the best of you. Many airlines sponsor fear-of-flying courses that include education classes and a test flight at graduation. You can also find programs and support groups on the Internet. And finally, your doctor can prescribe anti-anxiety drugs if your fear is making a real mess of your life.

Place Your Throwing Star in the Bowl, Please

You might be 100 percent certain that an international terrorist conglomerate is going to hijack your flight to Wichita and demand that all parrot smugglers be freed from American prisons, but it is still illegal in this country to pack a sword in your carry-on baggage. Other items to leave behind include ...

➤ Firecrackers, gunpowder, sparklers, blasting caps ... and oh yeah, loaded firearms.

➤ Dry ice in excess of 4 pounds.

➤ Bacterial cultures, vials of viral organisms, pesticides, rat poisons, insecticide, and thermoses filled with anthrax.

➤ Throwing stars, knives with blades longer than 4 inches, sabers, or machetes.

➤ Cans of gasoline, spray paint, CO_2 cartridges, lighter fluid, bleach, and nitric or hydrochloric acid.

You might be wondering why the detour through the obvious canal, but you would be surprised how many everyday folks can't even survive the mandatory trip through the metal detector. This is a full-service guide to survival and if you never get on the plane how are you suppose to know what to do when it goes down in the ocean?

Splashdown!

Don't lie. No matter how experienced a flier you are, there's probably been a time when you were flying over the ocean and considered what it would be like to make an emergency landing in the deep blue sea. Let's say your deepest fears become a reality, and the water is rapidly approaching as you make a hellish descent towards Earth. What can you do to increase your chances of survival?

First, realize that it *is* possible to survive a plane crash in a large body of water because more often than not such crashes involve smaller, low-flying airplanes and not the thunderous collision of a major passenger jet and the ocean. So, don't assume this is the end of the line and just give up. Aren't you glad now that you paid attention to the flight attendants' routine emergency announcements at the start of the flight? If so, you know where the lifejackets are located and how to operate the inflatable vests. (Don't jump the gun and activate the inflatable vests inside the cabin until you are told by the flight attendants, however. It will make maneuverability that much more difficult and it may impede the survival efforts of other passengers.)

Here's what else you should do, as directed by the flight crew:

➤ Remove any loose items that might cause problems upon impact, like knap-sacks, CD players, and dentures, except for eyeglasses, which should be secured on your body so you can spot a deserted island later.

➤ Listen to the emergency announcements until the pilot orders you and the other passengers to get into crash position. Once you are in crash position, con-centrate on staying calm and focused. Don't lift your head up to take a peek around.

➤ Stay in crash position until the plane completely stops, at which time the plane may be ripped open or apart, depending on the severity of the impact, and will begin to fill with water and/or sink. It's time to inflate your life vest and, ideally, a raft.

➤ Get away from the plane as quickly as possible because you don't want to get hit by debris or caught on part of the aircraft as it starts to sink. If you don't have a raft and a chunk of wing floats by, grab it, but don't sit inside the cabin because it will be nearly impossible to escape once it fills with water.

Adventures of a Lifetime

The ugliest situation you can imagine might be if you see fellow passengers in a cabin call-ing for help as the cabin becomes submerged by the ocean. Is it worth going back to try to save others? This is an ethical dilemma with no simple answer, but keep in mind that airplanes can sink almost without warning and you may be pulled back into the turmoil by a passenger clinging to anyone in a feeble attempt at avoiding a watery grave. If the water is too deep, the smoke is too thick, or the fire is too hot—get out.

➤ Remember that you were on a plane that just went down, so search teams will be in the area very soon. Unfortunately, if you aren't in a raft and it's a frigid body of water, hypothermia will kick in and freezing to death is a likelihood, but at least you survived the crash, right?

A pilot and a radio operator are picked up after they ran out of fuel and had to make an emergency water landing three days after Pearl Harbor, December 10, 1941.

(Photo courtesy of Captain Fair J. Bryant/National Oceanic and Atmospheric Administration [NOAA].)

Turbulence Happens

"Good evening, this is your captain speaking, we are currently cruising at about 30,000 feet, so relax and enjoy—what do you mean it's stuck—Oh good heavens, that's the Pacific Oce-- ....

The preceding announcement is unlikely, because before many crashes comes turbulence. We've all been in a jet that starts to shake, rattle, and roll, and the worst that usually comes of it is an exciting story to tell your friends. Still, turbulence is the cause of many injuries and the occasional death over the course of a year, so you should know how to handle the tilt-a-whirl in the sky.

SOS

Don't ignore the "captain requests you put on your seat belt" warning or the illuminated, universal sign for buckle up. Nearly all turbulence injuries and deaths due to turbulence occur when the passenger isn't wearing a seatbelt and should be.

➤ Turbulence often hits with little or no warning, so if you're kicking back in your chair, buckle your seat belt so as not to inadvertently jab a flight attendant in the eye.

➤ If it gets rough, put your head between your legs and place your hands on top of your head.

➤ If your stomach is doing flip-flops, breathe deeply into the paper bag provided in the seat pocket in front of you. As the turbulence subsides, you should start feeling better. Don't feel self-conscious about getting sick either, because you'll feel a whole lot better after the turbulence subsides—but don't forget to replenish the food you lost.

Adventures of a Lifetime

Major plane crashes aren't always fatal, so it pays to act like a survivor even if it appears you'll be checking out. According to airsafe.com, between 1978 and 1995 there were 164 fatal accidents (causing at least one death) in large jet transports designed in the United States and Western Europe. In a little more than half of the crashes, 90 to 100 percent of passengers died, but in 37 crashes, fewer than 10 percent of the passengers died.

Economy Class Syndrome: Deep Vein Thrombosis

Beyond the cramped quarters, $5 headphones after a $350 ticket, cardboard pillows, dry chicken, and the loud fat guy telling you the two-hour saga of his bunions, a new terror has beset the weary travelers behind those first-class curtains: deep vein thrombosis. It is a condition in which a thrombus or blood clot forms within a deep vein, often in the region of the thigh. The clot can obstruct blood flow, and in the most severe cases it will detach from a vein wall, make its way to the lung, and block an artery, which can lead to death. Deep vein thrombosis is caused by blood pooling in the vein, which sparks blood clotting. Sedentary behavior can lead to deep vein thrombosis and the tight squeeze in coach class can kickstart clotting.

You can recognize this "economy class syndrome" by harsher degrees of the standard aches and pains you experience in a typical coach seat, cross-country flight. If you feel strong tenderness, pain, swelling, or cramps where veins are located, or intense soreness in your joints, it may be the onset of deep vein thrombosis. Other symptoms include fever, fast heartbeat and/or sudden, uncommon, powerful coughing. The chances that you will be affected by deep vein thrombosis increases if you are pregnant, obese, using oral contraceptives, over the age of 55, a smoker, a recent surgical patient or accident victim, or have a family history of clotting or heart problems, or have suffered from past coronary artery disease.

Here's what you can do to avoid deep vein thrombosis:

➤ If you're in the high-risk category, say a 60-year-old, 350-pound smoker with two heart attacks and clotting problems, check with your doctor before flying.

➤ If you're on a long flight, take regular strolls up and down the aisle at least once an hour to stretch your muscles. It may seem equally uncomfortable, but make them move the beverage cart (it's a health issue here, people).

➤ While in your seat, roll your ankles, lift your thighs, flex your feet, and wiggle your waist—dare to be funny-looking.

➤ Drink lots of water throughout the flight. This will also send you to the lavatory more often, keeping the circulation up and running.

➤ Remember that alcohol consumption while in flight can dull your senses and you might not notice that *you can't feel your legs.*

Survival Kit

Clothes can make the man or woman—and the survivor—in the event of an emergency landing. Natural fibers like denim, cotton, or leather (get that Elvis jumpsuit out of the closet) are more likely to offer you some protection if a cabin fire breaks out on the plane. Wear long sleeves and pants in case you have to slide to freedom, and keep the high heels and Birkenstocks at home. Footwear and nylons that can get caught on the slide will have to be ditched, opening your feet up to broken glass, so don sneakers, boots, or thick work shoes.

"Good Luck and We're All Counting on You"

What if your airplane is headed straight towards the Rocky Mountains? And passengers are screaming for you to take the controls but your feet have fallen asleep and you collapse in the aisle and the last thing you see is a beleaguered flight attendant looking down and shaking his head in sorrow as everyone meets their maker? You could have saved the day with some basic calisthenics … and a crash course (pardon the expression) in how to land a plane.

A neophyte, plucked-from-row-16 pilot having to land a plane filled with howling passengers in the midst of chaotic weather is as intense an experience as any poor sucker could ever face, but it can be done. How do I know that? Because, like the majority of my readers, I learned everything I need to know about emergency landings from the classic movie *Airplane!* Yes, I'm serious … and stop calling me Shirley.

The thought of stepping into the cockpit might start you sweating profusely and mumbling incoherently, but you can land the plane! All it takes is patience, calm, a few deep breaths, and the following directions.

Take the controls, which may require unfastening the pilot's seat belt and dragging him or her into the cabin (and believe me, this will unsettle your fellow passengers).

Find the communications device, be it a CB-style microphone or the headset, and start yelling "Mayday! Mayday!" Hopefully, someone will respond and assist in bringing you in, but even if no one answers, try to describe what's happening and give the plane's information, which should be posted right on the instrument panel (akin to your car's dashboard).

Survival Kit

Before you start panicking at the thought of landing a plane, be aware that all commercial flights are required to have two pilots, either of whom can operate the aircraft alone and bring it down safely, so what we're talking about here is more of a fanciful, "what if" scenario.

Steady the airplane with the throttle (akin to the gearshift in your car),which increases speed when pushed toward the instrument panel and vice versa when pulled back. Use the yoke (akin to the steering wheel) to level the aircraft horizontally so that the nose is roughly 3 inches below the horizon. We'll assume there is enough fuel because flights are overstocked, but if not, an emergency landing becomes imminent.

When prompted, begin your descent, or if nobody is there to guide you, start scanning for an area large enough to bring down the aircraft. Obviously airport landing strips are best, but large fields, highways, and flatlands will also work. There is no ideal spot, so plan for a turbulent landing. Pick as flat an area as possible and go with it. At this point, you should begin deploying the landing gear, which is located near the throttle and has a round handle that looks like a car tire. Some airplanes have permanent, fixed landing gear, which takes care of itself and makes your job easier.

While reducing speed with the throttle, the nose will drop, but don't let it fall below 6 inches. As you descend to 1,000 feet on the altimeter (the dials measuring altitude), gauge the landing strip by the tip of the right wing because the front view of middle horizon is going to disappear.

In the final approach, pull back on the throttle to reduce speed. The airplane should be approximately 100 feet above the emergency landing strip and the rear wheels will touch down first. At this time, the plane should stall, and that is a good thing because unlike a car engine, it means you are losing air flow over the wing, not that the engine is conked out. Pull all the way back on the throttle, but keep the nose from dipping to the ground, level it out with the yoke.

You have to reduce your speed on the ground, after all if you made it this far, you deserve the title of survivor. Use the pedals to slow the airplane. The upper pedals are brakes and the lower ones steer the nose, right pedal moves right, left moves left, so straighten 'er out and slow, slow, slow ... down.

Once the plane has come to a stop, get everyone out of the plane right away in case there has been structural damage that could start a fire. Run from the plane until you and the other passengers are at a safe distance and collect the well-deserved accolades of those you saved. And go rent *Airplane!* so you can look back and laugh.

Terror in the Skies

Plane hijackings aren't an everyday occurrence, but they do happen, particularly in countries with unstable governments and/or political unrest. Don't you worry, though, dealing with hijackers can be as pleasant as a trip to the DMV. The main three-pronged rule to remember when dealing with terrorists in any arena is: *Don't agitate them, do what they say, and keep your mouth shut.* Here are some other things to keep in mind:

➤ Know the political climate of the region in which you're traveling, especially if you've never made the journey before.

➤ Hijackers will often ask Americans to identify themselves, but don't assume it means anything more than a high-profile scare tactic.

➤ Even though the hijackers may have advanced knowledge of technology, weaponry, and the airplane itself, they are still going to be scared, so follow orders to the letter. If you don't understand the demand because it is in a foreign tongue, don't argue, just keep cool.

➤ Unless you are absolutely sure you can overpower a lone hijacker, don't be a hero. A suicidal nut may get his revenge by killing the pilots (although if you carry this book with you at all times ...).

➤ Address the hijackers with respect, but don't make excessive eye contact or give off the impression that you could care less about their culture, cause, religion, or ideology. (Treat the situation like a high-pressure job interview for a position you don't really want.)

➤ If a hijacker tries to connect with you on a human level, engage him or her, because it could mean the difference between living and dying. Studies of hostage situations have shown that friendly rapport builds the relationship and makes you more human and sympathetic (baby pictures, anyone?).

➤ Allow your picture to be taken and to be the group spokesperson, stressing how you and the other hostages just want to get back home to your families; it makes you more of a person than an object. Don't get clever and try to send out "secrets," though, because it will make it onto the news, which the hijackers might watch and thus make you their first target.

Once the drama comes to an end and you can get off the airplane, go back home, kiss the spouse and kids, pop open a cold brew, and reflect on your bravery in surviving the experience.

The Least You Need to Know

➤ Even if you're afraid of flying, if you're a calm, relaxed passenger you'll have a lower stress level and will be better prepared for air travel.

➤ If you're in a plane that crashes into a body of water, inflate your life vest and get away from the plane.

➤ Sedentary behavior can lead to deep vein thrombosis, and the tight squeeze in coach class can kickstart blood clotting.

➤ People are injured every year as the result of turbulence, so keep your seat belt buckled at all times.

➤ The best way to deal with hijackers is by doing what they say, keeping your mouth shut, and not agitating them.

Working on the Railroad

The locomotive is as vital in American history as the cotton gin, light bulb, or personal computer, but it seems, if you will pardon the pun, to have lost most of its steam since the ubiquitous automobile came into vogue. It's a shame that trains have become a small fish in a big sea of highways, because they were the ones that first linked the coasts and made this country whole. Commuter and commercial trains are still a valuable asset to the national economy and Amtrak still gets people where they need to be, but it will never be the same as the locomotive glory days, when the citizenry got to know one another while riding the rails.

Trains are one of the safest ways to travel. Machines being what they are, however, derailments and fatalities do occur. So let's deal with the question at hand: How do you survive a railroad emergency?

Why Did the Jackass Cross the (Rail) Road?

Any time is train time.

Let me repeat that for those who aren't paying attention and are starting to drive the family car across railroad tracks to beat the train.

SOS

Private train crossings aren't required to have advance warning signs or other designating markers and are found on roadways that aren't maintained by public administrators or employees. Be extra careful when traversing a crossing without warning signals, because that cranked-up Ozzy Osbourne CD may be drowning out the horn of an oncoming train.

SOS

If you're ever faced with the horrible situation of abandoning a car stalled on the tracks, remember to run *toward* the train. The chances of being hit by flying debris are lessened considerably if you head up rather than down the line.

Any time is train time.

This is the main warning in the train industry, yet it goes unheeded year after year, resulting in unnecessary fatalities. Trains are enormous, powerful machines that take a long time to stop. They will make mincemeat out of you, the other passengers, and that pantywaist hunk-of-tin you're driving if you're stupid enough to test a locomotive by ignoring the flashing signals or driving around the warning devices. Foolish behavior by motorists leads to fatalities again and again. You are 30 times more likely to die in a car collision with a train than with any other vehicle. There are roughly 300,000 public and private highway-rail grade crossings, so it isn't an anomaly to come upon one—but your foolish behavior may ensure that you never cross one again.

There probably isn't any reason for us to go into detail on why it isn't a good idea to race across tracks trying to beat a 10,000-ton train moving at 30 mph, but here are a few safety notes to obey at all times:

➤ If the signal lights are flashing at a crossing, drivers should leave at least 15 feet between the front of their car and the train when it passes.

➤ If your car ever breaks down on the tracks as happens in so many nighttime soap operas, get out of the car immediately! This should be a no-brainer, but people are killed every year because they keep trying to start the engine instead of bailing out.

➤ Drive defensively to be sure that traffic, or the automatic arm coming down at a crossing, doesn't box you in on the track.

➤ Never trust your headlights wholeheartedly. Nightfall or inclement weather can play tricks on the eyes and you may overdrive (think you can see farther ahead than you really can) your headlights—right into Casey Jr.

➤ If you're crossing a train track on foot, pay attention to the middle and outside tracks. Trains may be coming behind a stationary locomotive or in the opposite direction. There have been instances of pedestrians seeing the first track idle and stepping right into the path of a train.

➤ Recognize the warning signs emanating from the train itself, usually a shrill, high-pitched whistle blown a quarter-mile before a public crossing, and repeated until the train is on the crossing.

These heads-ups may sound self-evident, but collisions of this sort are common and generally the cause of more fatalities each year than any other type of train wreck.

What would have become of the famous Chicago Daily Tribune headline "Dewey Defeats Truman" if Truman's train had T-boned a car full of drunken teenagers not paying attention at a private crossing instead of giving 'em hell on his accident-free whistle-stop campaign of 1948?

(Photo courtesy of the Harry S Truman Memorial Library.)

A Nervous "Brake" Down

Imagine you're cruising down a railway in style, sipping a Manhattan in the bar car while carrying on a witty, urbane conversation with a stranger on a train. Suddenly a conductor yells out, "The engineer just dropped dead, someone has to stop this train before we all die!" You spring into action, consumed by the will to survive and save your train brethren.

Anybody can start a train, but it takes someone with calm, cool poise to stop one. The momentum of a train is strong, and the steel tires on a steel track aren't conducive to "locking them up," which only produces a long skid and a damaged locomotive. The trick to stopping a train is to lessen the rotation of the tires over a longer period of time. This is called *dynamic braking*. Toy with the brakes until you find a comfortable zone; it's

Tactical Terms

If you have to stop a train with a lot of cars in tow, **dynamic braking** is essential because there is space between each car and the line needs to be kept taut so that they don't collide into one another This is called the "accordion" effect.

all in the wrist and the timing. To stop the train, you can also apply the emergency brake located in the train cab. This is referred to as placing the train into "emergency."

Adventures of a Lifetime

If you've always harbored dreams of driving an 80-ton, coal-burning steam engine, the "Your Hand on the Throttle" program of Essex, Connecticut, is calling your name. According to the company Web site (essexsteamstation.com), for $350 you can be a guest engineer and drive a locomotive on an 8-mile stretch through the scenic Connecticut River Valley. You must be at least 18, in good health, physically able, willing to sign a general release, and have a yearning to learn all about steam engines and driving safety. The program requires that you register in advance. For more information call 860-767-0103 or send an e-mail to engineer@valleyrr.com.

Getting Back on Track with Amtrak

You may not be aware of this, but the United States of America has a national railroad system. Maybe it's not as widely utilized as the Eurorail, but it can get you where you need to go … or close enough to hop on a bus for the rest of the way. Despite the occasional high-profile crash that gets replayed ad nauseum on the news, train travel is less risky than traveling in cars and airplanes, and Amtrak has a solid safety record. Amtrak also has bigger seats and more legroom, so you can sleep through your journey in greater comfort than you can in the sardine-style, coach class seats of an airplane. If, however, you end up in an emergency situation and have to evacuate, the following sections should help you out.

Freeing Yourself by the Doors

The standard Amtrak car is a single-level coach with eight exits you can use in the event of an emergency. There are the basic interior entrances on the north and south ends of the car; the ones you walked through on the way to purchasing snacks. You may have to walk the length of the train if your end is sinking into the bog, so patiently, but expediently, march to the front or rear of the train.

Each coach car also has two doors along the side of the south end of the train. You will recognize these exterior doors because they are the ones you went through upon the call of "all aboard" (at least in old movies). Most survival situations depend on locating the doorways, so find them when you sit down (train travel doesn't include the emergency procedures rundown we all know and love from flying). To open a locked door, find the red plastic handle above the exit and pull down; it should open to the outside instantaneously.

Or Try the Windows ...

Let's say your Amtrak car is being attacked at either end by two man-eating dragons and you want to get out through the window. In the single level coach there are four windows, two on each side, that can be used as emergency exits. The windows have a red plastic handle you pull toward you and use to tear away the rubber molding. There is another metal handle on the window you pull toward you to remove the pane. The window will pop right out. Before exiting, look down the track to ensure no other trains are barreling down the line. Once you're out of the car, move away from the train to a safe distance.

One last safety note: Unless you're a stuntman, a fugitive, a daredevil, or just plain stupid, it should go without saying that you should never leap from a moving train.

Don't Sweat the Personal Possessions

Along those should-go-without-saying lines, don't worry about your luggage in an emergency situation. If possible, grab some identification, but personal items can be replaced and you may be endangering someone else's life by trying to get to your luggage.

Survival Kit

Longer routes have personal sleeper cars and viewing cars with see-through roofs on an upper level, so check the safety brochure for exiting basics if you find yourself on an overnight journey.

SOS

Always look down at the ground before exiting the train. In the event of a natural disaster there may be jagged debris, broken glass, or downed power lines at your feet and escaping from a train is enough excitement for one day. And don't forget, some trains run along cliffs, and unlike the cartoons, if you fall from a cliff you won't hang in suspended animation.

Sit Tight and Wait for the Experts

If the train stops but there is no immediate danger, sit tight and wait for instructions from an Amtrak employee. If the electrical power goes out at night, crack a long-lasting, neon light stick at the middle. They are found in the emergency equipment locker, but it's better to ask a conductor to bring you one.

Adventures of a Lifetime

An earthquake recently caused a train traveling 65 mph to derail near Barstow, California. Fortunately, none of the 24 cars or four engines overturned and a few didn't derail. While the passengers waited for instructions, cellular phones were distributed for folks to call their families and friends, and breakfast was served in the dining car. Buses were dispatched to take passengers to their final destination. It pays to follow the instructions of the crew because emergency management runs a lot smoother without passenger panic. Sometimes being a survivor is all about shutting up and taking orders when they come.

In May 1931, a train bound from Seattle to Chicago was knocked off the tracks by a tornado.

(Photo courtesy of the National Oceanic and Atmospheric Administration [NOAA].)

I'll close this chapter on train safety with this nugget of wisdom: The infamous "third rail" of the New York City subway system is real. Never jump down on the tracks and touch the third rail, the one with the top cover, unless you want to be fried faster than a clam strip at Coney Island.

The Least You Need to Know

➤ Private railroad crossings aren't required to have advance warning signs or other designating markers and are found on roadways that aren't maintained by public administrators or employees.

➤ If you're trying to stop the train, the trick is to use dynamic braking, which impedes the rotation of the tires over a period of time instead of locking them up, which won't work.

➤ Always look down and examine the ground before exiting the train during an emergency because there may be jagged debris, broken glass, or downed power lines at your feet.

➤ If you're on a train that derails, sit tight until you're instructed to leave; then exit using the doors or the windows with the red handles.

➤ Understand that following the instructions from the conductors is the most important survival technique—but also know that trains are the safest way to travel.

Chapter 14

Escaping a Towering Inferno or a Plunging Elevator

In This Chapter

➤ How to handle hazardous material

➤ When all's not well in the stairwell: how to survive a high-rise fire

➤ A tragic tale that led to safety innovations

➤ What to do when you're not "going up" or "going down"

➤ It really was "the bomb": what to do if you receive a suspicious package

Back before Thomas Alva Edison illuminated the world with the light bulb, people weren't forced to work late. They packed up at sundown and called it a day; there was no such thing as reviewing legal cases or rewriting reports until the wee hours of the morning, except for the companies that employed the candle-holder. If a master needed light, he ordered the apprentice to hold a candle for him while he toiled away after hours (in much the same fashion as when you command the intern to make copies). Those apprentices who had trouble handling the taper, or just weren't as talented as the overachieving indentured assistant next to them, were seen as inferior and would be saddled with the label that they *can't hold a candle* to others in their position.

But what if that candle was dropped in the penthouse of a skyscraper, filling the offices and stairwells with smoke, prompting you and your fellow employees to concoct a contingency survival plan? Would you know what to do?

The Hazards of Chemical Dependency

As a nation—check that, as a *world*—we are all chemically dependent. We are all addicted, hooked, habitual abusers of chemicals who are jonesing for our next fix and wouldn't live a day without the synthetic agents. Don't believe me? Try envisioning a world without gasoline, or hair spray, or weed killer, or deodorant, lighter fluid, Tide with bleach, chlorine, antifreeze, car polish, transmission fluid, or any other of the infinite varieties of chemicals that are used in everyday life. The fact of the matter is that around the globe, chemicals are an essential part of existence. Many chemicals are natural and benign, but hundreds of thousands are the enemies of living things and very dangerous.

Chemicals spills, industrial mishaps, and the occasional meltdown are all potential threats to our survival. Pretend you work at Mr. Burns's power plant and one day Homer is too hung over to notice the spill leaking out of sector 7-G and poor Lenny and Carl are trapped in a room filling with toxic ooze, what would you do to save them? It's high time you consider this life-or-death scenario.

Here is what you should do in the event of a major emergency involving hazardous materials, which are most often due to accidents involving transportation or malfunctions at plants:

➤ **Listen to the authorities**. Chemical emergencies conjure up horrible images of Chernobyl, but they are rarely unmanageable. Keep cool and treat it like a natural disaster by listening to the radio or watching television and follow the emergency instructions for your community.

➤ **Get away as soon as possible.** You would probably evacuate instinctively, but the less exposure to the hazardous material, the better. You could be breathing in the toxins without even knowing it, so get out of there without touching any of the chemicals on the ground. Hurry up, because the potential for an explosion is wafting through the air.

SOS

Large-scale chemical spills are frightening, but the small household products should be of greater concern because they cause many more problems. Keep all chemicals locked away from children and pets and contact the Environmental Protection Agency for information about potentially harmful domestic products and their antitoxins.

SOS

If you come into contact with dangerous chemicals, do not touch your eyes because they are highly susceptible to permanent damage. If it's too late, and assuming there has been no official decree on not using water, flush the eye out thoroughly with lukewarm water and seek medical attention immediately.

➤ **Cover your mouth and nose.** Make sure your mouth and nose are tightly covered with a handkerchief, bandanna, surgical mask, or thick cloth. Your mantra should be, "I didn't inhale," because some chemicals can instantly scald your lungs. The best place to regroup is upwind, upstream, upriver, uphill or up, up and away--it will lessen the chances of contamination.

➤ **Don't automatically drag others to safety.** As tough as this may sound, you shouldn't touch anyone who has been affected by hazardous material until those in charge say it is all right. Yes, it's hard to watch a loved one roll around in nuclear waste, but you don't want to contaminate yourself for a hug.

➤ **Ditch contaminated clothes.** Once the high-sign is given that you can touch the afflicted, soak them in cold water to ease any burns. Seal their garments in a leakproof plastic bag and throw it in the garbage. Let's assume all readers of this book are smart enough not to burn underpants or any other items of clothing that have been soaked in hydrochloric acid.

➤ **Cover the vents.** If you are stuck in a building with a noxious gas leak, cover the vents with whatever you can find—electrical tape should do the trick. Turn off all fans and air conditioners as well. Breathe through a wet towel, assuming the water supply is undamaged, and try to take deep inhalations of fresh air from a window.

➤ **Seal the windows.** The opposite holds true if the chemicals are seeping in from outside. Use the tape to seal off all openings to the outside like the windows, doors, or laundry vents. Many chemicals are heavier than air, so go to the top floor and find a room with a single door and no windows.

If you are contaminated by an accident involving chemicals, it is best to see a doctor within 24 hours, even if there are no visible symptoms. If you are buying a house near a manufacturing plant, you should take the time to have your property inspected by an environmental expert. Sound like overkill—paranoia run amok? Maybe so, but Johnathan Harr's excellent book *A Civil Action* (Random House, 1995) would give anyone pause about the dangers of hazardous materials.

"You're Fired!"

It's the two-word sentence no worker ever wants to hear, but even worse is when your boss comes racing down the halls of the 89th floor of the corporate high-rise, yelling, "Fire!" He's trying to tell you that the building is burning, and first-degree burns or massive smoke inhalation trump a pink-slip and an unemployment check every time.

The primary way to combat skyscraper fires is through prevention. The combination of modern technology and stricter building codes have made building fires a rarity in the industrialized world, but they still occur. Old buildings are always at risk as well, because safety precautions weren't as uniform or enforced as they are today.

Unfortunately, almost every innovation and prevention measure comes as the result of a fiery tragedy, such as the widespread installation of smoke alarms and sprinklers in hotel rooms after more than 80 guests died in the 1980 fire at the MGM Grand. Often mistakes are revisited. The ancient Romans used a water pump to combat blazes, but its usage vanished for roughly 1,000 years in which, one could surmise, many unnecessary deaths could have been prevented. Progress is built upon the graves of those who perish in towering infernos.

A 1979 research photo of a fiery oil spill in the Bay of Campeche, Mexico.

(Photo courtesy of the National Oceanic and Atmospheric Administration [NOAA].)

Adventures of a Lifetime

If you've never seen the 1974 disaster classic movie *The Towering Inferno*, it's worth a look and it steamrolls all the ridiculous recent disaster movies, even *Titanic*. For starters, it features an all-star lineup: Paul Newman, Steve McQueen, William Holden, Fred Astaire, Faye Dunaway, Richard Chamberlain, and a man who would find himself in a different kind of heat years later, O.J. Simpson. It's the story of the survival (of some) and daring rescue of people trapped in a burning San Francisco skyscraper. The fire department can't reach the upper floors where the blaze broke out because of cheap, faulty wiring. It's got great special effects, suspense … and did we mention Paul Newman and Steve McQueen? Enough said.

Safety codes now include fire escapes, numerous escape routes, fire alarms, fire-resistant construction materials, and sprinkler systems. Fire-fighting equipment is better also, with pumps that can shoot water over 200 m.p.h. In the United States, the chances are slim of a repeat of the horrific 1942 fire at a Boston nightclub, the Coconut Grove, in which 492 people died in less than 20 minutes. The high number of fatalities primarily stemmed from the fact that the only way in and out was a revolving door, which got jammed with panicked citizens. This tragedy led to the regular doors that now flank all revolving doors.

High-rise fires are still a reality, though, and many older structures still don't have sprinklers. In addition, globalization is sending white-collar workers all over the world, and many countries are ill-equipped to prevent or battle skyscraper infernos. The next time you go to the office, ask yourself these questions: Do I know where the fire extinguisher is? Do I know the escape routes? Are there sprinklers in this building? Do the smoke detectors work? You may have been with IBM since 1958 and never considered what to do in an emergency fire, but it might be worth finding out because prior knowledge of terrain makes survival all the more likely. Take the time to check the basics whenever you stay in a hotel as well, because you may wake to screams in unfamiliar surroundings, but your survivor memory techniques will guide you to safety.

Here's what to do if you get trapped in a high-rise fire:

➤ **Don't panic.** Unfamiliar surroundings make it that much harder to keep your cool, but start by checking the door to make sure it isn't hot. If it's safe to enter the hallway, leadership will be called for and all the strangers who are under duress want to follow you to safety.

➤ **Stay put.** If all stairwells are filled with smoke, shut the doors to the stairwells and head back into a room on the floor. Seal off the room as much as possible, putting wet towels or some kind of protection around the doors and over the vents. Crack any windows slightly at the top and bottom and make a signal for firefighters, like a large "HELP" sign in the window. If the phones are operational or there is a cell phone handy, call 911 and give the operator your exact location within the building because ladders don't reach the 92nd floor and firefighters are going to come looking for you.

➤ **Stay off the ledge.** Fire can move up the exterior of a building, so don't assume that standing on the ledge or a small deck of a building a couple of floors above the blaze is going to save your life. Besides, if you panic because of the fire, there's a good chance you will take a fall and won't survive. Protruding balconies or decks actually keep fires from vertically integrating, but they will get hot, so don't wait out the fire on one unless it is clearly the safest (or only) alternative.

Survival Kit

One simple fire-prevention check that often goes unnoticed and could come back to haunt is the clutter in the stairwells. Look and see if there are piles of junk in the stairwells at your place of work. If so, call maintenance and have them cleared, because it's a violation of the fire code.

Survival Kit

Don't be embarrassed to be the person who organizes a building-wide fire drill for your office, just like in grade school. It may seem corny, but no one will think so if a fire tears through the office and your coworkers know the escape route.

➤ **Stay off the elevator.** The worst decision you can make in a skyscraper fire is to try and escape via the elevator. For one, they tend to malfunction in 1,000° heat and the last place you want to be is stuck in a small compartment that may offer no means of escape and is situated in an area that could fill with smoke quicker than a large floor. Second, automatic sprinklers may cut off the power. Third, heat can trigger call buttons that will send you to the floor where the fire is devouring the office supplies and will literally be your last stop.

➤ **Don't use television shows as your point of reference.** It is virtually impossible to see during a fire, there is no bright flame to act as a guide like on television or in the movies. Be aware that fire spreads quickly and violently, so don't think fire will act like it does in Hollywood blockbusters. Get real, and don't test the powers of fire, even if it was a divine gift to humans from Prometheus. (I mean, come on, should you trust the gift of a guy whose regenerating liver is devoured by an eagle every day?)

➤ **If you can, get to the roof.** As a last resort, you may have to go to the roof of your building, but never consider that your first, safest alternative. It beats sitting in a room that's filling with smoke, but consider the roof a halfway point, not a complete safe haven. It may be possible to be rescued from the roof, but heat can make that impossible, or you could become trapped there. In a tragic Sao Paulo, Brazil, fire in 1974, 179 people perished. The fire was so hot that helicopters couldn't land on the roof to save those who made it to the roof trying to survive.

A Tragic Example: The Triangle Shirtwaist Company Fire

One of the worst workplace fires in American history happened in 1911 at the Triangle Shirtwaist Company in lower Manhattan. Shirtwaists were dresses of the times and the company employed approximately 500 people, mostly young immigrant European women. The job involved long, hard hours for little pay. Shortly before the end of the workday on March 25, a fire started on the eighth floor. The oil from the sewing machines, loose fabric, and other flammable materials set the upper floors ablaze within minutes. The fire department ladders didn't reach that high, and the upper floors became a deathtrap when the poorly constructed fire escape gave way under the weight of the women. A main set of exit doors on the ninth floor had been locked to keep the women working at their machines, and the employees were packed in tight. The stairs filled with smoke and the elevators broke as a result of an overload of passengers.

Women began climbing out on the ledge of the building and as the flames crept closer, they started to jump. There were nets, but many women missed them and soon the nets were ripped apart by the force of the impact. Other women hit the ground or were impaled on a fence as horrified onlookers watched. Bodies littered the street as 146 people died and another 70 were badly injured. The horror lasted less than 20 minutes, but had long-lasting implications for both fire safety codes and union organizing. It is unlikely that a survival situation that forces someone to basically choose between burning or jumping to death would arise in New York City today, in no small part because of the tragedy of the Triangle Shirtwaist Company.

Seeking Elevation

It's hard to imagine the industrial age without elevators. New York City is the prototypical urban elevator paradise. Literally millions of people rely on elevators to get to work every day in the Big Apple alone.

Add all those people up with all the millions of others across the U.S. who pile in every morning, punching buttons and trying not to look like they're staring at the people next to them. What do you get? An entire society that is dependent on these unnatural up-down machines. From the oldest dumbwaiter to the slickest computerized high-speed lift, if we didn't have the elevator—well, we probably wouldn't have skyscrapers (or three-floor walk-ups, for that matter).

My, how we put our trust in these machines. They are no more than large metal boxes held up by a group of steel cables and operated by a series of weights and counterbalances. Seems almost too simple, doesn't it? Too easy. Like the slightest weakness in any of these mechanisms could send us hurtling down toward …

Take the Plunge

Okay, maybe it's not so common. But an elevator dropping ranks up there with airplane crashes as one of the most common unrealized fears of the average person. Which means you can relax. Chances are, it won't happen to you. The following combination of factors would have to occur simultaneously for your elevator to drop full-speed to the bottom of the shaft:

➤ **Cable failure.** And we're not just talking about one cable holding up the car. Most modern elevators have six or more cables attached to them.

➤ **Power failure.** In this age of utility deregulation and power shortages, blackouts are more common. But don't sweat it. Most modern buildings have backup power sources and emergency lights.

➤ **Computer failure.** Modern buildings are computerized. In an emergency such as a fire, elevators can automatically be ordered to the ground floor.

➤ **Brake failure.** All elevators have brake systems in the event of the unthinkable.

SOS

The old saw goes something like this: If your elevator plunges, jump just before impact. Sure. Ladies and gents, if your elevator plunges from any height over two stories, it doesn't matter how high you can jump. You'll just look silly before you die, and who wants that?

What will most likely happen is your car will plunge initially and then be halted by one of the backup systems. So stay calm and control your panic.

On the other hand, elevator plunges do happen. What should you do? It depends on your situation. If it's a short drop—two, maybe three stories—you'll probably survive, although injuries are likely. Brace yourself for impact. Lying on the floor may help, but in the end, you're still in a rapidly moving vehicle without a seat belt. If it's a long fall—more than three stories—there really isn't much you can do. You're just a soft little creature in a big metal box going a hundred miles an hour. If you're lucky, it won't hurt.

If you do happen to survive an elevator plunge, tend to the wounded if you're able. But DO NOT risk injuring yourself further by moving. It's a proven fact that most complications from spinal cord injuries occur *after* an accident, when victims move themselves or others. So stay put and wait for help to arrive. And consider yourself lucky to have survived.

Fire in the Hole

If you happen to be in an elevator that somehow catches on fire, don't panic (assuming you're not personally on fire). Remember that you're dealing with a machine that doesn't care that it's on fire.

1. **Call for help.** Every elevator car is equipped with a communication system, a phone, buzzer, or intercom that will connect you with building officials. Sound the alarm, tell them what's up, and await instructions. In most modern buildings, security will be able to call the car to the ground floor.

2. **Punch buttons.** Assuming the elevator is still functioning, hit the button for the nearest floor. Hit ALL the buttons if you have to. The object is to get the car to stop at a regular floor and open its doors.

3. **Wait.** If all else fails, what other option do you have? The car will have to stop somewhere. A plunge is rare, as we said earlier, so just sit tight.

This last option is fraught with possibilities, such as the car filling with smoke, or the car stopping but the doors not opening. Use common sense as each complication arises. And don't take stupid risks, such as climbing onto the roof of the elevator. That's strictly for actor Bruce Willis, and he gets mad when other people do it.

Anybody Up/Down There?

What if you're in one of *those* buildings? You know the kind I mean. A little seedy. A little gritty. They wallpaper over the bloodstains and bullet holes without so much as an ounce of spackel. Your elevator car stops, the phone is broken, and no one is answering your screeches. What then?

Well, we could make a list as long as your arm of possible leisure-time activities, such as charades, transcendental meditation, and courtship with an attractive stranger. So far, we've enjoyed telling you what to do. But if you're in this situation, the only thing we can do is tell you what *not* to do:

➤ DON'T try to "pry" open the elevator doors. Even if you manage to get both sets open (the car doors and the floor doors), you're at risk. The car could start up again without warning, and you don't want your hands and arms anywhere near an open elevator door when that happens. You'll understand very quickly just how fast these vehicles move.

➤ DON'T try to jump out between floors, say, if you pry those doors open and you have a small window to safety. Again, the car could start up when you're halfway through, crushing you and your hopes.

➤ DON'T climb onto the roof. Again, Mr. Willis could be up there. And he'd be mad. But seriously, what will you do once you're up there? Shimmy up the greasy steel cable system? Or shoot one cable and ride another all the way to the top floor like Keanu Reeves and Carrie Anne Moss in the movie *The Matrix*? Whoa—wrong answer, dude.

Best advice: Once again, stay put and wait for help. Even in one of *those* buildings, someone's eventually going to want to use the elevator.

And check your pocket. You might just have a cell phone in there that you forgot about ....

Bombs Away

The Bruce Willis heroics in the *Die Hard* movies were, without question, impressive, but don't forget that he was a trained professional—one of New York City's finest. Battling terrorists, waging a one-man war, and saving humanity is best left to experts. For average couch potatoes like us, we should consider our sole responsibility to be identifying the bomb and allowing the virtuosos of explosion management to handle the defusing and removal.

Survival Kit

Most well-equipped bomb squads use robots to destroy bombs these days. One of the ways the robots destroy explosive devices is by shooting them in a mechanical, Wild-West show-down.

SOS

If you receive a package that you think is suspicious, DON'T OPEN IT. Call the local bomb authorities to inspect its contents. It may turn out to be nothing, but get it out of your hands, because a little paranoia will ensure you have those very hands and fingers for the rest of your life.

We all became familiar with the "mail bomb" when the ugly antics of the Unabomber (Theodore Kaczynski) were splashed across the front page of newspapers across the country in 1996. Copycats are always a threat and the Internet has made it all too easy to find crude, rudimentary bomb-making techniques. Unfortunately, bombs can be delivered in almost any way, shape, or form, so there is no stereotypical example to use as a standard. Here are some tips on how to recognize a possible mail bomb:

➤ It's unusual to receive a package from an unknown company that includes a handwritten address label and no identifying stickers, letterhead, decals, etc. from the sender. Make sure the company is legitimate before tearing open the package.

➤ Most bombs are delivered by their creators, so if you get a mysterious package, try and write down everything you can remember about the person who dropped it off. Ask around and see if anyone else noticed anything that might aide authorities down the line.

➤ Brown paper packages tied up with string might make Julie Andrews smile, but it should bring a frown of suspicion to your mug. String or twine just isn't commonly used anymore, but woodsy nomads who haven't had contact with the human race in two decades might be unaware of modern packaging tools.

➤ Be wary of packages with odd greetings like "Herrrrreeere's Johnny," "Die, Pig, Die," "This Package is Da' Bomb," or "Gotcha!" In all seriousness, many terrorists have a God complex and want to go down in history, so they leave clues or identifying marks. An odd, cryptic greeting becomes their signature. The Unabomber "autographed" many of his bombs with the initials "FC."

➤ Packages with the following are also suspect: incorrect spellings; scribbled, unreadable handwriting; no return address; stains and leaks; protruding wires; *confidential* instructions, or an excess of postage on a package (which indicates the package wasn't weighed at the post office).

➤ Any time a strange-looking package is delivered, followed by a phone call asking if it was received, and by whom, it is worth taking a second look. Gently check the package for bumps, swellings, protrusions, or any other unusual bulk. If there's any doubt, call the authorities and let them check it out.

Just a Threat?

One afternoon you might innocently answer the receptionist's phone while he's out having a smoke or a doughnut and hear an ominous voice say, "There's a bomb in the building and I'm going to detonate it if I don't get ten million dollars in unmarked bills by end of business today." Okay, maybe the caller won't want a wad of cash, but bomb threats are becoming a regularity. Do you know how to survive the possibility of an unwanted surprise?

If you take a call, try to keep the caller on the line as long as possible and ask for specifics in case it's not a hoax:

1. **Start with the basics:** Where is the bomb? When is it going to go off? What type/style of explosive device is it? How could it be identified? How can it be disarmed?

2. **Move to the personal:** These details may help the authorities find out who is behind the threat. What's your name? Why did you place a bomb in the building? Where are you calling from?

3. **Take notes:** Write down anything that you notice, such as vocal patterns, accents, gender, background noises, mental state, and any other details you think may be relevant (and they all might be relevant).

Once the bomb threat has been issued, call building security and begin evacuation. Alarms won't be sounded for fear of setting off the device, so calmly walk outside and get at least 500 feet from the structure. If you happen to see the bomb on the way out the door, DON'T TOUCH IT. Alert the experts, gather your co-workers and after all that ... call it a day and hit the nearest happy hour.

The Least You Need to Know

➤ If there is a major chemical spill in your area, follow the instructions of authorities, get away from the accident, cover your mouth and nose, and don't touch anyone who may have been contaminated.

➤ The best way to combat hazard materials coming in from the outside is to go to the top floor and find a room with a single door and no windows, because many chemicals are heavier than air.

➤ The worst decision you can make in a skyscraper fire is to try to escape via the elevator.

➤ The Triangle Shirtwaist Fire of 1911 and other tragic fires led to the installation of safety measures such as smoke alarms and sprinkler systems in buildings.

➤ Most elevators are equipped with communication and safety systems, so if you're stranded, the best thing to do is to sit tight and contact building officials.

➤ Most mail bombs are delivered by their creators, so if you get a suspicious package, don't open it and try to write down everything you can remember about the person who dropped it off.

Part 4
Natural Disasters

You've probably heard the saying, "If mama ain't happy, ain't nobody happy." But what about Mother Nature? When Mother Nature is not happy, no one knows better than survivors of tornadoes, hurricanes, earthquakes, and volcanoes.

The chapters in this part will give you the most powerful tool to survive Mother Nature's wrath—knowledge. Nothing will protect you more than recognizing the signs and understanding the facts of what you are about to face. You'll learn how some of Earth's biggest storms are formed, how they're detected, where they occur, and how weather experts classify them.

From there you'll learn what you need to have on hand should the storm be headed your way, and how to survive in your home or car, or—heaven's to Betsy—if you get caught outdoors.

Chapter 15

It's a Twister!
It's a Twister!

In This Chapter

➤ What is a tornado and how does it form?

➤ How you can prepare for a tornado

➤ The difference between a watch and a warning

➤ Fact or fiction? Some common myths about tornadoes

➤ Mapping out a safety plan

American movies have a sneaky way of becoming the reference point for all things. Newspapers describe the rich, powerful, and lonely via *Citizen Kane,* and Ronald Reagan's missile defense fantasy is known as *Star Wars.* The Walt Disney-owned Anaheim hockey franchise co-opted one of its owner's products in a stirring display of corporate synergy when it named the team The Mighty Ducks after its owner's movie. And, of course, there is the famous example of film imagery that is instantly conjured whenever those infamous funnel clouds rip through the Midwest, wreaking havoc and sucking bovine and tractor alike in its voracious swath. That film, of course, is the Helen Hunt/Bill Paxton epic *Twister.*

Oh, right, there was that *other* cinematic classic that was kicked off by a fantastic tornado. If you haven't figured out what it is, here's a hint: "I'll get you, my pretty, and your little dog too!"

If you've ever experienced a tornado, though, you know it isn't the romantic notion *Twister* and *The Wizard of Oz* made it out to be. There are some key strategies everyone in Tornado Alley should know about when preparing for those big winds.

Auntie Em, What's a Twister?

Although tornadoes (also known as twisters) are usually associated with the flatlands of the United States, they can happen anywhere. Tornadoes have whipped through forests, swamps, mountains, deserts, and states from Alaska to Florida and everywhere in between. A tornado is defined as a fiercely rotating column of air extending from a thunderstorm to the ground. In order for a vortex to be officially classified as a tornado it has to be in contact with the cloud base and the land. The picture in your head of the ominous funnel cloud isn't always the case because some tornadoes don't have a visible funnel; however, the powerful rotating winds associated with tornadoes are a reality and can reach speeds of 250 mph or more. The average tornado is less than 50 yards wide and touches down for a short time, but a violent tornado can damage anything in a path 1 mile wide and 50 miles long.

Survival Kit

Don't take violent tornado warnings lightly; they constitute only 2 percent of all tornadoes but are responsible for 70 percent of deaths.

Born of a Thunderstorm

Tornadoes germinate from severe thunderstorms in warm, moist, unstable air along and ahead of cold fronts. In addition to tornadoes, these thunderstorms may generate large hail and damaging winds in a rough-weather smorgasbord. Winter and early spring tornadoes are often associated with strong frontal systems that develop in the central United States and then head east. Strong springtime weather patterns often support tornado development and major outbreaks rip through the heartland. During the late spring in the Central Plains, thunderstorms with the potential for tornadoes form along a "dryline," which separates very warm, moist air to the east from hot, dry air to the west. Tornadoes also develop along the front range of the Rocky Mountains southward into the Texas Panhandle, as unstable air from the ground flows "upslope" to higher ground.

A horizontal spinning effect is created before thunderstorms develop when winds change direction and ratchet up their speed and height. The rising air in a thunderstorm shifts the rotating air from a horizontal to a vertical plane, which becomes an area of rotation that spreads throughout the thunderstorm. The atmospheric conditions required for the formation of a tornado include extensive thermal instability, high humidity, and the convergence of warm, moist air at low levels with cooler, drier air aloft. The most destructive and lethal tornadoes occur from supercells, rotating thunderstorms with a well-defined radar circulation called a mesocyclone.

Adventures of a Lifetime

Tornadoes also develop in tropical storms and hurricanes as they move over land. Tornadoes are usually to the right and ahead of the path of the storm center as it moves ashore. In 1967, Hurricane Beulah caused the second largest tornado outbreak on record, spawning 115 tornadoes. As if that wasn't enough, there are weaker tornadoes called waterspouts that develop over warm water, common in the Southeast and along the Gulf Coast. These aren't officially tornadoes until they hit land, but they can still cause extensive damage.

A tornado tears through farm country.

(Photo courtesy of the National Oceanic and Atmospheric Administration/National Climatic Data Center [NOAA].)

Interestingly, the size of a tornado is not related to its strength. Slender, destructive "rope" tornadoes can inflict more damage than a big, bloated, half mile-wide "wedge" tornado.

155

The 10 Deadliest Tornadoes in United States History

Area(s) Hit	Date	Number of Fatalities
Tri-state: Missouri/ Illinois/Indiana	March 18, 1925	695
Natchez, Mississippi	May 6, 1840	317
St. Louis, Missouri	May 27, 1896	255
Tupelo, Mississippi	April 5, 1936	216
Gainesville, Georgia	April 6, 1936	203
Woodward, Oklahoma	April 9, 1947	181
Amite, Louisiana/Purvis, Mississippi	April 24, 1908	143
New Richmond, Wisconsin	June 12, 1899	117
Flint, Michigan	June 8, 1953	115
Waco, Texas	May 11, 1953	114

There is no rock-solid scientific explanation as to why tornadoes dissipate, but it has to do with a loss of instability like heat or the loss of its strong rotation. There are numerous systems in and around a thunderstorm that could weaken a tornado. Scientists have noted how tornadoes frequently die when their mesocyclones become engulfed in outflow air, which is the flow of wind out of the precipitation area of the thunderstorm. The severity of tornadoes, as a measure of the damage they cause, is rated on the *F-scale* (Fujita scale).

So now that you know what a tornado is, what can you do to keep from getting swept away to Oz?

SOS

Don't assume that certain properties define a tornado. While wind, rain, hail, and lightning can certainly be a part of a tornado, they are not a reliable predictor of a tornado, even though large hail is frequently a good indicator that a twister is on its way. Characteristics vary from storm to storm and can change at any turn or at any time.

Preparing for a Tornado

Tornadoes are normally smaller than other natural disasters like hurricanes or earthquakes, but they still wreak havoc, and death and destruction can be part of their makeup. There are lots of old wives' tales when it comes to combating tornadoes, but there are also simple ways to prepare for the mighty, and not so mighty, twisters. If you follow these simple preparations, your chances of severe damage will be greatly reduced.

Tactical Terms

Meteorologist Tetsuya Fujita created the **F-scale,** which ranks tornadoes from F0 (light: 40 to 72 mph winds and minor damage) to F4 (devastating: 207 to 260 mph and walls ripped from homes) to F6 (inconceivable: 319 to 379 mph with cars flying through the air like missiles). Although the F-scale is the most widely used gauge of a tornado's strength, wind speeds are an untested, estimated guess, and damage ratings are an arbitrary judgment call.

Know the Likelihood of Tornadoes in Your Area

We have already established that tornadoes can occur in any state, but there are spots in the United States where they are more common. "Tornado Alley" is the nickname for the broad swath of high-risk tornado occurrences across the Central Plains. If you are a resident of Oklahoma City, congratulations, you live in the city hit by the most tornadoes.

In the northern states, peak tornado occurrence is during the summer, while in the southern states, March to May is the peak time. In western states, the total number of tornadoes may be undercounted because of the patchy population of many areas.

Tornadoes Don't Come Out of Nowhere

Different communities have different warning systems, but no matter where you are there will almost always be ample time to ready yourself for the onslaught of a tornado. First off, pay attention to the National Oceanic and Atmospheric Administration (NOAA) Weather Radio, TV's Weather Channel, or any local media outlet for ongoing updates. Warnings from Weather Service personnel are relayed to local emergency departments and public officials and they in turn let the communities know, many via outdoor sirens. Not all communities use sirens, but all counties and parishes will be announced over the radio when a tornado warning has been issued.

Survival Kit

Although tornadoes can strike at any time, they are most likely to occur between the hours of 3 to 9 P.M.

Know the Storm Categories

It is also important to familiarize yourself with the four storm categories, so you know roughly how the situation is progressing. A *severe thunderstorm watch* means that thunderstorms are possible in your area. A *severe thunderstorm warning* means that they have begun in the vicinity. Tornadoes can develop in areas where there are severe thunderstorm watches and warnings, so monitor their development. A *tornado watch* means that tornadoes are possible in your area, and a *tornado warning* means a twister has been sighted or picked up on weather radar in your area, and it's time to get into safety mode. Having a detailed regional map handy is also helpful to track the storm as reports become available.

Look to the Sky

Once a tornado warning has been issued, the best indicator of a potential tornado is the threatening sky, which will become dark, and often green, a natural phenomena due to hail. There may be a lowering of the base of a thunderstorm (a wall cloud) and if it's rotating, it's telling you that a tornado is brewing. We have mentioned funnel clouds and large hail, which are a reliable, but not foolproof, indicator of tornadoes and the same can be said for a loud roar that is often likened to the sound of a freight train.

Survival Kit

A swirling cloud of debris can mark the beginning of a tornado, even if there is no visible funnel cloud.

Once tornadoes develop, they may not be visible to the naked eye, so don't rely solely on the binoculars in your tackle box. Some tornadoes are formed on the trailing edge of a thunderstorm and readily visible, as are the clear, sunny skies behind them. Other times, tornadoes may be encased in rain and you won't see them at all. Now would be a good time to keep the safety kit(s) handy that I mention in Chapter 1, "The Will to Survive," and the tearcard at the front of this book. Keep your battery-operated radio tuned in to updates on the storm. With tornadoes it pays to stay glued to weather reports because they often change speeds, direction, and intensity faster than you can click your heels three times and say "There's no place like home."

Ready the Ol' Homestead

The Federal Emergency Management Agency (FEMA) recommends enhancing building construction to minimize property damage to homes in areas prone to moderate to severe tornadoes. FEMA's advice includes …

➤ Use common connections in wood frame buildings, such as anchors, clips, and straps to provide a continuous load path for all loads—not just gravity loads.

➤ Reinforce masonry walls that provide structural support to a building to resist gravity, lateral, and uplift loads.

➤ Because garage doors are highly susceptible to wind damage, retrofit existing garage doors to improve the wind resistance, particularly double-wide garage doors. Use of retrofits and installation of new reinforced doors should better resist wind forces and, as a result, reduce roof and wall damage.

➤ Secure your chimney. Masonry chimneys that extend more than 6 feet above the roof or have a width of 40 inches or more, should have continuous vertical reinforcing steel placed in the corners to provide greater resistance to wind loads.

➤ Install permanent foundations with double-wide manufactured housing because it performs better than both double-wide and single units on nonpermanent foundations. Of those manufactured houses on nonpermanent foundations, double-wide units appear to offer a greater level of protection. This is because these units are harder to overturn and have interior rooms, while rooms in single units all have at least one exterior wall.

For more suggestions on how to reinforce your house for protection against tornadoes, check out FEMA's Web site www.fema.gov, which also features news, public service announcements, photographs, archives, and more of the organization that handles the aftermath of natural disasters.

Hit or Myth?

For whatever reason, superstition abounds for how to handle tornadoes. Here are a few of the standard myths and what you should *really* do in the presence of a tornado:

➤ **Myth #1: Get into the southwest corner of your house for safety.** Not true. The southwest corner isn't any safer than other corners. In fact, debris tends to collect in the corners and it is best to get in a small room, like a bathroom, away from windows, on the lowest level, in the center of the house.

➤ **Myth #2: If you are driving and see a tornado, turn and drive at right angles to the storm.** Ummm, don't do that. Tornadoes don't necessarily travel in a straight line. You might not be able to determine where the storm originated, and there could be another tornado within the rains of the thunderstorm. The worst thing that could happen is you could drive onto a road that curves right into the tornado and you will be dropped off a good 100 miles from home. People in automobiles are in the greatest danger, so get out of your car and head for the closest building or house. If there are none to be found, lie down on the ground in an area that won't flood and cover your head and neck.

➤ **Myth #3: You'll be safe as long as you are at a high altitude on a mountain.**
No you won't. Just so you know, in the late 1980s, a violent tornado in the
Grand Tetons of Wyoming kicked nature around like a rented mule at 10,000
feet above sea level.

➤ **Myth #4: If a tornado is coming, open the windows because the air pressure
will cause your house to explode.** Pressures are not strong enough to blow up
your house, but the powerful winds and the flying debris will ruin your good
drapes (and a whole bunch of other stuff) if you leave the windows open. Make
sure you and your family take cover far from any windows in case broken glass
starts whipping around the living room.

➤ **Myth #5: Tornadoes can skip across the pavement like a schoolgirl.** Tornado
"skipping" is often mentioned but always inaccurate. To be a tornado, the vortex must touch the ground; when it isn't touching, it isn't a tornado. If there is
a brief separation it means that there are multiple tornadoes because each time
one touches down it is a separate twister.

➤ **Myth #6: A hill or river offers a town protection from a tornado.** This is a
tall tale told by townsfolk to teeter the truth, but even if it's heartfelt, it's not
true. If you reside in a lower-risk area, consider yourself lucky, but nothing
more. The deadliest tornado in history, the infamous tri-state tornado of 1925,
scoffed at the Mississippi River and brought its appetite for destruction across
the Old Muddy.

Adventures of a Lifetime

If you are really craving the adventure of a lifetime, go to www.stormchasers.org. This is
the group that drives around after tornadoes, even if they are nowhere near as reckless as
the Hollywood hot shots in *Twister*. The best way to become a member of the group is
to take a serious interest in meteorology and hook up with scientists devoted to the
weather. There are also spotter meetings (for those who watch and don't chase) at the
National Weather Service office near you. The stormchasers' Web site is loaded with all
the information you'll need to get as up close and personal with a funnel cloud as you
care to be.

A Storm's a'Brewin': Your Safety Plan

Before a tornado comes knocking at the front door, it's best if you and your family have already mapped out a safety plan and held drills practicing what to do during the perilous weather situation. Once again, the primary gathering location should be the designated area in the lowest level of your house away from the windows. You are probably familiar with those wooden storm doors in farmhouses that lead to underground shelter, but your remodeled basement will do just fine. The key is to put as many walls as possible between yourself and the twister. The closer the walls in the room, the better, because they provide more support to the roof. In a violent tornado, the floor of a downstairs closet, bathroom, or pantry is a good place to lie down and take cover.

Here are a few other pre-storm suggestions:

➤ If you live in a mobile home, skedaddle, even if it is just over to the trailer park's designated shelter. Mobile homes are very vulnerable to high winds and prior to 1994, most manufactured homes (similar, but anchored to a permanent foundation) weren't built to handle winds either.

➤ Make sure your children understand that taking cover in a school, dugout, or restroom is the most important thing if they are ever caught outside (in a playground, at an amusement park, on a baseball diamond) and a tornado is approaching. Tornadoes are unstable and can move very quickly. Flying debris is a major concern, so stay away from trees or areas filled with objects, like a junkyard. Make sure they cover their heads, even indoors, with whatever they have at their disposal. It is also a good idea to teach them to get under a large piece of furniture and hold on tight if they are in a room with a lot of windows or heavy objects.

➤ Check with your child's school to ensure that every teacher knows the tornado policy, which is usually to bring the students into the inner hallway. Every school should be inspected, and designated tornado shelter locations should be assigned by a registered engineer or architect. Ask whether the school's alarm system is electric, in which case a battery-powered megaphone, a compressed air horn, or a loud, high-pitched whistle should be considered the alarm during power outages.

Adventures of a Lifetime

If you are feeling a bit paranoid about the upcoming tornado season, be glad it isn't April 3–4, 1974. In a 24-hour span, 148 twisters touched down in 13 states (one in Canada), with 23 rated F4 and seven rated F5. Three hundred nineteen people perished overall in the greatest outbreak of tornadoes in recorded history.

➤ I can't say this enough: If you and your family are in a car and you see, or hear on the radio, that a tornado is imminent, *get out of the car now!* Automobiles are death traps in tornado winds. You will be much safer lying flat on the ground and letting the flying debris pass over your head. A common and sometimes fatal mistake people make is to try to outrun a tornado in their cars.

However, if traffic is light and the tornado is still far enough away, you can probably drive out of the tornado's path. Watch the twister intently for a few moments compared to a fixed object in the foreground (such as a billboard, lamppost, or tree). If the tornado appears to be moving to your right or left, it is not moving toward you. If the tornado appears to stay in the same place, growing larger or getting closer and isn't moving horizontally in either direction, it's bearing down, baby, and you best hop out of your car and take cover.

➤ Long before a storm encroaches your personal space, make a list of outdoor items that are likely to get tossed through the wind like a Nerf football. Keep it handy so things like firewood, birdhouses, lawn gnomes, gardening tools, and so on won't be overlooked when you're securing the house. Removing dead branches allows for better wind passage and keeps them from breaking off and crashing through the bay window. Installing permanent outdoor shutters might infringe on your Saturday afternoon college football-nachos-and-Heineken routine, but it's time well spent. They can be closed in a hurry and can be a godsend in protecting windows.

A tornado hits Alfalfa, Oklahoma, on May 22, 1981.

(Photo courtesy of The National Severe Storms Laboratory.)

➤ Do not take shelter under a bridge or an overpass, because the bridge may well collapse in a tornado. People also suffer severe injuries when flying debris zips through the spaces between bridge and grade. It is understood why grabbing onto a girder would seem like a solid idea, but a powerful gust under a bridge could send you into the tornado itself and someone will probably find your body in the next town over. Folks on bridges have also been known to get plowed over by truckers attempting to beat the tornado to the next town … which wouldn't make for a half-bad country tune.

➤ Make sure your NOAA Weather Radio has an alarm tone alert to keep you abreast of all tornado watches and warnings in your area. All media outlets relay the same information, but the tone alert automatically lets you know what is happening (unless you forget to install fresh batteries as a backup or that darned squirrel chews through the cord).

Although the science for predicting tornadoes has become much more efficient and reliable in recent years, tornadoes are still unpredictable forces of nature in many ways. They often leave behind a wide swath of destruction and the property damage bills have reached nine digits on more than one occasion. If you follow the directions in this chapter, your home may sustain damage, but you and your loved ones will be safe and sound … and somewhere over the rainbow you can always go see the wizard about rebuilding.

The Least You Need to Know

➤ A tornado is defined as a fiercely rotating column of air extending from a thunderstorm to the ground.

➤ Tornadoes are very common in the Central Plains, but they have touched down nearly everywhere at one time or another.

➤ Take cover in the lowest level of your house away from any windows when a tornado pays a visit.

➤ Automobiles are the worst place to be in during a tornado. If you see a tornado that's bearing down on you, get out of your car, lay flat on the ground in a spot where you won't have to worry about drowning, and cover your head.

➤ Make sure you and your family have an established safety plan in the event a tornado strikes.

Chapter 16

The "Eyes" Have It: Surviving a Hurricane

In This Chapter

➤ Here comes the story of the hurricane

➤ The eerie calm of the eye of the storm

➤ Hurricane watch or warning: what's the danger?

➤ Where to take shelter

Do the following names strike fear in your heart? Andrew, Hugo, Frederick, Juan, Alicia, Betsy, Agnes (*Agnes*, for plum's sake?)?

Of course these common monickers wouldn't scare anyone, right? But put the word *hurricane* in front of them, and suddenly tragic memories of loss, death, destruction, and the brute force of tropical cyclones give these innocent names a whole new meaning.

In this chapter you'll not only learn what causes those names to instill fear in the hearts of even the bravest, but what to do if you find yourself stuck in the middle of swirling wind, water, and horrible flooding.

What's Depressing About the Tropics?

The word hurricane is derived from Spanish and Caribbean words for evil spirits and massive winds, which sums up the awesome force that these storms unleash on Earth. A hurricane is the strongest type of tropical cyclone, which is the standard term for all circulating weather systems over tropical waters. There are three classifications of tropical cyclones:

Tactical Terms

Trade winds are any of the nearly constant easterly winds that dominate most of the tropics and subtropics throughout the world, blowing mainly from the northeast in the Northern Hemisphere, and from the southeast in the Southern Hemisphere.

1. **Tropical depression.** This is a system of clouds and thunderstorms with a specified circulation and winds that don't exceed 38 mph, or 33 knots. (It is not the feeling Midwesterners get when they hear a Jimmy Buffet ditty in mid-January.)

2. **Tropical storm.** Depression begets anger, and the tropical storm is also a depression except it has winds of 39 to 73 mph, or 34 to 63 knots.

3. **Hurricane.** A tropical storm that turns into an intense weather phenomenon is known as a hurricane in the Atlantic Ocean, Caribbean Sea, or Gulf of Mexico; a typhoon in the western Pacific; and a cyclone in the Indian Ocean. These intense storms feature well-defined circulation and severe, sustained winds that exceed 74 mph, 64 knots, and can even get as high as 200 mph.

Hurricanes are solidly coiled weather systems that arise from the tropical waters and the atmosphere. Hurricanes start over the oceans as a collection of storms in the tropics. The low-pressure center takes in moist air and thermal energy from the ocean surface, convection lifts the air, and high pressure upwards in the atmosphere pushes it outward. Hurricanes are driven by the easterly *trade winds* and the temperate westerlies, as well as their incredible, internal energy.

Tactical Terms

The **eye** of the storm is the very center of the hurricane, a place that is incredibly calm with little precipitation and light winds.

A mature hurricane is almost a perfect circle and can grow to encompass an area of 500 miles. Near the core of the hurricane, winds grow with greater velocity, producing violent seas. The surface air spirals inward (counterclockwise in the Northern Hemisphere and clockwise in the Southern Hemisphere), converging on a circle of about 20 miles in diameter that surrounds the hurricane's center. At the hub of the tropical cyclone, however, is the *eye* of the storm, an area of light winds with little precipitation and a total calm.

A storm surge is a large dome of water often 50 to 100 miles wide that sweeps across the coastline near where a hurricane makes landfall. The surge of high water topped by waves becomes a waterlogged wrecking crew, especially in a strong hurricane and shallow water. If the storm surge arrives at the same time as the high tide, the water height will be even greater. A storm tide is the clash of the storm surge and the basic astronomical tide, which, let's say, adds 12 feet to a standard 3-foot tide, creating a devastating 15-foot embankment of water. A few sobering examples: In 1969, Hurricane Camille produced a 25-foot storm tide in Mississippi. This was nearly matched in 1989, when Hurricane Hugo produced a 20-foot storm tide in South Carolina. And in 1970, 300,000 people died mainly by drowning from a Bay of Bengal tropical cyclone.

Torrential rains, tornadoes, and flying debris are other hazards that arise when hurricanes descend upon landlubbers.

The Saffir-Simpson Hurricane Scale

Most tropical storms never become hurricanes, and even fewer strike the United States coastline because they die out over the ocean. Scientists predict that roughly five hurricanes will hit the U.S. every three years, and only two will develop into full-blown major hurricanes by the definition of the Saffir-Simpson Hurricane Scale.

The Saffir-Simpson Hurricane Scale rates hurricanes from categories one through five in order of increasing intensity based on the conditions of four criteria: barometric pressure, wind speed, storm surge, and damage potential:

➤ **Level 1—Minimal:** Has winds of 74 to 95 mph and a storm surge of 3 to 5 feet. It can cause minor damage to unanchored mobile homes, trees, and shrubbery.

➤ **Level 2—Moderate:** Has winds of 96 to 110 mph and a storm surge of 6 to 8 feet. It will knock down some trees and cause extensive damage to mobile homes, and flooding of coastal roads and low-lying exit routes.

➤ **Level 3—Extensive:** Has winds of 111 to 130 mph and a storm surge of 9 to 12 feet. It will cause structural damage to some small buildings and trigger the evacuation of coastal areas.

➤ **Level 4—Extreme:** Has winds of 131 to 155 mph and a storm surge of 13 to 18 feet. Significant damage to homes is likely, with possible flooding of low-lying areas as far as 6 miles inland.

➤ **Level 5—Catastrophic:** Has winds greater than 155 mph and a storm surge higher than 18 feet. A hurricane of this magnitude will destroy small buildings and require the evacuation of all residents in low-lying areas within 5 to 10 miles of shore.

A hurricane watch is issued when there is the possibility of hurricane conditions within 24 to 36 hours. A hurricane warning is issued when hurricane conditions, 74-mph winds, and/or rough and high seas, are expected in the designated area within 24 hours. As soon as a hurricane reaches level 3, start preparing for the potential of a level 5.

Satellite photo of Hurricane Camille in 1969.

(Courtesy of the National Oceanic and Atmospheric Administration [NOAA]/ National Climatic Data Center [NCDC].)

A hurricane can last from 24 hours to a full month. The danger posed by hurricanes is less today than it was in previous generations because of advances in forecasting and emergency preparedness.

Name That Hurricane

Hurricanes are assigned proper names because it's easier to identify and understand their movement with a short, distinctive handle. Once a name is used, that name is retired and never used again. For many years, hurricanes in the West Indies were named according to the saint's feast day on the day of the storm. Eventually, a nineteenth century Australian weather scientist, Clement Wragge, began referring to tropical storms by women's names, which was standard practice until 1978, when manly names were assigned to Eastern North Pacific storm lists. In 1979, both sexes were represented in lists for the Atlantic and Gulf of Mexico.

Adventures of a Lifetime

Only two level 5 hurricanes have ever hit the United States since the advent of keeping records of the storms. In 1935 a Labor Day hurricane devastated the Florida Keys, killing 600 people, and in 1969 Hurricane Camille pounded the Mississippi coast, killing 256 people, causing damage estimated at $1.4 billion, and providing a bountiful shrimp haul for everyone involved.

Costliest U.S. Hurricanes

Name	Area Hit	Year	Estimated Damages (Rounded to Closest $100 Million)
Andrew	Florida/Louisiana	1992	$30,500,000,000
Hugo	South Carolina	1989	$8,500,000,000
Agnes	Northeastern states	1972	$7,500,000,000
Betsy	Florida/Louisiana	1965	$7,400,000,000
Camille	Mississippi/Alabama	1969	$6,100,000,000

Deadliest Recorded Western Hemisphere Hurricanes

Name	Area Hit	Year	Estimated Deaths
Great Hurricane	Martinique/Barbados	1780	22,000
Mitch	Honduras/Nicaragua	1998	11,000
Texas	Galveston Island, Texas	1900	8,000
Fifi	Honduras	1974	8,000
Dominican Republic	Dominican Republic	1930	8,000

Preparing for Hurricane Season

The time to plan for a hurricane is not when a gale blows in the front door, or even when the first storm-watch bulletin is issued from some well-coifed local news anchor. The time to prepare for a hurricane is a month or two prior to the tropical storm season, say April or May, when the sun is shining and all is right with the world.

When planning for any possible hurricane here are some things to consider:

➤ **Learn the history of hurricanes in your area.** Looking at the past can help ensure your future, because weather patterns are often relatively similar from year to year. Check to see what the surge of the storm was like in your neighborhood in years past and whether the local elevation is high enough to avoid danger.

➤ **Pinpoint the safest escape routes.** Ask those who have evacuated the area during previous storms to find out if there are roads less traveled. It is also important to have an up-to-date map in case alternative routes become necessary. Many coastal regions have exploded during the last decade and a hand-drawn chart of the Confederate States of America won't cut it.

Survival Kit

If you plan on staying at a shelter, make sure that it's on the up-and-up. Checking it out beforehand is recommended, but if that isn't possible, find an official shelter run by a reputable organization like the Red Cross. Unfortunately, there are always a few con artists who view a natural disaster as Mother Nature's cash cow.

SOS

When a hurricane watch is issued, be extra prepared to evacuate if you live in a mobile home, along the coast, on a small island, in the immediate vicinity of a river or a flood plain, or on the upper floors of a high-rise building. Hurricane winds are fiercer at higher elevations and don't care if you live in the lap of luxury.

➤ **Select an evacuation destination.** Have a few places in mind in case you need to evacuate. Hotels, motels, friends' inland homes, or nearby relatives are all logical places to head during a hurricane, but have a contingency plan in case all the motels are booked or your friends are not home.

➤ **Shutter those windows.** Buy hurricane shutters or half-inch plywood boards to cover the windows of your home and business. Stocking up beforehand is important because there is always a run on plywood when a hurricane warning is issued. Make sure to install braces or anchors for the plywood, and drill holes in the wood so it can quickly be fastened when the conditions worsen. While you're at it, check the rain gutters and down spouts to make sure they're secure. Unclog them so they don't get backed up and weighed down.

➤ **Check your trees.** Go through the trees in your yard and remove dead and diseased branches. Trimming dead or weak branches will allow the wind to blow through the tree and lessen the chance of damage to your home and the tree itself.

The Hurricane Watch

Now that you're generally prepared for the hurricane season, let's break it down to the specifics. Once the National Oceanic and Atmospheric Administration (NOAA) Weather Service issues a hurricane watch, it will be repeated on TV's Weather Channel, local television and radio stations, over the Internet, or by every neighbor within shouting distance. Keep close tabs on how the hurricane is progressing. It's during the watch-and-wait phase that taking precautionary measures is most important. By the time the hurricane watch is upgraded to a hurricane warning, it may be too late to do anything. With that in mind, make sure to ...

➤ Gas up (and service) the family car.

➤ Bring in lawn furniture, garbage cans, Christmas decorations (which you really should have taken down months ago anyway), hanging plants, wind chimes, tire swings—anything that could get caught up in the gales and inflict property damage.

➤ If you live in a mobile home, check the tie-downs, but keep in mind that mobile homes are relatively unsafe in high winds no matter how well you batten down the hatches.

➤ Begin covering your windows, doors, and any other openings with shutters or the plywood a weather-wise person like yourself cut in advance for the impending hurricane season (see the previous section). Make sure all sliding glass doors are securely wedged.

➤ If you have a boat, anchor it (use extra lines) in a protected cove or arrange to have it hauled out and stored inside a building (such as a boatyard). You should make arrangements with the boatyard ahead of time to do this, as space will fill up fast before a hurricane.

SOS

Don't tape your windows. Tape won't keep the glass from breaking, and it's an enormous pain in the neck to get off. Ever tried to remove duct tape residue from a windowpane?

➤ Move vehicles such as motor homes, motorcycles, or cars (unless you plan to use them to evacuate) inside a garage or other building.

➤ Stock up on bottled water, candles, batteries, medicines, prescription drugs, canned food, and first-aid supplies (review the emergency kit suggestions in Chapter 1, "The Will to Survive," and the tearcard at the front of this book). Put aside some cash, too.

The Hurricane Warning

Once a hurricane warning is issued, it's time to get serious, because the storm is going to hit within a day's time. The most important thing to keep in mind is, *if official bulletins are issued urging evacuation, then leave.* Some lifelong dwellers of coastal regions think it's better to stay put and ride out the storm rather than get stuck in traffic while fleeing a hurricane. Proximity to the ocean and how high you live are the most important considerations, because residents of either category are more susceptible to damage. Even so, it's somewhat mind-boggling how many citizens refuse to follow evacuation orders and stay at home to take on the hurricane *mano a mano.* Whether to leave or not is up to you, but an evacuation order should never be taken lightly.

If you do evacuate, try to leave early in the morning to ensure the maximum hours of daylight.

During a hurricane warning you should also do the following:

Survival Kit

Never drive down flooded roads; if you come upon one, turn around and find an alternate route. If you happen to get stuck on a flooded road, get everyone out of the car and follow Stevie Wonder's advice: Keep on running until you reach the higher ground.

➤ Move all valuables upstairs.

➤ Fill as many containers as possible (bathtubs, basins, jugs, piggy banks, balloons) with drinking water, unless you bought out all the bottled water at your closest Wal-Mart.

➤ Take out all the candles and blankets in your home in case the electricity is knocked out or shut down at the source. Turn up the refrigerator to maximum cold so food will keep as long as possible and open the refrigerator only when necessary.

➤ Turn off all minor appliances, propane tanks, and utilities when officials order you to do so.

➤ Make prior arrangements for the family pets in the event of an evacuation.

➤ Move the family to the downwind side of the house and make sure everyone *stays away from the windows*. Tornadoes can spring up during a hurricane, so it's best to stay in the center of your home. As the winds get stronger, go to an interior first-floor room or the lower floors of a high-rise.

Gimme Shelter

For argument's sake, let's assume the majority of citizens is sharp enough to obey the evacuation orders and take cover at a designated shelter. Shelters provide many necessities, but there are still preparations that you should make to ensure the smooth transition from home to shelter. The hurricane will end, but in the meantime, your stay at the shelter will be more pleasant if you take a few simple steps:

➤ Notify a family member of your plans before leaving so he or she can update loved ones.

➤ Put out ample food and water for your pets, because public health regulations forbid pets at public shelters. Many hotels and motels don't allow pets either, so if you want to ensure your pet's safety, put it in an animal shelter or take it to stay with friends or family well before the hurricane hits.

➤ Lock up the house, because believe it or not, looters have been known to refer to dastardly winds as divine windfalls.

➤ Bring valuable papers with you, especially *insurance forms!* Trust me, insurance will provide more comfort than a Green Beret's jungle-strength raincoat. It's also a good idea to bring enough water for three days, food that won't spoil, and a sleeping bag, change of clothes, and an extra pair of shoes for each family member.

➤ Besides the essentials, don't be afraid to take cards, board games, and books to the shelter in case you and the other hurricane homeless end up having to kick back for a few days or weeks.

➤ Relax, relax, relax. Once you and your family are safe and sound at the shelter, let Mother Nature run her course and wait until the hurricane loses its energy and becomes a puny rainstorm.

Adventures of a Lifetime

Here's an amusing Hurricane Andrew anecdote that won't be found on any Red Cross recommendations list. A Dade County couple were put out of their home in 1992 and went to stay in their local shelter. What did they contribute to the community chest? Eight cases of Budweiser, which may not be an "essential," but was probably the most welcome sight this side of the National Guard.

The Calm During the Storm?

When a hurricane touched down in Springfield (state unknown), Homer J. Simpson of TV's *The Simpsons* walked outside his house and noted that it was "eerily calm," and he was right. Homer was smack-dab in the eye of the hurricane. Always be aware that the eye is deceptive and can lull the unsuspecting homeowner into a false sense of security. In fact, the most dangerous part of a hurricane occurs after the eye passes over and winds quickly pick up and blow from the opposite direction. Damaged property, wounded trees, and objects that were broken during the first go-round can be totally decimated or knocked around, like a kitten bats a ball of yarn, during the second go-round.

There Went the Story of the Hurricane

Once the hurricane has subsided and been downgraded to an annoying (but welcome) downpour, you aren't out of harm's way just yet. Even if you have severe cabin fever (and a strong urge to shower) try to wait until NOAA Weather Radio and local officials ensure that it is safe to return to a specific area. Some other things to keep in mind while taking the long way home are ...

Adventures of a Lifetime

One of the ways you'll know things are getting back to normal is if you see an ibis flying overhead. According to folklore, the ibis is the bird other birds look to for guidance during a hurricane because of its natural instincts. The *ibis* is often the last sign that dangerous weather is upon us— and the first bird to appear after a hurricane to welcome the clear skies.

➤ Avoid weakened bridges and flooded areas. It takes only a few inches of moving water to knock you off your feet. Plus, standing water may be charged from downed power lines.

➤ Keep an eye out for dangling and downed electrical wires on the road, in the yard, and on the roof of your home.

➤ Use flashlights, not candles, when first examining your home for gas leaks and other damages.

➤ Don't tie up telephone lines unless there is a serious emergency you need to report, because people with graver situations may not be able to get phone service if everyone jumps on the horn to tell cousin Johnny how *awesome* the hurricane was.

➤ Don't drink or cook with tap water until you know that it's not contaminated, and check all food for spoilage.

Hurricanes make a statement, that's for sure, but the awesome fury created by tropical cyclones can be handled with a little preparation, some solid window shutters, and an umbrella made of Kevlar.

The destruction wrought by Hurricane Andrew.

(Photo courtesy of the National Oceanic and Atmospheric Administration [NOAA]/National Climatic Data Center [NCDC].)

The Least You Need to Know

➤ A hurricane is the strongest type of tropical cyclone (74 mph winds and up), which is the standard term for all circulating weather systems over tropical waters.

➤ Making preparations during the off-season will lead to fewer worries as hurricane watches turn into warnings and then into massive storms.

➤ Pay close attention to reports by the National Weather Service. When you are told to evacuate, leave!

➤ Don't be fooled by the calm eye of the hurricane; dangerous weather will return before you know it.

➤ When you return home, keep an eye out for downed power lines and don't drink or cook with tap water until you know for sure it isn't contaminated.

Chapter 1

Quaking in Your Boots

In This Chapter

➤ What's an earthquake?

➤ Preparing for the big shakedown

➤ When you find yourself in the midst of it all

➤ Cleaning up after the shock

Residents of the Shaanxi Province of China crawled into bed on January 23, 1556, ready to catch 40 winks before rising to face another long day. No one suspected what would happen. Eight hundred and thirty thousand people would die that night in the most intense natural disaster in history. An earthquake, registering an 8.0 on the Richter scale, hit the densely packed area around Xian, literally bringing down the house.

To put the severity of the disaster in perspective, think back to the 1989 Bay Area earthquake that hit while baseball fans everywhere tuned in to the World Series between the Oakland A's and the San Francisco Giants. The image of the collapsing section of the Bay Bridge is unforgettable. What's unbelievable, though, is that fewer than 70 people died as a result of that massive earthquake. Much of this has to do with modern preparation techniques, because the sheer power of an earthquake is still an awe-inspiring vision of the dominant force that can be unleashed from underneath.

In this chapter you'll learn how to ready yourself for, combat against, and recover from even the most powerful earthquake.

It's Not Your Fault ... Yet

Earthquakes occur when energy is released deep in the Earth, along the *fault* lines where the mammoth plates that make up the Earth's crust have split apart. Stresses in the Earth's outer layer push the sides of the fault together. The majority of faults are the result of numerous displacements over extended periods of time.

Stress builds up on the fault and the rocks that make up the fault slip suddenly, releasing energy in waves that travel through the Earth's crust and cause the shaking felt during an earthquake. Earthquakes happen when the Earth's crustal plates grind and scrape against or along one another. Usually, the focus point (the point of origin) of an earthquake is tens to hundreds of miles underground, which is why humans cannot produce major quakes. The outermost plates of the Earth are tectonic plates and their movement, called plate tectonics, is the cause of earthquakes, and the process that forms volcanoes, mountains, and canyons.

Whenever you hear news reports of an earthquake, you are going to hear about the epicenter. The epicenter is the point on the surface of the Earth directly above the point inside the Earth's mantle that is the focus of the earthquake.

Tactical Terms

A **fault** is a fracture in the Earth's crust along which one side of the fracture has been displaced in respect to the other side in a direction parallel to the fracture. It is a thin area of crushed rock between two solid pieces of rock. A fault can range in length from a few millimeters to thousands of kilometers.

Shock It to Me

Aftershocks are smaller earthquakes that occur in the same general area, within one or two fault lengths, during the days to years following a major quake. Aftershocks are generally a readjustment along the fault line. The deeper the earthquake, the lesser the likelihood of aftershocks. There are also "foreshocks," earthquakes that precede bigger earthquakes in the same location. Unfortunately, there is no scientific methodology for predicting earthquakes, so foreshocks can't be used as a red flag to get yourself out of town.

The probability of an earthquake can be calculated with some success. Scientists have estimated that the chances of a major earthquake in the next three decades are 60 percent in sunny southern California, and upwards of 65 percent in the San Francisco Bay area.

Survival Kit

If you're afraid of earthquakes, the deadliest and least understood natural disaster, you should probably tell your travel agent to avoid the Pacific Plate area known as the Ring of Fire, where two-thirds of the world's largest earthquakes occur. The Ring of Fire stretches up the western coasts of North and South America through Japan, the Philippines, Indonesia, and New Zealand.

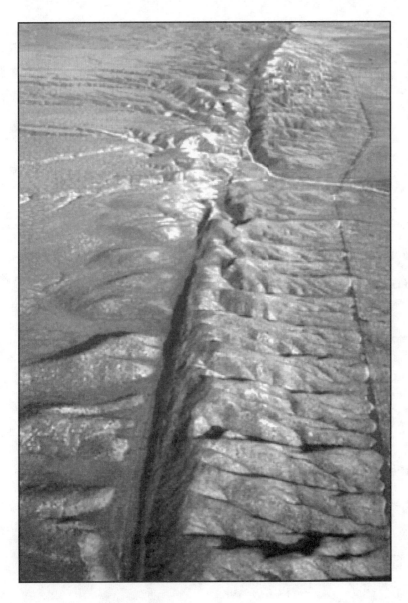

The San Andreas fault in central California is over 650 miles long and roughly 10 miles deep.

(Photo courtesy of the United States Geological Survey.)

The Richter Scale

The magnitude of an earthquake is measured by the *Richter scale*, developed in 1935 by Charles F. Richter of the California Institute of Technology. The Richter scale is a logarithmic scale that measures the size of the earthquake at its source by the amplitude of the largest *seismic wave* recorded.

179

Tactical Terms

The **Richter scale** is the term of measurement used for earthquakes. A **seismic wave** is a vibration within the Earth caused by an earthquake (and occasionally an explosion or the impact of a meteorite). A **seismograph** is a device for measuring and recording the vibrations and can often be found in the corners of art museums.

The United States Geological Survey's definition of the Richter scale says that earthquake magnitude is a logarithmic measure of earthquake size. In simple terms, this means that at the same distance from the earthquake, the shaking will be 10 times as large during a magnitude 5 earthquake as during a magnitude 4 earthquake. The total amount of energy released by the earthquake, however, goes up by a factor of 31.

An earthquake magnitude of 2.0 to 2.5 is very minor—it happens all the time and usually isn't felt—but it will be picked up by a *seismograph*. On the other hand, an 8.0 occurs only once every 5 to 10 years and can decimate communities near the epicenter. A large-scale earthquake can be measured on a seismograph anywhere else in the world. There are about a hundred strong earthquakes a year, 6.0 to 6.9 on the Richter scale, and those are the ones that cause a lot of damage in heavily populated regions.

Intensity scales, such as the modified Mercalli scale, factor in the damage an earthquake does and are better indicators of lives lost and property ruined. For instance, a 1964 Alaska earthquake between Anchorage and Valdez registered a whopping 9.2 on the Richter scale, but only 100 people perished and the damage didn't rank with the worst earthquakes because it hit hardest in uninhabited areas, thus registering lower on the intensity scale.

The Five Greatest Earthquakes in the United States

Area Hit	Date	Measurement on the Richter Scale
Prince William Sound, Alaska	Mar. 27, 1964	9.2
Andreanof Islands, Alaska	Mar. 9, 1957	8.8
Rat Islands, Alaska	Feb. 4, 1965	8.7
East of Shumagin Islands, Alaska	Nov. 10, 1938	8.3
Lituya Bay, Alaska	July 10, 1958	8.3

The Six Greatest Earthquakes in the Continental United States

Area Hit	Date	Measurement on the Richter Scale
New Madrid, Missouri	Feb. 7, 1812	7.9
Fort Tejon, California	Jan. 9, 1857	7.9
Owens Valley, California	Mar. 26, 1872	7.8
Imperial Valley, California	Feb. 24, 1892	7.8
New Madrid, Missouri area	Dec. 16, 1811	7.7
San Francisco, California	Apr. 18, 1906	7.7

Your Earthquake Disaster Kit

If you live in an area prone to earthquakes, it's wise to have a ready-made preparedness kit at your disposal at all times. Unlike hurricanes, tornadoes, snowstorms, or dinner with the in-laws, earthquakes are disasters that don't come with any advance warning. Even if you scour the seismology reports, monitor the strange behavior of your pet lizard, and keep close tabs on Grandpa's trick knee, there is no way to know precisely when an earthquake is coming.

Your emergency kit should contain the following items:

➤ A first-aid kit and basic medical handbook, along with the knowledge of basic procedures

➤ A decent supply of whatever medications your family members need

➤ Lots and lots of bottled water—figure on enough for five days for each family member, roughly a gallon a day

➤ Water purification tablets

➤ A battery-operated police scanner/radio and flashlights (and plenty of extra batteries)

➤ Canned, dried, and packaged foods, enough for a week—and don't forget a manual can opener

➤ Wrenches—pipe and crescent—to turn off the gas and water lines if you smell gas, have a water leak, or want to prevent your water supply from getting contaminated

SOS

Contrary to the delusions of many, there is absolutely no correlation between geological activity and atmospheric conditions. Earthquake weather does not exist, so don't be suckered in by anyone claiming that the time is ripe for a quake.

➤ Waterproof bags for waste

➤ Blankets or sleeping bags, including waterproof bedding (such as rubber sheets)

➤ Heavy-duty ponchos, changes of underwear and socks, and extra clothes for each family member

➤ Fire extinguisher

Ask yourself, *What do I need in an 8.0-scale earthquake?* and assemble your earthquake kit with that in mind. See Chapter 1, "The Will to Survive," and the tearcard at the front of this book for ideas on what else to include in your kit. Even though massive quakes are rare, it is, as the cliché notes, better to be safe than sorry.

The Never-Ending Off-Season

High school football coaches constantly harp on the axiom that it is the work that goes into the off-season that pays off during the regular season. Earthquake season is usually between the months of January to December, so the moral of the story is: You have to be prepared at all times.

Let's take a look at what your overall game plan should be:

Survival Kit

Keep food, water, comfortable shoes, and flashlights at your place of work (and know where the nearest fire extinguisher is). During an earthquake, transportation may be down and a 40-hour workweek might become a 72-hour sleepover.

➤ **Know where to go.** First and foremost, make sure everyone in your family knows where to go in the event of an earthquake. Designate a safe meeting place to regroup after the earthquake passes. If the earthquake hits during the day it may be trickier. Check with your children's school or day care to make sure they are adequately prepared. Explain to your kids why they should wait at school until you can come and get them.

➤ **Secure your home.** Reinforcing the physical structure of your home can go a long way in preventing extensive damage. Start by securely fastening bookshelves, large pieces of furniture, heavy equipment, water heaters, and gas furnaces to the walls or bolting them to the floor. Mr. or Ms. Can't-Fix-Its should buy a basic home-repair book or hire someone to help.

Many young children are injured during earthquakes by large falling objects. Have a supply of plywood on hand to cover broken windows, entryways, and other openings. Store heavy objects such as iron cooking skillets and bowling balls close to the floor instead of in overhead cabinets, latch cupboards, and put flammable liquids in a place where they can't tumble and spill. When constructing or remodeling your home, make sure the house is securely bound to a strong foundation and add extra bracing against horizontal pressure points.

➤ **Examine the bigger picture.** Although earthquake predictions aren't available yet, earth scientists are constantly developing new techniques for combating quakes, so keep up on the latest research. Keep a record of previous earthquakes in your area, so you'll know if your house is susceptible to flooding, wildfires, or landslides. It's worthwhile to support local organizations that encourage stronger building codes, less development along active faults, and the removal or rehabilitation of unsafe buildings. The more you understand earthquakes, the more aware you will be of how to handle the calamitous situation when it arises.

SOS

In an area prone to earthquakes, never place beds near large glass windows. You don't want a pane in the neck.

Adventures of a Lifetime

Contrary to popular belief, earthquakes tend to be very short, with minor ones lasting only a few seconds. The 1989 San Francisco earthquake lasted only 15 seconds, while the 1964 Alaska earthquake went on for three minutes.

Whole Lotta' Shakin' Goin' On

You will recognize when an earthquake hits because the ground will shake, jerk, sway, and move to the funky beat of plate tectonics. The duration of the shaking depends on the magnitude of the earthquake, the distance from the epicenter to your location, and the makeup of the ground under your feet. Softer sediments last longer than a strong bedrock, but either one will be quite frightening, especially to the uninitiated. Keep the following precautions in mind the next time the sidewalk you're standing on suddenly gets a mind of its own:

➤ **Drop, cover, and hold on.** Just drop to the floor under a desk or table, cover your eyes by pressing your face into your arm, and hold on. If there is no table available, sit against an interior wall, but make sure there is nothing heavy that can topple on you because the greatest danger is falling debris. The Red Cross encourages parents to teach their children this technique in the event of an earthquake. It should become an automatic response.

SOS

Many believe the best place to be during an earthquake is in a doorway, but that isn't entirely true. In old adobe houses doorways are much stronger, but in most modern homes they are no stouter than any other part of the dwelling, and you could get hit by a swinging door.

Survival Kit

If you're enjoying a camping trip in the mountains and an earthquake interrupts the wonders of nature, keep an eye out for falling rocks and trees. Look for a safe clearing where there's nothing above you.

➤ **If you're at home ....** If you're indoors, stay there, but move out of the kitchen, away from windows, and go to a relatively empty area like a hallway. If you happen to get awakened from a deep sleep (I once jumped out of bed during a quake, convinced a thug had broken in *to violently shake my apartment*), stay put, hold on to a bedpost if you can, and cover your head with a pillow.

➤ **If you're in a building ....** If you're in a building, the best advice is to stay put. Don't run outside unless it's a life-saving necessity; falling debris is especially common around buildings. Don't rush for stairways or exits, because they get jammed with panicky types. Stay off the elevators—they often automatically stop functioning during fires or other situations. And don't be surprised if the electricity goes out while the fire alarms and sprinkler systems are activated. Breaking glass, screaming, bells, and other alarms will sound, but try to block out the noise and keep your cool.

➤ **If you're outside ....** If you find yourself in the great outdoors, get away from power lines, trees, and buildings and lie flat on the ground in an open space. If you're in the heart of Manhattan and can't escape the buildings, step into the closest building doorway to avoid the debris raining down from above.

➤ **If you're in a car ....** If you're getting your kicks on Route 66 and your car starts shaking like a blender, either you're driving a Pacer or you're in the middle of an earthquake. Carefully reduce your speed and pull the car as far away from traffic as you can. Don't stop under an overpass or bridge, and stay away from trees, power lines, traffic signs, light posts, or anything hanging from above. Remain inside the car until the shaking stops, but when you resume driving remember to watch for cracked roads, downed power lines, fallen rocks, bumps at bridge approaches, and broken pavement.

Don't panic if you feel more than one jolt. Different seismic waves, first the P-wave, then the S-wave, stem from the same earthquake. Also, don't forget about aftershocks, which can come right away or days later and often level or destroy structures weakened in the original earthquake.

Back on Steady Ground

Once the earthquake has ended, there are still many hazards that must not be ignored, even if it's natural to feel a great sense of relief. One of the greatest dangers is the effects of ground displacement, which includes mudslides, landslides, avalanches, and devastating oceanic waves, such as a tsunami (see Chapter 8, "Yo Ho Ho, It's the Island Life for Me"). But you already took these potential disasters into account and aren't in any imminent danger, right?

The first thing to do after an earthquake is the same thing you'd do after any other natural disaster—hug your family and your pets while listening to an NOAA broadcast or another local station for an assessment of the damage in your area and any reports of aftershocks. There are other steps to follow after the "Big One" or a "Little One," because the aftermath of either poses problems:

➤ Don't use the telephone unless there's a medical or fire emergency, because the lines could get tied up and people in real dire straits should have first priority.

➤ Check yourself and your family for any injuries, but don't attempt to relocate or move anyone with serious injuries. Cover the person with a warm blanket and call 911 for help.

➤ Before surveying the house for damage, put on a thick, long-sleeved shirt, pants, work gloves, and strong, thick-soled shoes in case you encounter broken glass. Bring along the fire extinguisher and put out any small fires first, and if you rely on a wood-burning or coal-burning stove, make sure that it didn't tip over.

SOS

If you're on a lake, beware of a seiche following an earthquake. This is an oscillation of the surface of a lake that can act like a scaled-down tsunami and flood the shoreline.

SOS

If you smell gas or suspect gas is leaking, shut off the gas right away. When investigating a gas smell, always use a flashlight, not a candle. More people die from candle-related blazes after a natural disaster than from Mother Nature's handiwork.

➤ Don't go on a town tour to survey the damage; take care of problems at your own home first.

➤ Inspect the area around your house for downed or broken power lines, utility wires and pipes. If your house is in serious jeopardy, get your family out and to a safe open area.

➤ Be prepared to *drop, cover, and hold on* while you check on your house, because aftershocks will most likely be forthcoming.

➤ If your family is safe and your home secure, call a relative or family friend to spread the word that everything is all right, if possible. You then may want to go over and see if the neighbors or a nearby church, school, community center, store, or retirement home need any assistance. Anywhere people are frightened and need help is a good place to be.

Adventures of a Lifetime

If you are a Southerner perusing this book, you might be saying to yourself, "Why in tarnation do I need to worry about earthquakes?" Well, in 1886, the city of Charleston, South Carolina, was hit by the most damaging U.S. earthquake east of the Mississippi River, and its effects were felt from New York to Cuba. Roughly 110 people died and almost all of the brick homes in Charleston were damaged, as well as homes within a 200-mile radius.

Earthquakes are colossal, jaw-dropping displays of the raw force of nature at its primordial best. The movement of the Earth's crust can't be predicted and no other natural disaster carries the potential for the carnage an 8.0 earthquake can unleash. Still, there are ways to prepare so that you and your family survive the experience.

The Least You Need to Know

➤ Earthquakes occur when energy is released deep in the Earth, along fault lines where the mammoth plates that make up the Earth's crust have split apart.

➤ There is no scientific way to predict when an earthquake will hit, and there is definitely no such thing as "earthquake weather."

➤ The easiest thing to remember during an earthquake is to *drop, cover, and hold on.*

➤ While examining your home for damage, don't forget that an aftershock may soon be forthcoming.

Chapter 18

It Must Be
the Gods

In This Chapter

➤ All about asteroids

➤ The anatomy of a volcano

➤ How you can be prepared for a volcanic eruption

➤ Protecting yourself and your family during an eruption

Many of us wasted away our adolescence pumping quarters into a machine to destroy oddly shaped critters that threatened to blow up our little spaceship before we could vanish into hyperspace. Just what were those asteroid things, anyway? Well, asteroids are for real and they crash into our planet from time to time, occasionally doing great damage along the way. It's a good thing we've got big brother looking out for our best interests, because we won't be able to do one thing to escape the consequences if a large asteroid were to hit the Earth. Fortunately, the National Aeronautics and Space Administration (NASA) has a plan for our survival.

And then there are volcanoes—more fire and brimstone for us to worry about. But at least these wonders of nature give us some warning so, while we may not be able to control them, we have a good chance of getting out of their way. In fact, they're quite beautiful to view from a safe distance.

Let's see what we can learn about surviving rocks from heaven and fire from Earth.

Asteroids: Minor Planets

Asteroids are metallic, rocky bodies without atmospheres that orbit the Sun but are too small to be classified as planets. Known as minor planets, tens of thousands of asteroids huddle in the main asteroid belt: an enormous ring located between the orbits of Mars and Jupiter. They are believed to be organic, primordial material that was prevented by Jupiter's strong gravity from growing into a planet at the germination of the solar system some 4.6 million years ago. Scientists have estimated that the mass of all asteroids combined would be roughly half the size of the moon at roughly 930 miles in diameter. There are several hundred thousand known asteroids and new ones are continually being discovered.

Asteroids in the main belt tend to follow stable orbits, revolving in the same direction as Earth and coming full circle around the Sun in three to six years. The majority of asteroids are one of three types:

1. **C-type (carbonaceous):** Includes more than 75 percent of known asteroids. They are very dark with a low *albedo* and a composition believed to be close to the Sun, minus hydrogen, helium, and other gases. C-type asteroids inhabit the main belt's outer regions.

2. **S-type (silicaceous):** Make up a little more than 15 percent of asteroids and are relatively bright. Their composition is metallic iron mixed with iron- and magnesium-silicates and they dominate the inner asteroid belt.

3. **M-type (metallic):** Relatively bright with a composition that is apparently dominated by pure nickel iron. M-type asteroids inhabit the main belt's middle region.

Adventures of a Lifetime

In 1801 Giuseppe Piazzi discovered the first asteroid, Ceres. It is also the largest asteroid at 600 miles in diameter—just a shade under the distance between Atlanta and Miami. Sixteen asteroids have a diameter greater than 150 miles, which would be more than enough to wipe out the area between Chicago and Milwaukee.

Tactical Terms

Albedo is an object's reflective power, the intrinsic light of the surface or body.

How Close Are They to Earth?

Asteroids with orbits that bring them to within 121 million miles of the Sun are known as near-Earth asteroids (NEAs). It is believed that most NEAs are pieces thrust loose from the main belt by a combination of asteroid crashes and the gravitational influence of Jupiter. NEAs fall into three categories as well: Amors, which cross Mars's orbit but don't quite make it to Earth's; Apollos, which cross the Earth's orbit in over a year's time; and Atens, which are under a year.

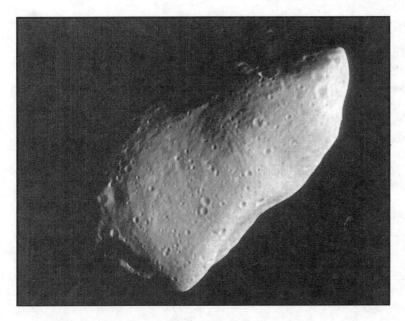

The asteroid Gaspra; the photo was taken by the Galileo Spacecraft.

(Photo courtesy of the National Aeronautics and Space Administration [NASA].)

Many asteroids have struck the Earth's surface and it is an accepted theory by many scientists that an asteroid may have hit 65 million years ago (evidence places it in the Caribbean region) and led to mass extinction of life forms, including the dinosaurs, that marked the end of the Cretaceous period. In 1908, an asteroid with a diameter of a scant 330 feet hit a part of Siberia and wiped out a half-million acres of forest. In 1989, one came within 400,000 miles of Earth, and it was hauling at 46,000 mph and weighed 50 million tons. Scientists estimated that only six hours separated the Earth and ... can you say mass destruction?

Survival Kit

Although asteroids can't be seen by the naked eye, they can be viewed through strong binoculars or a small telescope.

We Don't Want to Go Out Like the Triceratops

Since it is impossible to know for sure what the impact of a massive asteroid would do to the Earth, other than plunge us into darkness, let's look at what NASA is doing to prevent that from happening. Assume that if we are going to be hit by an asteroid, the best course of action would be to get far, far away from where the estimated point of impact is, but if it's a large asteroid it won't make any difference. If that isn't enough comfort, well, it's probably best to leave it up to the boys and girls at NASA, who are currently working on an Armageddon (or *Armageddon* for all you Bruce Willis fans) scenario.

If a large asteroid were to impact Earth, the scenario could play out as follows:

➤ Life near the impact would be totally vaporized from the high pressures and rising temperatures.

➤ Huge amounts of dust and gas would infiltrate the atmosphere, which would more or less block out sunlight, plunging the globe into a nuclear winter that few life forms could survive. With the massive depletion of food sources, we could all say good night, Gracie.

Survival Kit

Other defensive plans include anchoring a solar sail or a rocket engine to an asteroid to change its course. Not anything you can do yourself, but it's good to know somebody's working on it on your behalf.

The impact of a major NEA is believed to be equivalent to an explosion of a million megatons of TNT. Even smaller asteroids could vanquish an entire community, but wouldn't lead to the end of the world as we know it. As if this isn't bad enough, the chances of a collision are increasing, and according to the first line in a NASA news release by Leon Jaroff, "When it comes to asteroids wreaking disaster on Earth, the real question is not if, but when."

Scientists have been working on a variety of early warning detection systems, however, and the crash isn't necessarily inevitable. Astronomers have been mapping the main asteroid belt for a long time. The more they learn about the number of asteroids and their orbital planes, the better chance they have at recognizing when an asteroid is jarred from the belt. There are giant asteroid-finding telescopes and the Air Force has launched micro-satellites to better the detection efforts. If a major NEA is detected years in advance, spacecraft can be sent up to examine the properties of the beast. If scientists track a whopper of an asteroid early enough, there are plans to use nuclear explosions in space to destroy smaller ones or send larger ones off course— yes, just like in the movie *Armageddon*.

Let's be honest, there aren't a whole lot of ways to prepare for the end of civilization; but you should take comfort that we are in the capable hands of astronomers, the military, and NASA. There's no need to worry about asteroids because collisions with the Earth are rare. Besides, if an asteroid hits, you won't feel it—unlike the pain you'll feel being buried alive in a pile of volcanic ash.

It's Always Good to Vent

There are two "v" words that always precede a powerful, loaded word with a definition that isn't open to a wishy-washy interpretation. The latter word is "erupt[ed]" and the former words are "violence" and "volcano." Coincidence?

Deep within the bowels of the Earth, rocks become so hot that they melt and become a flowing molten rock, called magma, which weighs less than the rocks in its vicinity.

A volcano is a vent or a fissure through which the magma escapes to the Earth's surface; once the magma leaves the volcano, it's called lava. The intensity of a volcanic eruption depends on the makeup of magma because it is the gases within the molten rock that are the determining factor. If the magma is runny or diluted, gases have no trouble escaping and the lava will flow out of the volcano. If the magma is dense and sticky, gases are unable to escape and pressure builds until there is a violent explosion. Large-scale volcanic eruptions release not only lava, but clouds of hot *tephra* that can roar down the mountain and destroy whatever is in its path.

Tactical Terms

Tephra is from the Greek word for ashes, and it is solid material ejected during a volcanic eruption and transported through the air. Tephra can range in size from tiny pebbles to huge boulders.

Ash that is shot into the sky via the cone of the volcano returns to earth, literally drowning humans and animals in a blanket of ash. Ash can also contaminate water supplies, knock down power lines, collapse roofs, disrupt all sorts of communication and flight control systems, and even gum up jet engines.

Another major hazard is a mudflow called a lahar, which forms when the hot lava melts ice and snow, or mixes with mountain streams, swallowing communities near the volcano in a sea of mud. Lahars can reach speeds of 30 to 40 mph or more and often contain a large amount of rock debris. At the steepest heights of Mount St. Helens, lahars reached the unbelievable speed of 90 mph and reached heights higher than a five-story building.

The 10 Deadliest Volcanoes in History

Area Hit	Year	Number of Deaths	Primary Cause of Death
Tambora, Indonesia	1815	92,000	Starvation
Krakatau, Indonesia	1883	36,417	Tsunami
Mt. Pelee, Martinique	1902	29,025	Ash flows
Ruiz, Colombia	1985	25,000	Mudflows
Unzen, Japan	1792	14,300	Volcano collapse, tsunami
Laki, Iceland	1783	9,350	Starvation
Kelut, Indonesia	1919	5,110	Mudflows
Galunggung, Indonesia	1882	4,011	Mudflows
Vesuvius, Italy	1631	3,500	Mudflows, lava flows
Vesuvius, Italy	A.D. 79	3,360	Ash flows and falls

Information from the Volcano World, University of North Dakota

Mount St. Helens, May 18, 1980.

(Photo by Austin Post, courtesy of U.S. Geological Survey (USGS)/Cascades Volcano Observatory.)

Let It Flow, Let It Flow, Let It Flow

More often than not, lava doesn't explode out of a volcano, but it can still be deadly and cause incredible amounts of damage. Hawaiian volcanoes are usually marked by their lava flow and not by a violent eruption, but a steep slope can send lava on a rapid journey and it can travel a great distance. The intense heat demolishes everything in its path, even if it slowly creeps across the land at 2 or 3 mph.

SOS

If you go to watch a lava flow (which we'll get to shortly), don't be fooled into thinking that lava flowing into the ocean will be cooled down. When hot lava touches the ocean, it evaporates some water, forming an impressive steam plume that can also contain bits of glass and a corrosive acid. The steam plume heats the surface water to temperatures capable of causing third-degree burns, and spectators have been scalded by waves.

Volcanoes are rife with residual consequences as well. Earthquakes, flash floods, landslides, wildfires, rock falls, and electrical storms are all possible effects of a volcano. The basic realm of all living organisms is changed in a violent eruption because the ecology of the region is fundamentally altered. Trees are snapped like twigs, animals that dwell above ground are killed, and birds, plants, and insects die when they can no longer find their source of nourishment. A tragic loss of human life due to starvation has been an aftermath of huge volcanic eruptions.

Adventures of a Lifetime

When Mount St. Helens erupted on May 18, 1980, in Washington state, a plume of ash reached 12 to 15 miles above sea level and went on for over nine hours. The ash landed at least as far away as Billings, Montana, dusting the town in a haze of white. Twenty-four square miles of valley was filled with debris, and 250 square miles of land was damaged by a lateral blast. In Yakima, Washington, ash so darkened the skies that lights had to be kept on 24 hours, and it took roughly 10 weeks to clean the streets of ash.

How Does a Volcano Grow?

There are three types of volcanoes, defined by their shapes:

1. **Stratavolcanoes** are formed by their eruptions, unlike mountains, which are pushed up from the ground. Volcanoes are built on the surface through the accumulation of layers of its by-products from the eruptions, namely lava, tephra, ash flow, and mudflow. Stratavolcanoes are the symmetrical cones with steep sides that most people associate with peaks like Mount St. Helens.

2. **Shield volcanoes** are flatter, broader volcanoes with lesser slopes, and are formed by flowing lava.

3. **Cinder cones** are smaller, cone-shaped volcanoes that develop when lava fragments into smaller bits, which cool and harden into cinders that pile up around the primary vent.

Preparing for an Eruption

It's impossible for scientists to predict exactly when a volcano is going to erupt. The best they can do once volcanic activity starts is to estimate how many hours or days until eruption. Scientists predict volcanic eruptions through constant monitoring of changes in the volcano itself. Instruments that track changes in the movement of magma usually give ample time for warning the public. Outdoor alarms are instantly sounded, so it's important that every member of your family knows what the alarm means. Whenever you're indoors, National Oceanic and Atmospheric Administration (NOAA) Weather Radio has a tone-alert feature that will let you know when the earth feels like it's going to spew.

Here are some other things you can do to prepare:

➤ **Explain to your children what volcanoes are and why they erupt.** Unlike other disasters such as hurricanes in Florida, tornadoes in Kansas, or earthquakes in Los Angeles, volcanoes might have a violent eruption only once in many generations, so your children may have no previous experiences to draw upon.

➤ **Conduct safety drills.** Your family probably won't have volcano drills like they would with more common calamities. To ease the tension and fear, let everyone know what safety measures should be taken.

➤ **If you live in a high-risk area, keep close tabs on the volcano.** The people in the most danger are those who live at the base of a volcano and won't have much time to evacuate if they don't monitor the details. Keep in regular contact with the U.S. Geological Survey representatives monitoring the volcano and look for a summary of their findings in the local newspaper.

➤ **Take care of insurance paperwork.** Pay a visit to your friendly neighborhood insurance representative to find out what your policy will cover in the event of a volcanic eruption.

➤ **Find a map of the hazard zones.** When the event happens, you don't want to rush your family into an area that is ripe for a mudslide, rock fall, lava flow, or extreme ash fall. The maps of hazard zones are drawn by volcanologists (scientists who study volcanoes) and show the areas destroyed during previous eruptions. Maps of hazard zones are based solely on geological data and should not be a substitute for the evacuation maps that are available from local emergency officials.

Survival Kit

In addition to the items in your earthquake disaster kit (see Chapter 17, "Quaking in Your Boots"), include a pair of goggles for each member of the family and have a healthy supply of disposable surgical masks in case there's a heavy downpour of ash.

➤ **Trust the authorities (to a point).** Whenever evacuation orders are issued, carefully follow the emergency plans developed by officials, but have a backup plan for your family's safety if things go haywire. Volcanoes offer so many potential problems that the standard means of survival may go out the window. It will be up to you to remain calm and implement a Plan B. Having a plan for handling mudslides, a second plan for earthquakes, and a third plan for falling ash, for example, could mean the difference between living or becoming ashes. It's best to follow the directions from emergency experts, but be prepared for a variety of dangerous situations that could result from a violent eruption.

➤ **Don't consider yourself immune.** Violent eruptions like Mount St. Helens send the wrath of the nature gods a long way from the cone, so don't assume you are out of harm's way. Check the status reports of volcanoes within 1,000 miles of you, just to be on the safe side. Even if you can't see the volcano erupt, the lava and ash might land on your doorstep, so jeepers creepers, don't rely on just your peepers.

Watch Out, She's Gonna Blow!

What can be done once the volcano erupts? Plenty, starting with the key to surviving all natural disasters: *Try to remain calm.* Easier said than done when the sky is turning black and Armageddon appears to be upon us, but there are ways to handle even the most powerful show of the forces of nature, the kind that reminds us all that the planet is a whole lot tougher than the inhabitants who are trying to destroy it.

Adventures of a Lifetime

Perhaps the most famous volcano in history is Mount Vesuvius, which is roughly 4,000 feet at the top of the main cone and part of the backdrop of Naples, Italy, to the southeast. Mount Vesuvius erupted in A.D.79 and buried the cities of Pompeii and Herculaneum under piles of ashes, cinders, and mud. It has erupted many times since and is the only *active* volcano on the European mainland. In a gesture that apparently thumbs its nose at the gods, the townspeople built a railroad at the base of Vesuvius.

Here's how to increase your chances of survival:

➤ **If mud is headed your way, get to higher ground.** Mudflows are one of the primary killers after a volcanic eruption, so the easiest way to approach them is to not approach them at all. If the water level seems to be rising in the creek behind your house, get to higher, stable ground. Avoid overpasses or bridges because they can be wiped out by a strong mudflow. Also stay out of ravines, river valleys, and streams because more of the potential dangers are found in low-lying areas.

➤ **Stay away from the "down"-town.** Downstream, downwind, down-slope, down *anything* is not a good place to be because it's the route most of the volcanic eruption hazards will be heading. (Okay, a down coat or a down comforter might be handy in the situation, but if you're downwind you will need them both to keep the ash out of your lungs.)

➤ **Stay inside.** It's better to be safe and sound inside than anywhere outdoors. If possible, go inside right away and seal up any windows, doors, chimneys, and dampers that would allow ash to become an unwanted guest. Put cars and machines in the garage and cover them with tarps or their guts will fill with ash. Also, you'll want to shovel the ash off your house as soon as possible, because ash can be heavy and cause a collapse.

➤ **Don't forget the animals.** Bring family pets into the house, and shelter horses and livestock in the barn with plenty of food and water. Seal any barn doors, windows, and crevices to prevent ash from getting in.

➤ **Protect your body.** Volcanic ash contains fine, glassy particles that can do serious damage to your lungs, face, eyes, and skin. Cover your arms and legs, wear gloves, goggles, glasses (as opposed to contact lenses), and a surgical mask or a damp cloth over your mouth at all times. It's important to remain indoors, but it's imperative if you or anyone in your family has bronchitis, asthma, respiratory ailments, emphysema, or any trouble breathing in general. If you get caught outside unprepared, at least cover your mouth and nose and thoroughly wash your skin the minute you get inside.

➤ **Don't go for a leisurely spin.** Driving during an ash fall is a bad idea, because ash will get into the engine of your car and you will suffer major viscosity breakdown (according to the commercials). The engine will clog and severe damage may be done to the brakes, transmission, and pistons—in short, any moving part that can't handle a flurry of tiny abrasives.

You may want to watch slow-moving lava flow like a tortoise out of the volcanic landscape in places like Hawaii. It is majestic and safe as long as you exercise a little caution and follow suggestions such as …

➤ Stay away from steep cliffs because they break off regularly, and you can't climb up from the ocean if you fall in the drink.

➤ Be alert for loud noises and move inland immediately if you hear cracking or booming sounds, which can be explosions of rock and lava caused by the bench. (A bench is an area of unstable land that forms where the lava hits the ocean. Landslides often collapse the bench and cause violent explosions that send rock and lava flying through the air like projectiles.)

➤ Be aware of the heightened risk for sunburn, dehydration, heat stroke, and abrasions.

Be it down from the heavens or up from the depths of the Earth, asteroids and volcanoes are going to rear their powerful heads every now and again, so let's at least pretend like we're not going to take it by getting out of harm's way.

The Least You Need to Know

➤ Asteroids are metallic, rocky bodies without atmospheres that orbit the Sun but are too small to be classified as planets.

➤ It is a generally accepted theory that 65 million years ago, an asteroid hit Earth (evidence places it in the Caribbean region) and led to mass extinction of life forms, including the dinosaurs.

➤ A volcano is a vent or a fissure through which magma escapes to the Earth's surface; once it erupts from the volcano, magma is called lava.

➤ It is best to stay out of ravines, river valleys, and streams after a volcanic eruption because more of the potential dangers are found in low-lying areas.

There Goes the Neighborhood

These two natural terrorists are like an underground group that blows up an embassy and then proudly announces, "It was us! It was us!" They come right out and tell you who they are and what they do. There is no covert, dual, shadowy secret to their basic nature. They are quite proudly … landslides and wildfires, two compound words with nothing to hide.

So now that they've introduced themselves, what can be done to keep the land from sliding and the fires from getting too wild?

The Landslide Brought It Down

Technically, mudslides are a form of landslides, but we'll look at both in this chapter because they are geological dangers common to almost every state in the union. Landslides cause an estimated $2 billion in damages in the United States every year and they cause thousands of deaths throughout the world annually, yet they don't strike fear in the hearts of homeowners around the world like their powerful brethren the hurricane, the earthquake, or the tsunami. Perhaps it is because the last word in their names conjures youthful imagery of a twisty ride down a candy-cane colored slide at the playground, or the three-story, three-ticket trip on a burlap sack at the county fair. A landslide just doesn't sound very ominous, does it? It sounds like leisurely erosion. But if you've ever lost your home to a wall of mud or debris, you gain a whole new respect for this natural disaster.

Landslides are driven by gravity, which pulls earthen material down a slope. Landslides can be slow and gradual, or they may move at high speeds, which are the kind that result in the greatest loss of life. Landslides are triggered by a variety of things, including ...

➤ Earthquakes.

➤ Volcanic eruptions.

➤ Heavy rainstorms that result in the saturation of the ground.

➤ Human modification, alteration, or construction of the land.

➤ The freezing/thawing cycle.

➤ Steepening of slopes due to erosion.

➤ Fires.

Adventures of a Lifetime

If you live in an area prone to earthquakes, don't forget about the not-so-friendly neighborhood landslide. The 1994 Northridge earthquake kick-started over 10,000 landslides in southern California. An earthquake in Montana in 1959 sent the entire side of a mountain sliding into the Madison River gorge, forming a new lake in the process.

Landslides generally coincide with periods of heavy rain or a warming trend that brings a quick melting of the snow. Landslides are often a sneaky offshoot of the main problem and can exacerbate flooding in regions that are already beset with an overflow of water, or they can form because of loose material due to drought or areas that have recently been overtaken by fire.

It's a safe bet that if a landslide happened once in a particular area, it will happen again because many landslides have taken place over the same terrain since prehistoric times. Repeat performances are always a strong possibility, no matter how stable the land appears to be.

Muddy Waters: Types of Landslides

Landslides are classified in a variety of ways, but for our purpose, we'll stick to classification by sediment size:

➤ **Debris flows.** Debris flows are also called mudflows, mudslides, or debris avalanches, and are literally rivers of earth saturated with water. They develop after rain or snow and include rock, sand, mud, trees, earth, and so on, but typically less than 10 percent clay and silt. Debris flows are fast-moving and can range from watery to chunky, depending on what they engulf as they make their way down a slope. Debris flows tend to start out as shallow landslides, but they accumulate more liquid and accelerate to speeds of between 10 to 30 mph. Often, two or more debris flows will combine into a destructive force, swallowing boulders, cars, telephone poles, whatever gets in the path. The volume grows, and when the debris flow reaches flat land it can cut a wide swath and severely damage inhabited areas. In the mountains, debris flows often fill up the channels and reservoirs before overflowing and making their way downward.

SOS

Mudflows often sweep through canyons or down the sides of mountains unabated because there is little or no vegetation to slow the erosion of earth. If you are hiking on a hill or mountain and a rainstorm hits, be aware that if there are few plants, rocks, or trees around, the place is ripe for a humdinger of a mudflow.

➤ **Earth flows.** Earth flows consist predominately of sand, silt, and clay and tend to move slower than debris flows. Earth flows, though, can roll over lower slopes and slowly infiltrate and destroy highways, water supplies, and oil reserves. Earth flows aren't as dangerous per se, but they can inflict long-term damage on homes and property that can cost a bundle to repair. Humans, with their underground septic tanks that lubricate underground clays, have instigated earth flows.

➤ **Rockslides.** Rockslides are technically debris flows, but they can cause so many problems that they are often mentioned in their own category. They are the rapid movement of a mass of large and/or small rocks with little or no hydraulic lubrication. Rockslides can be extremely dangerous and can steamroll cars, trains, animals, and humans as if they were nothing more than an inconvenient speed bump.

This Landslide Is Your Landslide

As mentioned earlier, landslides tend to find their way down the same slopes as their prehistoric ancestors did. The most important thing is to respect, dissect, and inspect past landslides: Respect the fact that they have been there before and they will be there again, not just once in a generation. Dissect what happened during landslides of the past few decades and see if the geography/topography/geology has been altered and how that will affect the next landslide. If possible, inspect the previous landslide grounds themselves and see if there is anything that can be done to shore up the terrain before the next one.

Survival Kit

If the trees in your backyard gradually bend, or the rocks on the hill above your home move every time a storm hits, you're in a prime spot for a landslide because the small storms are already stronger than the natural objects.

Areas other than existing landslides that are potentially dangerous are ...

➤ The base of a steep slope, mountain, or hill, especially if it happens to be at the bottom of a volcano.

➤ The base of any drainage area, particularly man-made channels, which can be weaker than natural drainage outlets.

➤ Hillside areas of residential development in regions prone to heavy rain, earthquakes, rapid snow melt, and wildfires.

➤ Anywhere water tends to accumulate in the ground.

Landslides can be predicted most of the time because they either follow another natural disaster such as an earthquake, or, more often, take a long time to develop such as during a heavy rainstorm. The problem is that too many people ignore the potential hazards of landslides and end up paying for it in the end. Don't be one of those people. Pay attention to the changes in the landscape around your home, particularly the areas where runoff water flows down-slope over soil. Simply being in tune with your surroundings can make a big difference.

You're Prepared ... by a Landslide

Here are some important tips to help prevent a landslide from causing serious damage:

➤ **Talk to professionals.** If you have no idea if you are in a landslide-prone area, talk to local officials or contact a geologist in your area. Geologists work for state geology surveys, forest services, departments of natural resources, or possibly the science department of a state or local university. There are engineers/contractors who specialize in earth movement and you may want to have them take a look at your house and grounds to see if it is up to snuff in the preparedness category.

➤ **Monitor the zoning laws.** In parts of southern California, landslides have become a regular occurrence and in some communities it is overzealous developing that must shoulder part of the blame. Houses go up where they shouldn't and regulating the building of homes in areas highly susceptible to debris flows is just plain common sense. Steep slopes, the mouths of streams, and drainage areas are not wise places to erect mini-malls, so keep your community abreast of local development through meetings, fliers, e-mails, and so on. And here's a helpful hint: If you are building a new home, make sure local builders use flexible pipe fittings, which tend not to break so easy.

➤ **If it's time to go, go.** You will be familiar with the rain patterns in your area after living there for a while and will probably be able to recognize a torrential storm from a standard one. If the National Oceanic and Atmospheric Administration (NOAA) Weather Radio is ordering an evacuation, it's time to hit the road. Even if the main storm has let up, the short, intense pounding of rain can fill the channels and spark a mudflow.

➤ **Be careful while driving.** Embankments are a landslide's best friend. The road may also be covered in debris, so keep an eye out for rocks, collapsed road, or pavement slick with mud, oil, or water.

➤ **Stay away from the slide.** Steer clear of the landslide even if it appears to be little more than a trickle. A rock could come barreling down and knock you out cold, which would then coincide with a strong secondary landslide. If you do get trapped in a slide of any kind, roll up as tight as you can and cover your noggin.

➤ **Remember that houses can be rebuilt.** Of course, by now you know to check for downed power and gas lines and to inspect the outside of your home and surrounding area for damage. Remember, houses can always be rebuilt, but this

SOS

If you hear unusual sounds, like rocks crashing into one another or trees being snapped, it may indicate that debris is moving and a landslide is headed your way. Another telltale sign is if the stream behind your house has a substantial increase of water flow that is muddier than normal.

Survival Kit

Just like on the golf course, replace your divots (the chunks of turf or sod that are lifted from the earth). Repairing ground ruined by hyper-erosion will prevent flash floods and secondary debris flows.

time consult a geology expert to help you evaluate your current landslide hazards and ways they can be avoided in the future.

Homes along the South Fork Toutle River destroyed by mudflows from Mount St. Helens.

(Photo by Lyn Topinka, courtesy of U.S. Geological Survey [USGS]/Cascades Volcano Observatory.)

USGS Photo by Lyn Topinka, July 19, 1981

Is It Clear-Cut That We're to Blame for Landslides?

Poorer countries often turn their backs on environmental concerns in favor of economic "progress," but are deaths by landslide a residual effect? The United States has infringed on nature in many ways, but the millionaires in Malibu who lose their private screening rooms to mudflows are going to be all right. However, the massive destruction caused by flooding and mudslides in places like India, China, or Mexico has negatively altered the lives of thousands of the world's underprivileged who don't have the resources to rebuild their lives. Many scientists lay the blame on the absence of forests on hillsides due to clear-cut deforestation. If there aren't any trees to block the flow of debris, guess where it's headed? If we continue to clear forests and woodlands in favor of "progress," the landslide may bring us down after all.

Five-Alarm Wildfire

Wildfires are probably the most common "natural" disaster and there are more than 100,000 every year in the United States. Large-scale wildfires are less common than small ones and account for fewer than 4 percent of yearly fires; but they account for over 94 percent of the woodlands (roughly 1.2 million acres) that burn annually. Wildfires are certainly disasters, but "natural" is a stretch because humans spark over 80 percent of them. Before we get into the ways humans ignore Smokey the Bear, let's look at a few types of fires:

➤ **Crown fire.** A crown fire is an intense fire that moves quickly through the top layers of foliage on trees.

➤ **Surface fire.** A surface fire is the most common type of wildfire; it spreads across the floor of the forest, burning vegetation.

➤ **Ground fire.** A ground fire is usually started by lightning and it burns organic matter below the floor in the root system.

Ideally, none of these fires will become a roaring *conflagration*.

There are many ways for wildfires to break out, but they often arise due to drought conditions. Any time there is a long dry season, especially if it follows a mild winter or spring and winds are high, be aware that your area is susceptible to wildfires. If you contact your local forest service, monitoring drought conditions is a snap because the United States Department of Agriculture (USDA) Forest Service Wildland Fire Assessment System has a drought index.

Tactical Terms

A **conflagration** is a large, destructive fire that is often fueled by strong winds and can change the local weather conditions.

Lightning storms can spark wildfires, but foolish human behavior is the worst culprit. If national forest fire-fighting services had to do battle with only Mother Nature's work, they would have a lot more free time to devote to their families.

Fifteen Ways You Can Help Prevent Fires

We all know the many ways that fires can be started, but here are 15 common-sense ways you can prevent fires:

1. Sweep your roof and empty the gutters on a regular basis.

2. Check your chimneys a couple of times a year to make sure the dampers are in good working order. Throw the local chimneysweep a bone every dry season.

3. Verify that the spark arresters on your ATVs, chainsaws, portable generators, and snowmobiles are functioning. If you don't know what spark arresters are, just know that all vehicles and equipment have to have them, and the local dealer or forest service can tell if they are working.

4. Make sure all gas-powered lanterns, stoves, or heaters are totally cooled off before they are refueled.

5. This should be old hat by now, but always keep at least one fire extinguisher in your home. Make sure it's in good working order and ready to use if you need it.

SOS

Don't burn any garbage or leaves without first checking the laws in your community. Some allow burning by permit only, at certain times or days, while others don't allow it at all.

Survival Kit

Don't crush out cigarettes or cigars on logs because ashes can stay lit and get into the wood, thus becoming an outdoor yule log spreading destruction, not joy, throughout the forest.

6. Don't burn leaves, grass, hay, wood, or anything organic. Use this material for compost instead.

7. If you burn your trash, put it in a safe receptacle, not on the ground. Fiery debris from burning trash can get carried by the wind and spark a fire.

8. Never burn aerosol, paint, oil, or gasoline cans. They can explode and flying material can spark wildfires.

9. If you are building a campfire (or any fire, for that matter), keep it well away from trees and bushes so that ashes and cinders don't spark any nearby dead branches. It's best to avoid building any fires during the dry season.

10. Never smoke while hiking on a trail, and for the love of Pete, don't throw a cigarette butt into dry grass. Grind it into the dirt to extinguish the butt, then carry it out with you.

11. Keep your campfire small and build it up slowly, starting with dry twigs, adding bigger sticks and then slowly pushing logs into the center of the fire at the height of the flame.

12. While you're at it, dig a circle around your fire and fill it with rocks, which will keep the fire contained while providing more heat.

13. Drown your campfire to put it out. Lift the rock circle to make sure there are no stray embers, add dirt and more water to the dying fire and stir it around until it is just a warm memory and a cool reality.

14. When discarding used charcoal, throw it into a big bucket of water. Soak it all the way through until it is a black pile of liquid sludge.

15. Don't shoot bottle rockets or fireworks out into dry canyons. In fact, if you want to see fireworks, it's best to stick to your local Fourth of July fireworks display. Leave it to the experts.

It all boils down to using good old common sense. If you're using fire and you think it might be unsafe (or stupid), you're probably right.

Fire in the Home

If you live in an area prone to wildfires, it's best to prepare the ol' homestead because the odds are almost even that you'll face one before too long. Like the old saying goes, an ounce of prevention will keep the fireman away ... or something like that.

Follow these tips to protect your home:

➤ Separate the house from any combustible vegetation by keeping a 25 to 100 foot buffer zone. If you live in a pine forest, stretch it to 150 feet.

➤ Install smoke alarms on every level of your home, especially near bedrooms; buy long garden hoses that can reach any part of the house; and install freeze-proof exterior water outlets on the side of your house.

> **Adventures of a Lifetime**
>
> In October 1825, loggers in the Northeast started a fire in drought conditions. The blaze raged from Maine through New Brunswick and burned three million acres of forest, but didn't have anywhere near the death toll of an 1871 Wisconsin wildfire that killed over 1,300 citizens in a single night.

➤ Build your roof with fire retardant materials such as rock, stone, stucco, or tiles, and consider building a rock wall or planting fire-resistant trees and shrubs, as a buffer from any dry area around the house (for example, a cornfield).

➤ Use strong, tempered glass in windows and doors and install mesh below porches, decks, and gazebos and on openings to the roof or attic.

➤ Continually prune dead branches; have the power company remove downed branches on electrical wires; remove limbs that are less than 20 feet from the ground; and stack firewood away from the house.

➤ If possible, install underground electrical wires, and set aside a fire kit somewhere readily available, which should include a fire extinguisher, axe, rake, bucket, shovel and a hand- or chainsaw.

Don't Yell "Fire" in a Crowded Theater (and Other Tips)

Once a wildfire comes blazing, there are plenty of ways to deal with the heat of the moment:

➤ If you hear evacuation orders on NOAA Weather Radio, leave; but make sure your family is thoroughly clothed from head to toe and their mouths and noses are covered with handkerchiefs, scarves, or towels.

➤ If time permits, turn off the gas, close the windows, doors, and drapes, move furniture toward the center of the room, open the fireplace damper and close the screens, leave all the lights on for added visibility through the smoke, un-hook outdoor propane tanks, and wet the roof with a hose or sprinkler.

➤ If you get caught in a wildfire, remember you can't outrun it. Kneel or crouch in a pond, stream or slow-moving river and cover your head, face, and upper body with wet clothing.

➤ If you aren't near water, lie face-first, flat on the ground and cover yourself with wet clothes. If you have no wet clothes to cover your body, use cold dirt and soil. You can also take cover in a cave, an area clear of trees, or a bed of rocks or rocky area.

➤ If you are driving, pay attention to road reports because wildfires often shut down standard passages. Avoid the fire hazards, and keep an eye on the changes in the direction and velocity of the smoke and fire.

➤ Always try to breathe through a cloth (preferably wet) and suck in the air closest to the ground because it is the least smoky.

➤ Stay down! Remember, smoke rises, so the more you stand, the more smoke you'll take in. Many more people are killed by smoke inhalation than they are by flames.

There you have it, landslides and wildfires, disasters that are kind enough to almost always announce that they're coming, so don't screw up the preparations.

The Least You Need to Know

➤ Landslides are driven by gravity, which pulls earthen material down a slope.

➤ Be careful while driving, because embankments are a landslide's best friend. The road may also be covered in debris, so keep an eye out for rocks, collapsed road, or pavement slick with mud, oil, and water.

➤ Humans start over 80 percent of all wildfires.

➤ If you get caught in a wildfire, try to breathe through a cloth (preferably wet) and suck in the air closest to the ground, because it is the least smoky.

Chapter 20

A Little Water Never Hurt Anyone

In This Chapter

➤ The 30-second flash-to-clap rule

➤ The safest places to ride out the storm

➤ Treating someone who has been struck by lightning

➤ The number-one weather-related killer: flash floods

Rain, rain, go away, come again another day ….

A child's yearning for a glimpse of the sun can take on dark, ominous tones when the simple request to the heavens becomes a call to alleviate the profound suffering that goes hand in hand with calamitous lightning storms and flash floods. These two disasters might seem benign when compared to the earthquake, but they are the killers of more United States citizens annually then their showy cousins.

Their peril might best be summed up in the cry of Texas blues guitarist Stevie Ray Vaughn and Double Trouble, who noted the basic aggravation of the showery season in his song "Texas Flood," saying there's "flooding down in Texas, all the telephone lines are down." The dangerous underbelly of rainy days was also captured by blues man Lightnin' Hopkins, who asked only that if he meets his namesake maker, "See That My Grave Is Kept Clean."

And the Thunderstorm Rolls ...

Both lightning and flash floods emanate from the thunderstorm, which needs moisture and unstable air to form. As the air rises, marked by towering cumulus clouds, a thunderstorm develops but usually doesn't produce rain or lightning yet. As it reaches the mature stage, this is where the magic happens: lightning, pouring rain, heavy winds, hail, and its violent offspring, the tornado.

Survival Kit

As a thunderstorm develops, skies can become murky and bleak, often turning dark green. The best time to watch the skies? During late afternoon and evening hours in the spring and summer months, but be forewarned that thunderstorms can occur at any time during the year.

Thunderstorms tend to last about 15 minutes and can form alone, in lines, or in clusters, and usually cover a range of about 15 miles. They are, on average, in and out within 30 minutes, and take place constantly around the globe; there are more than 15 million thunderstorms a year. About 10 percent of thunderstorms in the United States are classified as severe. According to the National Weather Service (NWS) guidelines, a thunderstorm qualifies as severe if it includes hail three-quarters of an inch or larger, has winds of 58 mph or higher, or includes a tornado in its repertoire.

Singular, stationary thunderstorms can be devastating because they pound the same area for an extended period of time. Air that quickly drops below a thunderstorm can reach dangerous speeds of up to 100 mph. Straight-line winds can wreak the same havoc as a tornado and have been known to knock over 18-wheelers like they were pins in Mother Nature's bowling alley. In western areas of the United States, thunderstorms often feature little rain with powerful winds that can stir up incredible dust storms.

Hail is another mark of the thunderstorm, and the size of hail can range anywhere from a tiny pebble to a softball. Hail forms when rising air within a storm updrafts and carries water to heights where liquids freeze. The pieces of ice get too heavy and fall out of the updrafts back to Earth as hailstones, which also can reach the century mark in miles per hour. Hail damage costs the United States over a billion dollars a year. Denver once rang up a staggering one-storm total of over $600 million.

The last fixture on the thunderstorm party circuit always electrifies the crowd.

Days of Thunder, Nights of Lightning

The soaring and falling air within a thunderstorm separates positive and negative charges, and lightning forms between roughly 15,000 to 25,000 feet above sea level where raindrops are turned to ice. A cloud-to-ground lightning charge germinates in this region, the result of a buildup and release of electrical energy. The lightning charge moves downward in 50-yard segments, known as step leaders, also known as the hard jagged lines we all drew with our yellow crayons when drawing a roaring thunderstorm. Lightning makes its way to the ground on the step leaders and creates a charged channel until it finds a suitable connection. Thus, the circuit is complete (created in under a half-second) and the charge has gone from cloud to ground. The current produces the radiant illumination we associate with lightning storms much more than the part that touches down. Most lightning occurs between cloud and ground or within the cloud itself.

Lightning is a wonder to behold and to be heard, because it produces its famous sidekick, thunder. Light travels faster than sound, so lightning always precedes thunder, which is caused by the abrupt enlargement of the air in the channel of the electrical discharge (AKA a shock wave). The old trick you used as a kid is a solid gauge of how far away the storm is: When you see a flash of lightning, simply count one Mississippi, two Mississippi, three Mississippi … until you hear a clap of thunder. Divide that number by five, and that's how many miles away the thunderstorm is.

The National Weather Service tracks thunderstorms and issues both storm watches and warnings:

➤ A **storm watch** tells the time and place of an upcoming thunderstorm and is issued primarily to raise public awareness when conditions are favorable for harsh weather. A severe thunderstorm watch expects the noise to arrive sometime within roughly the next six hours in an area ranging approximately 120 to 150 miles wide and 300 to 400 miles long. The National Weather Service issues that thunderstorm watch and the local NWS office issues the flash flood warning. Remember, lightning is occasionally a result of a developing thunderstorm and can come before it rains on the scarecrow.

➤ A **storm warning** is issued when severe weather has been reported by various weather watchers or advance *Doppler radar* readings. A warning indicates that a dangerous thunderstorm, often accompanied by tornadoes, is imminent, and it's time to get your family to safety.

SOS

Don't fall for that old nugget that lightning never strikes in the same place twice. Lightning can zap the identical mark repeatedly in a single discharge.

Tactical Terms

Doppler radar is advanced weather radar capable of looking at the heart of a thunderstorm and alerting scientists to severe weather conditions. Doppler radar can detect when a new thunderstorm develops along the leading edge of the storm's cooler air outflow.

Cloud-to-ground lightning flashes have been recorded and mapped in the United States since 1980, and there are over 20,000,000 strikes on continental soil every year. Lightning strikes kill over 90 people annually, lead to more than 300 injuries, and cause hundreds of millions of dollars in damage. According to the National Oceanic and Atmospheric Administration (NOAA)/National Climatic Data Center, between

1959 and 1994, over 3,200 people have died and 9,800 have been injured by lightning. Your chances of being struck hover around 1 in 600,000, but since the air around a lightning charge is heated to a temperature hotter than the surface of the sun, those odds may still seem too high.

Multiple cloud-to-cloud lightning strikes.

(Photo by C. Clark, courtesy of the National Oceanic and Atmospheric Administration [NOAA]/ National Severe Storms Laboratory [NSSL].)

Now That I Have Seen the Lightning

If you see lightning, count until the thunder claps, and the flash to clap time is under a minute, it's time to take cover. If the storm reaches 30-seconds flash to clap, you may find yourself in serious jeopardy. What else can be done to stave off the wrath of lightning bolts?

➤ **Get inside.** For obvious reasons, lightning causes the most casualties to people who are outdoors. Be it camping, swimming, golfing, hiking, boating, or mowing the lawn, staying outside in an electrical storm is a bad idea. Postponing outdoor activities is the smartest move you can make. Be sure to take cover at the first sign of lightning even if it's not raining, because just as many people get zapped before the rain begins.

➤ **Get out of the water.** During an electrical storm, get far, far away from the ocean, lake, pool, or any body of water because H_2O is a great conductor of electricity (as is the human body, which is basically a sack of saltwater). An electrical charge can zip through the entire body of water and injure everyone in it. If you're safe and sound indoors, take a deep whiff of the natural human scent, because nobody should take a bath or shower, or use running water for any other purpose during a storm. Metal pipes and plumbing can become ace conductors if they are struck by a charge. The same holds true for telephone lines, so use the phone only in an emergency.

➤ **Stay away from tall objects.** Lightning finds the tallest object around, so avoid trees, towers, telephone poles, street signs, gates, fences, Shaquille O'Neal, and so on. If you're caught in the forest, take cover under a clump of short trees, but never stand under an isolated tree of any size. Don't find yourself at the top of a mountain when lightning is in the area, unless you want a shocking end to your existence.

➤ **Put down the 9-iron and ditch the golf cart.** Don't make yourself easier to strike by clinging to lightning rods such as golf clubs, fishing poles, bicycles, tent poles, go-karts, sailboat masts, or anything else made of metal.

➤ **Take shelter in a sturdy building.** Large, enclosed, sturdy buildings that are made of stone or brick are the safest spots to wait out the thunderstorm. Avoid places like baseball dugouts, sheds, clubhouses, bleachers, gazebos, fire towers, rain shelters, and outhouses, because although they offer cover, they're small and attract lightning.

➤ **Protect your home.** During a thunderstorm watch, secure all lawn furniture and any other objects that could cause injury or damage. As a precaution, you might want to install sturdy shutters over the windows, and if you live in an isolated area, lightning rods to safely bring the electrical charges to the ground. Lightning rods will also provide protection against strikes to your house. During the storm, don't use electrical appliances, especially air conditioners, because power surges can destroy the compressors. Stay off the computer (it's best to unplug it) because if it gets zapped, you could lose information on your hard drive or suffer other damage.

Adventures of a Lifetime

One guy who stayed outside in a storm was Benjamin Franklin, who tested his theory that lightning is a channel of electrified air by seeing if it would pass through metal. In 1725, he attached a key to a kite and flew them up into the storm to get the proof he sought. Franklin also realized how dangerous lightning could be, so he came up with a protective measure, the lightning rod.

SOS

If you're on flatlands and your hair starts to stand on end, lightning is about to strike. Make yourself the smallest possible target by dropping to your knees and crouching up on your toes. Keep your hands on your knees and hang your head. Do not lie down horizontally—you may as well paint a bulls-eye on your stomach.

SOS

Don't worry about turning the lights on in your house during a thunderstorm. Motel 6 has nothing to fear; it's a myth that leaving the lights on increases the chances of lightning striking a building.

Survival Kit

Although someone struck by lightning can suffer severe burns, nervous system damage, and the loss of hearing or vision, the victim *will not carry an electrical charge* and can be touched, moved, and attended to right away.

➤ **If you're driving, pull over.** If you're driving and the storm hits, pull over to the side of the road, away from any trees or anything that could land on the roof, and turn on your emergency flashers. As long as you have a hard-topped, fully enclosed vehicle, you're safer inside your car than outside, even if it is struck by lightning, as long as you are not touching metal. Roll up the windows, sit tight, and keep in mind that rubber-soled shoes offer no protection whatsoever.

Caring for the Victim of a Lightning Strike

What if the unthinkable happens and your best mate gets struck by lightning? Start by dialing 911 immediately, because people can survive a lightning strike. However, a victim could end up with long-term repercussions like memory loss, dizziness, fatigue, mental strain, depression, and trouble focusing or paying attention for any length of time.

When the medical team arrives, be sure to tell them the victim was struck by lightning and wasn't electrocuted by household power because each of those situations involves a different treatment.

If you need to care for someone who has been struck by lightning, remain calm and follow these procedures:

➤ If the victim isn't breathing, start cardiopulmonary resuscitation (CPR). Check for a pulse and if there isn't one, begin cardiac compressions (see Chapter 4, "Lifesaving Skills 101").

➤ Move the victim to a safer location. Unless a person has had a bad fall, it's rare for a victim of a lightning strike to suffer severe breaks that would lead to paralysis, so don't worry about moving him or her. If you must move a person who isn't breathing, give the victim a few short breaths before you seek secure shelter.

➤ Hypothermia is a dangerous reality, especially if the victim has been pelted by rain, and it can hinder resuscitation. Put a buffer between the body and the ground, preferably a dry blanket.

➤ Administer first aid, check the victim for burns where the charge entered and exited the body, and look for other injuries that you can attend to.

Flash! (Flllooooooddddddddd) Wetter of the Universe

"I'll take natural disasters for $1,000, Alex."

"It's the number-one weather-related killer of U. S. citizens annually at roughly 130 fatalities every year."

"What are flash floods?"

Correct! But why are flash floods so dangerous? And how does flooding end up costing the United States over $3.5 billion dollars in damages every year?

Flooding occurs on flood plains after heavy, prolonged rainfall; short, violent rainfall; melting snow and ice; or tropical cyclones. For our purposes, we'll look at flash floods that are due primarily to a rainfall's intensity (rate of rainfall) and duration (how long the rain comes down). Topography, ground cover, and soil conditions also play a role. Flash floods happen quickly, between a few minutes and six hours of the violent downpour, or when a dam or levee breaks, or when water that was held by an ice jam bursts free. Most people don't consider heavy rainfall and the accompanying flash floods to be all that dangerous, but there is often little advance warning.

Most flash floods come from slow-moving thunderstorms, hurricanes, or thunderstorms hitting the same area for a long period of time. Flash floods can gain momentum and feature 25-feet heights. Flash floods can pick up debris (and jumpstart mudslides) along the way, while uprooting trees, rolling boulders, wiping out bridges, ruining buildings, and forging ahead in new channels of their own creation. Urbanization has lessened the Earth's ability to absorb rainfall, and the concrete jungle can turn into the asphalt Amazon.

Flood Flash: Get to Higher Ground

The number-one rule in battling flash floods is to *seek higher ground* ... right now! Even if it isn't raining and you don't see the flash flood, weather upstream may be worse. Don't wait until you hear the flash flood bearing down—unless you want to enjoy a natural log flume without the safety devices.

Adventures of a Lifetime

The worst flood in the history of the United States was the result of a dam break in Johnstown, Pennsylvania, on May 31, 1889. It left 2,200 people dead in a tragedy that could have been avoided. A massive flash flood that left the town swimming in its wake took place in Rapid City, South Dakota, in June 1972. Fifteen inches of rain hammered the city in just five hours, leaving 238 dead and over $160 million in damages.

Here are some other things to remember to keep you and your family safe:

➤ **A half-foot can sweep you off your feet.** It takes a mere 6 inches of fast-moving water to knock an average person off his or her feet, so never try to wade through a flooded area. Stay out of low-level areas like canyons, drains, culverts, and washes because they will fill up fast. As a rule of thumb, if the water is above your ankles, you shouldn't be in it. Make sure your children understand they have to get away from flash floods immediately because, while they may look fairly harmless, they can become powerful in mere seconds. Heed NOAA Weather Radio flash flood watches and warnings and follow all evacuation orders.

➤ **Is your home near a danger zone?** If your house is built near a stream, river, or creek, it's in harm's way if those bodies of water start to overflow. Some communities don't allow home building in floodplains, but if your home is there now, try adding a levee or a floodwall as a buffer against water getting inside the house. Move the water heater, furnace, and power sources to your attic. Waterproof walls, corners, and basement windows, because it can end up costing a fortune if water gets into the frame of the house or the plumbing.

➤ **The attic is better than the basement.** A flash flood can cause severe property damage in a short time, so when a warning is issued, get the house as secure as possible. Make sure there are no family members or pets in the basement because it can become a deathtrap if it becomes engulfed in water. Move all your valuables, family heirlooms, jewelry, and anything else you treasure to the upper floors of your house.

➤ **You guessed it—water.** Fill all sinks, tubs, jugs, and barrels with clean drinking water because floodwater can contaminate the pipes.

➤ **Driving, you crazy.** Half of all fatalities in flash floods are related to the foolish notion that cars are tougher than Mother Nature. It's a stupid notion, because the lateral force of moving water coupled with buoyancy can move almost any automobile in two feet of water. If your car stalls in the rising water, leave it behind and find higher ground because it will be swept away. It hurts to lose a 1968 Mustang, but what good is it if you're six feet under? Often, cars won't suffer much damage, so don't risk it—leave the car. Never drive around barricades, even if, God forbid, you have to take an alternate route home. Barricades are placed in front of roads by emergency officials for a good reason: The roads are flooded. And if you have to drive at night, use extra caution, because flood dangers will be harder to recognize.

➤ **Back at the homestead.** If you didn't prepare your home beforehand, you may be facing a hefty repair bill after the flash flood has subsided. Don't enter your house (or any other building) until someone has checked it out and given it a passing grade. Foundations can be weakened by water damage and floors have been known to collapse, and gas or power lines may be down. (And if lightning taught us anything, it's that water makes a fine conductor.) Call a plumber if the sewer lines are backed up and don't use the toilets. Servicing septic tanks or leaching systems as soon as possible is important because there are many health risks inherent in broken sewers. Lastly, don't drain all of the floodwater out of your basement or garage all at once, because pressure from the saturated soil on the outside could collapse the walls. Try pumping a quarter of the water out every day for four days.

Survival Kit

It's best to keep important insurance papers in a secure, waterproof box, but don't assume your insurance covers flood damage. Most insurance companies don't cover flooding in their homeowners' or renters' policies, so contact your source to see about acquiring flood insurance.

SOS

If you're outside during a flash flood or just after one subsides, be wary of poisonous snakes. Flood waters flush snakes out of their natural habitats and can sweep them into buildings, homes, streets, and sewers. It would be really awful to come out of a dangerous flash flood smelling like a rose only to get bitten on the leg by a coral snake.

Now that you know what to do when the flooding begins, think big. Load two of every animal you can find onto a giant ark built by hand … hey, it worked for Noah, didn't it? You've got the safety knowledge, so why not save as much of the animal kingdom as possible?

The Least You Need to Know

➤ Both lightning and flash floods emanate from a thunderstorm, which needs moisture and unstable air before it forms in the sky.

➤ Lightning causes the most casualties to people who are outdoors. Stay away from water of any kind, seek shelter in a reinforced building, and steer clear of any metal objects.

➤ Most flash floods come from slow-moving thunderstorms, hurricanes, or thunderstorms hitting the same area for a long period of time.

➤ If you're driving in a flash flood, leave your car and head for higher ground. It takes just two feet of water to float a car.

➤ Urbanization has lessened the Earth's ability to absorb rainfall, and the concrete jungle can easily turn into the asphalt Amazon.

Part 5

Getting Away from It All

Whether you're traveling at home or abroad, with family or friends, there is bound to be a moment when you'll need to rely on survival techniques. After all, I don't know about you, but it's rare that we've been on a family vacation where someone didn't end up bruised, scraped, or even in the hospital.

With that in mind, this part of the book is jampacked with information on what to do if you're ever kidnapped in a foreign country, how to stay calm when your roller coaster derails, how to disarm an attacker, and if you're traveling with a pregnant companion, how to help deliver a baby.

Chapter 21

Stranger in a Strange Land

In This Chapter

➤ You're the foreigner now: street smarts in a foreign country

➤ Was that gunfire?

➤ It didn't happen like this in *Midnight Express!*

➤ You don't have to be a "kid" to be kidnapped

➤ Hope floats, but boats sink

➤ When a cave becomes a cave-in

Anything can happen on a vacation. Usually this is a good thing: You bring back classic stories as well as cheesy souvenirs. But we say again, *anything* can happen on a vacation. Will you be prepared? Travel is dangerous anywhere you go, foreign or domestic. Letting your guard down in a place where you've never been before is a rookie mistake. Are you a rookie?

Granted, we're not saying you should stalk through Red Square low to the ground with two hands protecting your Darth Maul lunchbox. You still want to have a good time. Being vigilant doesn't mean being paranoid. It simply means being aware of your surroundings.

Which is harder than it sounds for some people ....

What Makes an Ugly American?

They call us Ugly Americans for a reason. We embarrass ourselves daily when we wear Hawaiian shirts with Bermuda shorts and Panama hats. We humiliate ourselves nightly as we guzzle umbrella drinks and do the rumba in our blindingly white slacks. We expect everyone to speak English just because we do, and we don't make an effort to learn the language and customs of the country we're visiting. Ours is a culture of assumption: We too often assume that everyone everywhere else does everything the same stupid way we do.

It just ain't the case.

When traveling abroad, you'll encounter any number of customs in any number of languages in any number of regions across the globe. Virtually any country (except for the United States' enemies *du jour* such as Cuba, North Korea, and Iraq) will have some kind of established tourism bureau that caters to Americans.

Why? Because Americans have money. Even foreign currency is a universal language, and these governments know that a good number of U.S. travelers like to go off the beaten path. "No Wally World this year, kids, let's do Southeast Asia!" Subsequently, these governments welcome Americans with open arms.

Which is fine. But once you're out of the airport, do you even know how to flag a taxi? Or, not how much that taxi will cost, but what it *should* cost? You'll quickly understand that these countries like American money a lot more than they like Americans.

Here are some general tips for traveling in any foreign country, whether it's an English-speaking land like Great Britain or a subcontinental island nation off the coast of Asia:

➤ **Dress down.** You're the foreigner now. Wearing loud leisure clothes and expensive jewelry is like wearing a neon sign above your head that flashes "American Fool and His/Her Money!" The two of you will be parted faster than two teens French-kissing at a prep-school mixer.

SOS

Wear "cabana wear" (such as the aforementioned Hawaiian shirts with Bermuda shorts) outside the cabana at your own risk. Nothing screams "tourist" louder than loud clothing.

Survival Kit

If you travel to a foreign country, research local customs and study a map *before* you arrive. Familiarize yourself with the local currency as well as the exchange rate in U.S. dollars. Also, become acquainted with the language and learn at least key phrases. Pick up a good guidebook and carry it with you on your trip.

➤ **Be discreet.** Keep your camera in a bag when you're not using it. And keep that bag attached securely to your body. The same goes for purses. Keep your wallet in your front pocket. And money clips? Money clips are for people who can afford to be ripped off. Don't display your vacation nest egg every time you buy an overpriced T-shirt. Use travelers checks instead of cash or credit cards. They can be replaced if they're stolen.

➤ **Learn the language.** Consider it a courtesy to your hosts. Try to pick up at least some basics: "police," the name of your hotel and what street it's on, "where's the bathroom?" and most importantly, "Royale with cheese."

➤ **Learn the terrain.** Study maps *before* you hit the streets. Know the basic layout of any region you plan to see and walk with purpose and confidence. Nothing screams "tourist" like a badly folded map and a well-scratched head.

➤ **Protect your passport.** It's your last, best lifeline if something bad happens. Keep it separate from your cash, camera, and chocolate bars.

As in any big city in the United States, the dumber you look, the more lowlifes will be attracted to you. But lowlifes in a foreign country have a huge home-turf advantage. Don't give them a reason to come after you. Show them that you know what you're doing, or at least that you look like you know.

"Coup d'État" Is Not an Appetizer

Here's a good rule of thumb while traveling in the third world: When someone says "a coup," don't answer "gesundheit."

Like hurricanes, earthquakes, and dinner theater, a *coup* (or *coup d'état*) ranks up there with the things you don't want to be a part of. Even tourist-friendly countries are susceptible to civil unrest, martial law, and riots, although obviously some countries are more prone to this kind of thing than others. You can't predict civil unrest, but you can take steps to be more aware of the possibilities.

It's safest to leave the country if any problems break out. If planes, trains, and automobiles are available, leaving is your best bet, especially if the United States is involved in any unrest. That tends to make Americans more attractive targets.

Tactical Terms

A **coup,** or **coup d'état,** is a sudden and decisive action resulting in a change of government illegally or by force. It usually comes with violence, riots, and tanks (and you're welcome!).

If you insist on staying, here are some points to consider:

➤ **Obey warnings.** The U.S. State Department routinely issues warnings to Americans traveling abroad when certain regions get hot. Pay attention.

SOS

Never go anywhere without your passport. It's your identity and your sole lifeline to the U.S. Embassy if something bad happens.

➤ **Watch the news.** CNN is everywhere. You can believe what they tell you more than you can believe what you hear from, say, the country's tourism bureau.

➤ **Listen to locals.** People who live in a certain area could know what's going to happen before it happens. Consider the source, of course, but if someone you don't know discreetly tells you that "this restaurant will explode," you might want to make new dining arrangements. Fast.

➤ **Ask questions.** Talk to your hotel manager and/or concierge. Ask a police officer. Call the U.S. Embassy. Get the facts.

➤ **Know your surroundings.** If the danger of violence exists, don't wander into unfamiliar areas. Stay alert. Note possible escape routes. And don't take unnecessary risks.

You're not Indiana Jones or James Bond, so don't act like either one. Your adventures should consist of taking cathedral tours and visiting local flea markets. No bullets, no bombs, no car chases. If disaster strikes, buy a six-pack of local beer, hole up in your hotel room, and watch it all on CNN. You can still brag to your friends that you were in town when it all went down.

Ka-Blooey!

And what if it does go down? What if you're out in the middle of it, caught by surprise like everyone else? Don't hesitate: Be a shepherd and get the flock out of there. Running is allowed.

➤ **Get to your hotel.** You have a room there, after all, and that's where your stuff is. Hotels also have emergency facilities, food, drink, beds, and all the wonderful things you'll need when you're pinned down by gunfire for several days. But seriously, a large hotel will probably have other Americans staying there. Which will lead to contact with the U.S. Embassy. Which is a good thing. And don't forget to demand a refund from management (they should at least upgrade you to a suite with a view of the tracer fire).

➤ **Get to the U.S. Embassy.** This is a good bet, for the embassy stands on U.S. soil. Just be sure to bring your passport so they know you're a citizen.

➤ **Get indoors as best you can.** If you're really stuck, take cover in whatever structure presents itself. Don't be shy.

➤ **Find a journalist.** Probably a long shot, but hot zones are crawling with them. At the very least, they'll know the area and can direct you to a safe place. And be dramatic—they might put you on TV.

You sure got a lot more than you bargained for on this trip. At least a lot more than if you had gone to Wally World. Hmmm. The moose ears aren't sounding too bad now, are they ...?

"You Can't Do This to Me—I'm an American!"

Coups could be tame compared to other possibilities, like getting busted in a foreign country. Is there any vacation plight that is more joked about, more dramatized, and more feared? Mexican jails are up there on the list. And Turkish prisons are even more famous than Turkish baths.

Why? It's every American's nightmare. Your freedom is stripped. But worse, every right that you take for granted in the United States—even while incarcerated—does not exist in most countries. If you get arrested in a foreign country, expect the unexpected. That way, if the treatment is less than what you expect, it might not seem so bad (how's that for positive thinking?).

Adventures of a Lifetime

If you actually committed the crime of which you're accused, be prepared to accept the consequences. Don't assume that because you're in a smaller country that they're stupid. Doing the crime is the real stupidity. Remember that some things we red-blooded Americans (especially younger ones) take for granted are considered very serious offenses in other countries: drugs (that harmless joint isn't worth it); explicit magazines and videos ('zines like *Maxim* and the *Sports Illustrated* swimsuit edition may be tame here, but not everywhere); bringing Cuban cigars into the United States; graffiti ... the list is endless. So be a good citizen, observe the local customs, and don't spit on the sidewalk (especially in Singapore).

Some Definite Do-Nots

If you get busted in a foreign country …

➤ *Do not* **expect to be allowed a phone call.** You're not in the good ol' U.S. of Attorneys anymore. In many countries, you're guilty until proven innocent. Expect no respect. Expect no help. And expect no contact with the outside world.

➤ *Do not* **expect fair treatment.** You're American, after all, and in some countries, taking an American down a few notches is grounds for promotion. Take whatever pleasantries are offered and consider yourself lucky.

➤ *Do not* **demand swift legal action.** No one will care who you are, where you're from, or who your daddy is. The process of foreign justice moves at its own pace, not yours.

➤ *Do not* **expect edible food.** If you don't like the local cuisine to begin with, imagine what the prison food will taste like. If no food is offered, remember that old saw about bugs being all protein.

➤ *Do not* **expect due process.** No lawyers, no pleas, not even a trial. Heck, you might just … disappear. In this case, a priest might be more useful than a lawyer.

Basically, it's going to be an all-around lousy experience. And it's the person with the survival mentality who will come out on the other side with a chance at returning home.

Do You Focus … or Fold?

Now's the time to forget everything about your previous life. Your new life *inside* has begun, and if you want to set yourself free, you need a firm plan. If anything, you'll have a lot of time to think about it.

Here are some do's:

➤ *Do* **get the word out.** Make sure someone knows where you are. Your traveling companions may already know you've been busted. But if not, or if you're alone, you need to get word to the U.S. Embassy of your plight. The only way you'll get help from the outside is if they know you are inside. This could be problematic if you aren't allowed a phone call, which is an even better reason not to travel alone or, at the very least, to let friends know where you are and how long you plan to be there.

➤ *Do* **find out your rights, if any.** Are you entitled to a trial? An attorney? How do you get to tell your side of the story? Can you make a phone call? If so, who will you call? Be ready at a moment's notice to take advantage of any opportunity.

➤ *Do* **keep a positive mental outlook.** You'll be alone, cut off, perhaps living in fear for your life. That's when survivors rise to the occasion and meet the hopelessness head on.

➤ *Do* **refuse to sign anything you can't read.** In fact, don't sign anything, period. This is the most basic, common-sense advice we can give. You'll end up signing your confession and the game will be over before the fat lady takes the stage.

➤ *Do* **learn the language.** Learn all you can, in whatever way you can. The more you understand, the more you can prepare. This also helps with the most rudimentary communication, such as with guards or fellow inmates.

➤ *Do* **think like a trial lawyer.** You are your best defense. And even if you have a fool for a client, you'll still defend that fool ferociously. Ask for the country's criminal code in English. Learn local laws. Try to figure out why you were arrested, and if found guilty, what kind of punishment you can expect.

➤ *Do* **be persistent, but courteous.** No one will much like you in your new home. You'll have to ask for everything. Just be careful, for while the squeaky wheel gets the grease, the whiny American gets smacked in the head.

In all, you're looking at a very rough time if you get busted in a foreign land. So leave the stupidity at home where it belongs. Your neighbor will be happy to feed your cat for a week to 10 days, but not for 20 years to life.

Another Use for Duct Tape

Here's another great vacation story: kidnapping! Like the T-shirt says, it happens. Heck, you don't even have to be traveling in a foreign country to be kidnapped. But we're on a vacation kick here, so let's run with it.

You're minding your own business trying to load your camera for another 24 Kodak moments when a van pulls up, the door opens, and the next thing you know your mouth is duct-taped, you're blindfolded, and everyone around you talks fast and smells like gun oil.

Congratulations! You've been kidnapped. But why? There are three primary motivations for kidnapping someone:

1. **Financial:** Someone thinks you're worth money.
2. **Political:** Someone thinks you're worth headlines.
3. **Pathological:** Someone thinks you look cute in that cabana wear.

If it's one of the first two, you're dealing with professionals. Which means that you can expect a certain level of, well, professionalism. It's business to them, not personal. On the other hand, if you're kidnapped for pathological reasons—be they violent or sexual or both—your life is in greater danger, because ransom is not part of the equation. We could say that you won't be dealing with the sharpest tool in the shed, but unfortunately, that just might actually be the case (like power tools or chainsaws).

Bad joke. But hey, a sense of humor is important at a time like this. At least you'll die laughing.

Let's look at these scenarios separately, shall we?

Kidnapped by "Pros" You Hope Will Soon Be "Cons"

Okay. Let's say you've been kidnapped by pros for what they hope will be a tidy ransom. It could be because your daddy runs a global financial conglomerate that sports a market cap greater than the gross national product of the country in which you're vacationing. Or maybe you have political connections. Or maybe you're just from the West. Sometimes, citizenship is pedigree enough.

Any way you slice it, you're now in the hands of people you will probably never understand. You think you have a hard time keeping your temper during a beer-laden debate about politics and religion at your local bar? What do you think will happen if you try to talk turkey with people who don't celebrate Thanksgiving?

You have several things in your favor:

➤ Professionals won't kill you … at first. You're worth something to them. They may rough you up to make a point, however.

➤ Professionals are "working." Which means appearances must be kept. So must timetables. Which means …

➤ Professionals want to get paid. Blowing the deal is counterproductive, so your captors will be walking a fine line between genuine and false threats.

Here's the real problem: Will the people on your end negotiate in good faith, or will they play games? The U.S. government doesn't have a great track record when it comes to Americans being taken hostage in foreign lands. You can only hope that everyone will be behaving as professionally as you. Because after reading this, you'll be one cool cucumber:

➤ **Don't panic.** Sure, it's a cliché. But survivors have such a long history of not panicking that they made it a cliché in the first place.

➤ **Listen.** No one can predict how you'll be treated. But keep an ear open as to the state of the operation, the stage of the process, and anything else that will shed some light on why this is happening to you.

➤ **Obey.** Do what they tell you without argument. Your captors will have their hands full with outside dealings. They don't need further hassles from self-righteous Americans with delusions of entitlement. You can demand to talk to the president, but trust us, the president really doesn't want to talk to you.

➤ **Take what's offered,** whether it's a smoke, a quick word on the phone, or half a chicken wing. Because whatever you're getting might be the best you're going to get—and it might not get that good again.

➤ **Don't play games.** You can try to escape. But by doing that, you aren't leaving your captors with a choice: They must either kill you or severely punish you. And whatever comforts you may have in captivity will disappear. Escape should be a last resort after it is clear that the wheels of negotiation have stopped spinning. Remember, there's only one thing easier than trying to escape, and that's getting shot.

There really are no moves to be made on your part—except exercising common sense. Either the deal will happen or it won't. All you can do is hope you're worth as much to your loved ones as you think you are.

Kidnapped by a Psychopath

What if your new host has no political affiliation and seems to enjoy sharpening kitchen knives instead? Well, you might want to rethink your position on nonviolent noninterference. You won't have time for complex psychological evaluations. Either your captor is a pro or not. Either he wants ransom and recognition or he wants ... er, whatever turns him on.

Suffice to say, you are now officially in it up to here. Whereas with professional kidnappers you can do things to facilitate the situation, you must now do whatever you can to un-facilitate it. You must now think about saving your not-yet-properly-tanned-because-I-was-kidnapped-in-the-middle-of-my-vacation skin. That means survival. Evasion. Escape.

Survival Kit

Decide quickly what a kidnapper's motives are. If you're in the hands of a psychopath who isn't interested in money, then you have to take action to protect yourself.

How to do that is up to you. We suggest using whatever means are at your disposal. You'll find some helpful hints in Chapter 23, "A Personal Attack." But whatever methods you choose, always remember one very important thing: This person wants to hurt you. That means, to paraphrase Patrick Swayze, that it's now time to "not be nice." That's our advice. Say it twice.

A Raft of Knowledge

Going from being kidnapped in a foreign land to drifting on a foreign sea is a real leap of bad luck. If it happens to you, think about staying home for the next 10 years. Rent some videos and follow local high school sports. *Do not* vacation anymore. You're a hazard to us all.

Fine advice, but not much help if you're already plopped in a raft in the middle of an ocean. Your only hope is rescue, AKA being spotted. So conserve any form of signal you have, such as a flare, until you're sure to be seen, especially during daylight.

In the meantime, you have to figure out what you're going to eat and drink until your dramatic rescue. Hopefully, you packed a case of Evian and half a side of beef jerky. But if you didn't ...?

Water, Water Everywhere

Two rules about floating on the ocean:

1. Without fresh water to drink, you'll be dead in less than 72 hours.
2. You can't drink sea water.

SOS

Do not set fire to your boat or raft as a signal unless it's a last-ditch effort. Sure, they saw the smoke on *Rescue from Gilligan's Island,* but if they don't see yours, you've just burned up your only means of floatation.

So ... if you don't have any fresh water with you, you're in a fix. The first thing you should do is erect some kind of shelter to protect you from the sun. The sun will make a raisin out of you right quick, so any shade you can provide yourself with will prolong evaporation and dehydration.

Second, you have to collect fresh water. Unfortunately, your only source is the sky, in the form of rain. If you're lucky enough to get a storm (one that doesn't produce waves big enough to kill you, that is), be ready for it. Some suggestions are ...

➤ Use your clothes to soak up rainwater. Strip buck naked and use every scrap you own. Cotton works best. Wring the water into your mouth or into any containers you might have.

➤ No containers? Use your shoes. They may not be watertight. And they may not be, um, tasty. But they can collect hard rain better than all of the things you *don't* have.

➤ Use your raft. Rubber rafts, unlike smelly shoes, are watertight. You're sitting in the best fresh-water collection device this side of Hoover Dam. Which is why you should also keep it clean.

Bottom line: If you're in the middle of the ocean without fresh water, your hopes of survival are as dry as your throat. In this case, we suggest singing show tunes until your time is up. Because no one will ever know ....

Food for Thought ... and Survival

If you're lucky enough to have a supply of fresh water, your next priority is food. If you have some, great. Conserve it. You don't know how long you'll be out there. Better to be found alive with leftovers than found dead surrounded by empty Snickers wrappers.

If you don't have any food, well, bummer, dude. If you're fortunate enough to have fishing tackle (or the primitive makings thereof), give it your best shot. Raw fish is a delicacy (and the protein won't hurt you, either). And if raw fish turns your stomach? Don't worry, your stomach will indeed turn the right way if it's empty enough.

Just remember this: Humans can live for a long time without food as long as they have water. Stay focused on survival. When you're rescued, you'll get all the chicken broth and lime Jell-O you can stand.

Can You Dig It ... Out?

After surviving that coup, breaking out of jail, escaping from that psycho kidnapper, and your glorious rescue from that one-person raft 700 miles from the nearest land, you must be exhausted. We have the perfect antidote to those post-vacation blues: *spelunking!* Cave exploration can be one of the most interesting excursions of your getaway. It can also be one of the most dangerous.

Cave-ins are to a spelunker what avalanches are to a skier or snowboarder. Obviously, for some daring adrenaline junkies, the risk is the reward. But how much risk can you stand?

Tactical Terms

Spelunking is the act of exploring a cave, usually requiring protective clothing and climbing gear.

Old abandoned mines present a huge risk. Just look at the words themselves: *old ... abandoned.* That means people don't go in there anymore. Cave-ins were a common occurrence when the mine was active, so do you really think your chances will improve with age? Not bloody likely.

Earthquake zones present an equal risk, since no one can predict when an earthquake will hit. Entering a cave on a fault line is about as intelligent as toasting an English muffin in the bathtub. That said, let's pretend you've just entered an old abandoned mine. On a fault line. With glee, you shout up ahead, "Duh, hello!" which echoes back three times as loud, just to prove our point. Hopefully, you went in prepared like a Boy Scout. Obviously, you don't want to travel heavy, but you don't want to travel stupid, either. Here are some suggestions for *before* you enter the mouth of madness:

➤ **Don't skimp on safety.** If there's climbing involved, use professional-grade rope with all the hardware trimmings. That includes protective gear—helmet, gloves, knee and elbow pads, and thick-soled, waterproof boots. Don't do any cave exploration without it.

233

➤ **Hire a guide.** Someone who knows how to climb. Someone who knows how to react in a crisis. And, of course, someone who knows the caves.

➤ **If you're going alone, tell someone where you're going and when you expect to return.** If you don't show up at the appointed time, that person will know there's been a problem and will organize a search for you.

➤ **Pack food and water.** Even if you're not hungry. This is strictly preventative medicine: A canteen of water and a power bar can keep you alive for days, if necessary. Like the man says, better to have it and not need it than to need it and not have it.

➤ **Bring a flashlight.** And pack extra batteries, just in case.

➤ **Bring a knife.** Because it's the greatest survival tool in the history of mankind.

Okay, you've got the stuff. Into the cave you go. About 50 yards in, the ground starts to tremble and the whole world comes down on the tunnel behind you. Now what? For our purposes, we'll assume you're alone. Right about now you're pining for that tiny jail cell back in the third world. But that was kid stuff. What you need to do now is assess the situation:

➤ **Are you hurt?** First aid comes first. If you're seriously injured, do the best you can to stop any bleeding and prevent the onset of shock.

➤ **How bad was the cave-in?** Can you see any light through the debris? Can you hear anyone trying to get through to you? If not, you may be sealed in airtight. That's bad, but don't panic. If you're packed in airtight, you'll need all the oxygen you can get.

➤ **How is your equipment?** Do you have everything? Good. You'll need it.

Survival Kit

If you hear rescuers through the rubble, don't scream. Conserve your air. Instead, use a rock or metal device to tap out Morse code and alert them to your position: three short taps, three long, three short for SOS.

If no one knows you're down there, you can assume no one will be coming for you (that's why it's a good idea to tell someone where you're going). If so, you might have to dig yourself out. Be aware, though, that if you start digging it could bring down more dirt and rock, making possible rescue even more difficult. It could also trigger another cave-in.

If others know that you're trapped, let them do the digging. Concentrate instead on doing the following:

➤ **Assemble your communication devices:** rocks or metal objects for tapping out Morse code. Don't use the butt of your flashlight; it might break.

➤ **Stay put.** Assuming rescuers know roughly where you are, that's where they'll be searching.

➤ **Conserve everything.** Air. Water. Food. Energy. Batteries. And above all, hope.

When that daylight finally hits your face ... wow, what a feeling. In fact, it feels so good that you might even book next year's vacation immediately. Maybe one with the family this time. Which means we'll need another chapter to help get you through it. Read on!

The Least You Need to Know

➤ When visiting another country, you are the foreigner. Have an understanding of local customs, laws, language, and landscape before you get there.

➤ If violence breaks out in the country in which you're traveling, retreat to your hotel and contact the U.S. Embassy for instructions.

➤ If you're arrested in a foreign country, do everything you can to let someone know where you are. And remember, American laws do not apply.

➤ If you're kidnapped for ransom, be cooperative. You're worth something to your captors. If kidnapped for pathological reasons, do whatever you have to do to protect yourself.

➤ If you're stranded on a raft at sea, your priorities come in this order: fresh water, shelter from the sun, and food. You must survive to be rescued.

➤ If you're trapped in a cave-in, don't scream. Conserve your air and tap out Morse code SOS signals with a rock or metal object.

Chapter 22

Family Bonding

In This Chapter

➤ Parks and resorts are not all fun and games

➤ Roller coasters are *supposed* to be scary—but not deadly

➤ When the ski lift stops lifting

➤ Ready for a riptide?

You've had enough of the foreign prisons. And kidnappings are *so* last year. This year, when it comes to vacations, you and the kids want a little more Great, a little less Adventure. What better way to enjoy oneself than to savor the fruits of domestic travel: the good ol' U.S. of A. and all that she offers.

Traffic. Toll roads. Car exhaust. Body odor. Road rage.

No, we mean the good stuff. Theme parks. Ski resorts. Beaches. The things you remember fondly as a child. But since this is a book about survival, and since your vacation luck last chapter was about as good as bad gets, you can expect some trouble on these trips.

And we wouldn't have it any other way ….

The Roller Coaster Ride from Hell

Fear sells. People will pay good money to be scared out of their wits. That's the sole reason for the roller coaster and other thrill rides. Generally, the world's roller coasters are safe. Every year newer, faster, and more daring rides debut, begging for your amusement dollar. These aren't the rides you have to worry about—they've been built in the Lawsuit Era, and are designed to prevent just that. But the ancient wooden coasters that have been standing for 50 years? A few questions about replaced lumber, track, and cars might be in order.

But truly, anything can happen on any ride, no matter what the age or condition. The train could stall. Worse, the train could stall in the middle of the ride's "event," like a loop. Worst of all, the train could derail.

See? *Fear.* You could simply walk away and wait for your friends while they take the ride. Or you could just embrace the risk. After all, if the wood looks like it's about to collapse under the weight of the rails, that's free fear on top of the fear you're already paying for. What a deal!

Stalled for Time

Most roller coasters—from the ultra-new loopers to the classic wooden coasters—are chain-driven up the first hill, which explains the chuk-chuk-chuk sound as you move (and which also helps build suspense). After that, the ride is gravity-driven. Just a fast train "coasting" on narrow tracks.

If the train stalls on that first hill, the cars will still be engaged with the chain. The mechanism is designed to lock up at the first movement backwards, so if there is a power failure or stall, you're not going anywhere. Stalling is rare, but the most common problem among problems. Stalls can be caused by anything from a power problem to something mechanical.

Which brings us to the standing rule (or the no-standing rule, if you like): If the roller coaster stalls, *stay seated.* Simply remain in the car and wait for the stall to be corrected. Security guards are required to walk up the hill and advise you to stay put (and make sure that you do). Any information that you need will come through them. Most "normal" problems are corrected in five to 10 minutes.

Survival Kit

In the event of a roller coaster stall, always remain seated. Most problems can be cleared up in a matter of minutes. And do you really think you're better off standing on a roller coaster's infrastructure more than a hundred feet in the air?

That can seem like an eternity when you're 150 feet in the air. There will always be some acro/claustro/deathophobic individuals who will immediately try to get out of their cars. Don't do it. After all, if you're that afraid of heights, why would you want to stand on a 1-foot-wide deck at a wickedly steep angle with only a 2-by-4 wooden railing to hold on to?

In fact, if you're afraid of heights, why did you get on the ride in the first place? Safe fear, right? Secure thrills. Well, if you don't stay seated, you could get some insecure thrills. And they can be fatal.

Hanging Upside-Down

You've probably seen footage on some cheesy TV video segment. A carnival ride locks up and leaves its passengers hanging upside-down in the middle of the thrill. How unsatisfying.

This is extremely rare. However, if it happens to you, don't panic. In the case of a roller coaster, modern models with loops and twists and ribbons are what's known as "rail-locked" trains. Which means that the wheels are actually locked around the rails that the train rides on. So the train won't drop off the loop, okay?

SOS

Whether the ride stalls or is operating normally, never fiddle with the ride's safety harnesses, straps, belts, bars, or doors.

As for other carnival rides of various descriptions, being stuck in an uncomfortable position is better than falling. So we say again: *Stay seated!* Don't mess with safety mechanisms. Don't try to open doors, lap bars, or seat belts. Don't do anything except stay calm and wait for instructions. What kind of fool would want to get out of shoulder restraints while hanging upside-down, anyway? Chances are you won't be hanging there long. So sit tight and tell all those other people on the ride that you read this book. You'll instantly become the Gene Hackman in the *Poseidon Adventure* of their lives.

And that's cool.

Derailment Is Not Part of the Ride

As was stated previously, the more modern, loopy roller coasters are rail-locked, so derailment isn't really an issue for them. The classic wooden rides, however? They certainly *can* derail under the wrong circumstances (are there ever any right ones)?

Derailment can range from simply rumbling to a halt to flying right off the whole structure. In the former case, you should be just fine. Wait for the vehicle to come to a halt before disembarking. In the latter case? Well, you can flap your arms if it makes you feel better, but you're coaster toast. Hmmm, now that we think about it, this may be the only time where the "no-standing" rule can be broken (if you think jumping out will help).

The safest thing you can do is not ride the ride at all. Then again, it could derail and land on your head as you sit patiently waiting for your friends, who are about to arrive a lot sooner—and harder—than you think.

Bah. Take the ride with pride. After all, you paid good money for your fear. Enjoy every second.

Adventures of a Lifetime

An anonymous former amusement park employee tells his story:

"The worst accident I can remember was on a busy weekend when management decided—as they usually do on busy holiday weekends—to run two roller coaster trains at the same time. There are sensors on the tracks that tell the ride operator when the first train is halfway through, therefore the second train can begin. Sounds dangerous, but it makes for faster lines and more money. Well, the ride operators aren't NASA scientists. Somehow the first train came whipping through the last turn and through the gate just as the second train began climbing the hill. Both trains were full. The ride operator never stopped the first train and it slammed into the back of the second train. I can still hear the screams. I remember seeing a woman who was near the rear of the first train who had broken either her back or pelvis. She pulled a Linda Blair from *The Exorcist*, twisting full around. But the twist began at her waist."

Hangin' Out at the **Ski Resort**

If you ski, have you ever looked at the flip side of your lift ticket? You haven't seen that much fine print in such a small area since they started listing the ingredients on Twinkee wrappers. In a nutshell, it says skiing is an inherently dangerous sport and the ski resort cannot be held liable in the event of your injury or death. Good, stick-to-your-ribs lawyer-speak. Basically, they mean that your butt is in your own hands.

Naturally, if you break your leg, or back, or neck, it's probably because you were doing something that you shouldn't have been doing (double diamonds are great in poker, but bad for novice skiers). Come on, is meeting people at the lodge later that night really worth all that pain ("You want me to sign your cast *where?*")? But here's a good question: Does all that fine print cover mishaps that occur when your butt is somewhere other than in your own hands? Like say, on the ski lift?

We're not talking about getting on and off the lift (which can become an Inspector Clouseau-esque adventure in its own right). We're talking about dangling far above the slopes with nothing more holding you up than some frozen steel, a few bolts, and a thick cable.

Riding the ski lift is traditionally a time to relax, take in the scenery, and chat. Perhaps take a swig of cognac from your flask. Some of the nicer ski resorts feature fully enclosed, heated gondolas, which are essentially limousines to the top of the mountain.

But sometimes they just stop. If you've skied before, you know the feeling. *Ugh.* You just dangle there, bouncing gently up and down while the wind suddenly feels a lot colder against your cheek.

There are only two things that stop a ski lift:

1. Someone fell while getting on or off.

2. The machine broke.

Survival Kit

The same rule for roller coasters applies to halted ski lifts, too: *Stay put!*

If it's the former, the lift will start up again in a few seconds (after they clear away the human debris). But if it's the latter, you can expect a delay of anywhere from a few minutes to … well, a long time. However, long delays are rare. In fact, breakdowns are rare. But they do happen, and no matter how impatient you may be, no matter how much you need to ski, no matter how much you paid: *Stay in the chair!*

One rule. Bottom line. No shortcuts.

Well, that's not entirely accurate. There is one other possibility. You could jump. But if you're thinking of jumping, consider the following factors:

➤ **Height.** Only James Bond can drop from 50 feet and ski away into the arms of a female spy. Even a drop as little as 10 feet can hurt you, especially while wearing boots and skis. And you're not being shot at.

➤ **Depth of snow.** Deep snow can cushion your fall. It can also hide rocks, stumps, and the skeletons of other dead skiers.

➤ **Clear landing area.** Avoid jumping into trees. Also avoid rocks, stumps, and the skeletons of other dead skiers.

➤ **Your intelligence, or lack thereof.** Sensing a pattern yet? Jumping from a perfectly good—albeit broken-down—ski lift is stupid. Don't do it.

What's the worst that could happen on a disabled ski lift? The cable could snap, in which case you won't have time to do anything except fall. Or you could hang there for hours, freezing (but you're a smart skier and you dressed for the weather … right?). In that case, they'll get you down sometime, somehow.

Patience is your best friend here. Just keep in mind that the longer you hang there, the more free passes you can demand when you finally get off that cockamamie machine.

Something to Tide You Over

They're called beach "resorts" for a reason. The process of getting there and enjoying them makes you "resort" to screaming, fistfights, and firearms.

The beach used to be such a nice place. White sand. Clean water. The cloying scent of coconut oil. But now? If the traffic doesn't rip a fresh hole in your personal ozone ... if you find a parking space ... if you enjoy paying $20 admission to stake a claim to a little plot of sand ... if you don't mind thousands of angry, hairy, greased-up samples of humanity ... and if you don't get a hypodermic needle stuck in your big toe on your way to the surf ... well, you too can be eligible to enjoy the dangers of a *riptide*.

A riptide sounds worse than it actually is, but make no mistake, it is dangerous, especially if you've never experienced one before. One minute you're enjoying the rough surf. The next you're being swept out to sea—and it seems like there isn't a thing you can do about it. Not true.

Here's some common-sense advice to heed *before* you go in the water:

➤ **Know thyself.** Being a good swimmer is only a starting point. Knowing how fast, long, and strong you can swim can certainly save your life; but having the common sense not to take unnecessary risks can prevent putting your life in danger in the first place.

➤ **Never swim alone.** This is especially true if the beach has no lifeguards. The buddy system is one of the most common pieces of swimming advice for a reason. At the very least, have someone on the beach watching you.

➤ **Obey warnings.** Lifeguards and beach patrols issue regular warnings about rough surf and strong undertows. Listen to them.

➤ **Don't assume anything.** Thinking, "Oh, the lifeguards will rescue me if something bad happens," is one passage of the buck that could get you killed. Anything can happen. Don't put your life in someone else's hands unnecessarily—what if that person fails?

Swimming at the beach, while seemingly harmless and fun, is still swimming. Even if your feet can touch the bottom, don't forget that you're still standing in an ocean. Riptides happen unexpectedly, which means you'll be well on your way by the time you figure out you're actually in one.

If a riptide takes you …

➤ **Don't panic.** Conserve your strength and realize that, yes, you will be moving away from land at a frightening pace. That's what a riptide does. But if you know what you're doing, you can help yourself.

➤ **Call for help.** Alert the lifeguards. Good lifeguards will already see that you're in trouble. You can take steps to save yourself—as you'll see in a minute—but getting some trained professionals on the payroll is key.

➤ **Stay visible.** This is most important in an open-water rescue (whether you're floating at sea due to a riptide or some other mishap). If rescuers can't see you in the water, they can't help you. A colorful bathing cap is nice. But if the fashion police kept you hatless that morning, try your bathing suit. Either wave it around or put it on your head (assuming it's not black, dark green, or navy blue). Don't be bashful. No one can see your bottom half in the water. And if you're a female wearing a one-piece? Take it off anyway. Being visible is more important than modesty.

➤ **Swim parallel to the shore.** Don't swim directly against a riptide. Your first instinct might be to try to go back the way you came, but you're wrong. You'll effectively be swimming upstream in a powerful river. Riptides may be swift and strong, but they are usually narrow. Swim laterally, parallel to the shoreline, and you should make your way out of it.

➤ **If you get tired, tread water or float.** Slow your breathing. Calm down. Lie on your back and use slow, sweeping motions to conserve energy while you remain afloat. Panic is your real enemy here, so simply tell yourself that you're unsinkable and help will be there soon.

The most important thing to remember is that riptides, while frightening, are not killers. They don't bite. They don't suck you down to the bottom of the sea. They're just currents. People are the ones who get themselves killed. If you're a good swimmer, you should be able to escape a riptide on your own. And if you're not a good swimmer? Heed all tide warnings and never, ever swim without supervision.

After all, surviving means you first must live to tell the tale. Then you can tell it over and over again that night over a few well-deserved drinks.

The Least You Need to Know

➤ If a roller coaster stalls, always stay seated. Most problems are corrected in a few minutes.

➤ On a stalled carnival ride, never try to unlock safety restraints. Sit tight and wait for the problem to be solved or for help to arrive.

➤ The same "stay seated" rule applies to disabled ski lifts. Never jump from a stalled ski lift, no matter how close to the ground you think you are.

➤ If you're caught in a riptide, swim laterally until you get out of it. Never swim against the current.

➤ In an open-water rescue, the most important thing is to stay visible. If you're wearing a colorful bathing suit, use it to signal lifeguards.

➤ Never swim without trained supervision, or at the very least, a "buddy."

A Personal Attack

Self-defense is a wonderful thing. It's legal, for one, which means that when facing harm from another human, you are free to defend yourself with impunity, extreme prejudice, and even bad taste. In other words, you can do whatever it takes. And why wouldn't you? It's your body and it's your life we're talking about.

Alas, being physically assaulted is not what you would call your everyday gig (unless your first name is Indiana or your last name is Bond). When it happens, some people panic. That's not the survivalist mentality at its finest. You need to keep calm. You need to quickly assess the situation. And then you need to whip out this book and read the following pages to figure out what to do next.

A Note About Hollywood

Ah, Hollywood. The place of dreams. Only in a Hollywood story could a loser British secret agent with bad teeth and worse taste in clothes shag both Elizabeth Hurley *and*

Heather Graham. Only in a Hollywood story could two slightly more studly secret agents hit each other head-on after leaping off their motorcycles going 80 miles an hour—and live to beat the crap out of each other for another 15 minutes. But this is *Mission: Entertainment*, Mr. Hunt. Not *Mission: Reality*. And that's why this section may be the most important in a book full of dangerous "what ifs."

There's no doubt about it, human drama happens. These pages are filled with hundreds of instances of human drama. Any one of them could happen to you. That's why knowledge is the best medicine, so to speak. Basic knowledge might help you survive.

However—and this is a big, 10-foot-high *however*—between the time that a human drama happens and the time the rest of us hear about it, that drama travels through filters. And each filter—whether it's a news report or tell-all book or just a story told over a couple brews—amps up the drama. The more filters, the bigger the story, the more drama is needed to sell it.

SOS

Leave the Hollywood stunts to the professionals. If you're assaulted, running away is always the first, best solution.

That's where Hollywood comes in. Scan the table of contents of this book. You could probably name an existing movie for every chapter. Why? Because we relate to movies. They give us instant common ground. Instant images. Instant comparisons.

But we're about to talk about self-defense. And that's where you, dear reader, need to know one major thing: Hollywood is bogus. Dangerous, even. Hollywood, as entertaining as its movies are, deludes us into transference—letting us think that we can do whatever a hero does onscreen.

News flash: You can't. You won't. You'll get hurt if you try.

Everything in a film—from the biggest set piece down to the shortest scene—is choreographed. Nothing is left to chance. So when you see Jackie Chan twisting a gun out of Chris Tucker's hand in *Rush Hour*, or Jet Li yanking the slide off Mel Gibson's 9mm in *Lethal Weapon 4*, or Steven Seagal blocking a knife strike and breaking the perp's arm in *Above the Law*, know this: You've just seen more choreography than you'll see in a Janet Jackson video.

Bottom line: Disarming an attacker is one of the most dangerous things you could ever do. So if you have to try, rely on common sense, not your DVD collection. There really is only one acceptable film technique you can use when attacked. The film? *Monty Python and the Holy Grail*. The technique? "Run away! Run away!"

Unarmed Does Not Mean Unharmed

No one is unarmed. A potential "unarmed" attacker has many weapons at his or her disposal: fist, foot, elbow, knee, nails, and teeth, to name a few. And this attacker has many methods of delivering these weapons: size, strength, speed, and flexibility. Other factors affecting an attack include emotions, drunkenness, drug use, and whether or not you know the person. The unarmed attack, therefore, comes in many forms. It may be an anonymous man attacking a lone woman on a dark street. A brother punching a brother over a pool table in a bar. A wife attacking a deadbeat husband. The list is endless. But each situation has one common thread: someone defending him- or herself against aggression.

So how do you disarm an unarmed attacker? You could try wit, but you'd get hurt. No, it's time for action. You'll have to think fast, use what nature gave you, and absolutely *do not hold back*.

The Unarmed Assault

An unarmed attacker comes at you. What do you do? Remembering that you'll have only a second or two to act, your immediate options are to …

➤ **Escape.** Flee. Bolt. Common sense, right? Escape is always the first, best option. But that may not always be possible, depending on the circumstances. If escape is impossible …

➤ **Evade.** Dodge the attack. This could mean sidestepping a head-on charge or turning to one side to evade a punch. Like Mr. Myagi said in *The Karate Kid*: "Best defense, no be there." Evading an attack gives you precious seconds to regroup, to escape if possible, or to contemplate your counterstrike when you …

➤ **Engage.** Only a last resort. But if you must fight, don't fight to win. Fight to escape. Disable or delay your opponent (yes, that means hurt the person) long enough to allow yourself time to get away.

We'll discuss defense techniques in a moment. But you now have specific and immediate choices for that moment when most people think they have no choice at all.

Fight the Bad Fight

So how do you defend yourself when it's time to get physical? If you've had some training—be it martial arts, military, boxing, or law enforcement—you're better equipped for such situations. But what about the average Joe or Jane who lives his or her life like most of us movie-watching, munchie-munching creatures of habit?

To offer an entire course on self-defense in these pages would be irresponsible and dangerous. When it comes to getting physical, there is no substitute for hands-on instruction and practice. Get out there and take some classes at the local Y. Sign up for those tai-kwon-do lessons you've been meaning to investigate. Invite that black-belt, ex-Marine buddy of yours to show you some moves. The one problem with training is that it takes years to become a ninja. In the meantime, here's some common-sense advice on self-defense:

Survival Kit

If you're being assaulted, scream "Fire!" Strangers are more prone to respond, or at the very least, call 911 when faced with the possibility of a fire.

➤ **Scream.** Sometimes our first reaction to the insanity of an attack is silence. Shake it off. Scream until you're blue in the face. The sound will hopefully take your attacker by surprise and make him or her pause. If you scream "help" or "rape," people may be reluctant to get involved. If you scream "fire," however, they will react, or better yet, they will call 911. If you can, point at someone and demand action. "*You!* Call for help, now!" Once identified, people feel more obligated to do something.

➤ **Breathe.** Control the adrenaline dump and feed your brain oxygen by moderating your breathing. *Think* about breathing. During a confrontation or high-risk incident, your body forces blood from the extremities to the vital organs (the beginnings of shock), which can cause you to lose coordination—a bad deal for you in a physical confrontation. Steady, deliberate breathing can also help stave off panic.

➤ **Remain confident.** Keep telling yourself, "I will win this fight, I will not die." Sure, it sounds corny, but a positive mindset can be the difference between life and death.

➤ **Fight dirty.** If you have to fight, follow Clint Eastwood's advice in *The Outlaw Josey Wales:* "Get mean. Mad dog mean." This person wants to hurt you. Don't be gentle. Don't be polite. Don't be merciful. It's your life, and it's in your hands. Fight back with all you've got.

No Points for Niceness

When the gloves come off, so to speak, the rules go out the window, too. Which means that any one of the following areas of anatomy becomes an instant target of opportunity when dealing with an unarmed attacker:

➤ **Groin.** Pretty self-explanatory. Hit 'em where it hurts. This strategy may have to change if the attacker is armed with a knife or gun (to be discussed momentarily), but for an unarmed attacker, do your worst.

➤ **Eyes.** Make a fist. Extend your thumb slightly, allowing the nail to protrude. Jab it as hard as you can into your attacker's eye. Both eyes will close and if you're lucky, the perp will grab the wound with both hands, allowing you to escape.

➤ **Ears.** Grab hard and pull. Don't be shy about tearing. Also effective: slapping the ear with your palm.

➤ **Nose.** Strike someone in the nose and his or her eyes will water, blinding the person. It hurts a lot, too.

➤ **Mouth.** Your mouth, that is. Bite whatever presents itself.

➤ **Soft tissue.** The solar plexus (just below where the ribs meet in the center of the torso) and the throat are both vulnerable to hard blows. Again, don't be shy.

Remember, these tactics are a last resort when self-defense is the only option left. Do not attack someone unless it's in self-defense. That's felonious assault, and carries jail time. Critical times like these require sly intelligence, not bold stupidity.

The Edge Goes to the Bad Guy

What if your attacker has an edged or pointed weapon such as a knife, machete, sword, straight razor, box cutter, ice pick, screwdriver, or *shank?*

Don't underestimate these weapons. They are devastating. A box cutter can open a fatal throat wound. One blow from an ice pick can perforate your stomach, liver, or lungs.

The best defense against an edged weapon attack is twofold:

1. **Distance.** If it can't touch you, it can't cut you. Get space between you and the blade. If someone is charging you, use quick lateral movements and anything around you, which means …

2. **Obstacles.** Get objects such as chairs, garbage cans, or parked cars between you and your attacker. And *scream.*

   If there isn't time to get out of the way, you may have to block the attack. Sure, it sounds terrifying, but what kind of wound would you rather have? A gash across your face, or a gash across your hand?

> **Tactical Terms**
>
> A **shank** is a prison term for a homemade weapon used for inflicting deep puncture wounds. Shanks can be made of anything from a wire coat hanger to the sharpened handle of a toothbrush.

Someone attacking you with an edged weapon in public will want to be discreet. Most streetwise attackers jab quickly or slash upward, with the blade palmed and running parallel to their wrist or forearm. So if you sense an attack, look at the person's hands to see what's coming.

If you have to block, use whatever is available:

➤ **Heavy clothing.** Not many razor blades can cut through a good leather coat sleeve on the first try. Thick wool is good, as is fur. You can also wrap your hand in a winter hat or scarf. In warm weather, your plain old naked arm will have to do. Unless, of course, you have …

➤ **Luggage.** Not the big suitcases, mind you. But your briefcase, umbrella, satchel, handbag, backpack, or Darth Maul lunchbox would be delighted to take a hit for the team.

As always, escape is the best solution. But if you are given no choice, don't hesitate. Protect yourself. And remember just how dangerous that little Swiss Army knife can be.

Adventures of a Lifetime

When it comes to edged weapons, some law enforcement officers rely on the "21-foot" rule. An attacker armed with an edged weapon can close 21 feet before an experienced law enforcement officer can unholster a sidearm and discharge a round. A good comparison is the distance from the top of the key on a basketball court to underneath the rim. If a suspect is inside that 21-foot zone, a cop knows that some other mode of defense will have to be used. The lesson to you is, if someone's coming at you, get ready to dodge or fight.

Is an edged weapon worse than a gun? Yes, for a number of reasons. Edged weapons are …

➤ Cheap.

➤ Easy to obtain.

➤ Easy to conceal.

➤ Easy to use.

➤ Easy to dispose of.

➤ And worst of all, *silent.*

Guns get the glamour, folks. But chew on this: Any moron can go into a Home Depot and buy a utility knife.

Is That a Gun in Your Pocket, or ...

Guns have never been more visible in our society then they are now. Sure, per capita numbers favor the Civil War era, but they didn't have TV back then. If you've never fired a gun or been around someone firing a gun, beware of Hollywood fantasies. Here are some gun realities:

➤ When you fire a gun—even the smallest gun—it produces an explosion that you'll feel to your very core. Your ears *will* ring. You *will* flinch.

➤ TV guns don't kick. Real guns kick *hard*. Rapid-firing a semi-automatic 9mm pistol with accuracy is tough enough. Emptying the clip of a fully automatic sub-machine gun is like trying to hold down a jet engine.

➤ Handguns are heavy. Bigger guns can be cumbersome, as well. A .44 magnum revolver with an 8-inch barrel is a ridiculously impractical street weapon. You're more likely to encounter smaller semi-automatic pistols in a robbery. They're lighter, hold more ammunition, and can be fired more rapidly.

Unlike knives, guns are never underestimated. One pull of the trigger and you're toast. Your attacker knows what kind of fear a gun instills, and will use a gun because the he or she knows you will be afraid. And you should.

But should you be frightened to the point of inaction? Never.

When They Pull a Gun on You

Criminals aren't out there consulting psychology texts to figure out which weapon is more effective in a street crime. It's pure common sense: If a person pulls a gun, that person gets whatever he or she wants. It's about power.

You have two basic situations. Either you know the person with the gun, or you don't. *If you know the person:* Does your attacker have the stomach to actually fire the weapon? Everyone has a dark side, and you need to know just how desperate this acquaintance is. Talk to your attacker. Use whatever friendship you have to get your attacker to lose the gun. And if the attacker does give in, it's better to have him or her put down the gun so you can retrieve it, rather than for you to take it from the attacker (because the gun could go off, okay?). *If you don't know the person:* Assume the attacker will kill you as much as look at you. Don't play a Hollywood game and think you "see fear in his eyes." Of course you'll see fear. But eye contact is a sign of aggression and could get you killed. If the attacker is a stranger, assume the worst at all times.

Defending Your Life

The distance defense from our previous edged-weapon discussion does not apply to guns. You can't outrun a bullet. Hiding behind obstacles remains viable, however, provided you pick your shelter wisely. A car door will block a bullet. A car window won't. A brick wall will block a bullet. A drywall structure won't. Get the picture?

The best defense is hiding behind obstacles if you can find them. If you run, move laterally so you create a harder target. Think about it: If you simply turn around and run away from a gunman in a straight line, it's a straight shot to hit you in the back. But if you zigzag or run laterally? The perp would have to be a world-class marksman to hit you. And most thugs aren't even third-class.

The Absolute Last Resort: Disarmament

If distance, obstacles, and lateral movement aren't part of the equation, and your attacker is right in front of you or behind you, you may be left with no other choice but going for the weapon. If this is the case, you cannot make the decision half-heartedly. You cannot hesitate. You cannot use anything less than every ounce of strength in your body. If you compromise in the slightest, you'll be killed.

SOS

Never go with your attacker. If someone with a gun or knife tells you to "come quietly and you won't get hurt," the person is taking you to the site of your death. Why? The attacker obviously sees something wrong with the current scene and cannot commit the crime there for some reason (eyewitnesses, traffic, avenues of escape). This is a good time to scream your head off.

Be responsible with your life and the lives of those around you. Trying to disarm a gunman in a convenience store full of people—or in any crowd situation, for that matter—is reckless and stupid. An innocent bystander is likely to get shot.

An edged weapon can't shoot anyone, obviously, but the danger to your own life is still high. This is the time for the survival mentality. This is life-or-death time. Don't screw it up.

Some techniques that you may have seen in the movies—and that actually sound effective—are actually not. *Do not* attempt the following with an armed attacker:

➤ **Striking the attacker's forearm.** Yes, this can force the hand to open and drop the weapon, but the blow would have to be delivered with unbelievable force.

➤ **Striking the attacker's shoulder with a karate chop.** Might as well call this one the "Captain Kirk Technique." It just doesn't work. And you'll look stupid doing it.

➤ **Giving a bear hug.** Try it on a friend and you'll see that you can still get stabbed or shot.

➤ **Stomping on the foot.** It might hurt, but it won't do anything to disarm your attacker.

➤ **Kicking to the groin.** Again, it hurts, but chances are the attacker won't drop the weapon.

Control of the weapon lies in two places: the weapon hand and the attacker's overall balance. Think about the anatomy of the arm. The shoulder is a ball-and-socket joint. The elbow is a hinge. But the wrist? The wrist can move in nearly any direction and can be manipulated.

Adventures of a Lifetime

Any cop in the world will tell you that a great physical description is priceless, and a lot better than an attempt at becoming a hero. If it's a robbery, give up the goods. But catalog everything about the person: gender, age, skin and hair color, scars and tattoos, clothing. As for height, did you ever notice the height markers on the door frames as you leave a convenience store? Use any point of reference you can to establish height: a tree, a stop sign, a mailbox. Bottom line, the more information a cop has, the more reasonable suspicion a cop has for stopping a suspect later on.

So you've made your choice. You're going for the weapon. It's time to think systematically and act deliberately. Follow these steps:

1. Establish the location of the weapon hand. This is a no-brainer if the gun is against your head (no pun intended). But it could also be in your ribs, or pressed against your back. The latter is actually an advantage since it gives you a reference point for reaching, and a chance to plan while waiting for your *window of opportunity*.

2. If there's some kind of distraction and you're in close, you might actually feel your attacker's arm relax slightly. At that moment, go for control of the weapon hand. This does

Tactical Terms

A **window of opportunity** is the ideal time to take advantage of a situation and act. A distraction—a car horn, a person entering a room—can cause an attacker to pause, and give you a chance to escape.

Tactical Terms

A **pistol bite** occurs when an attacker's trigger finger is broken or ripped off in the process of being disarmed (or dis-fingered, as the case may be).

not necessarily mean taking the weapon. You are simply limiting the attacker's ability to hurt you.

3. In the case of a gun, clamp one hand over the weapon, one hand under the weapon. Always keep the muzzle pointed away from you. In the case of an edged weapon, clamp both hands on the attacker's weapon hand. In either case, *always use two hands.*

4. Crouch low with a shoulder-wide stance and pull the weapon toward you. That's right, towards you. You must get the weapon closer to your center of gravity. This will also cause the attacker to lose balance.

5. With a gun, remember that the attacker's finger will be on the trigger. As you twist and pull towards you, the pistol either goes off and misses you, or you break the perp's trigger finger. Or better yet, you pull the finger off (it has happened—this is called a *pistol bite*). *Be prepared for the gun to go off.* As we've said, gunfire is loud and the gun will kick violently. Don't let this distract or deter you.

   The two-handed, over-under squeezing of the pistol may disable the action of the gun. In the case of a revolver, the cylinder could be prevented from spinning or the hammer could be prevented from striking the round. With a semi-automatic, movement of the slide could be compromised.

6. When weapon control is obtained—or at least disrupted—begin the "unfair" fight and do whatever you have to do to gain the advantage.

7. *Do not* strike at the expense of relinquishing control of the weapon.

8. *Do* scream your head off the entire time.

Remember, these strategies offer no guarantees. We can't recommend enough the need for formal training in any physical confrontation. On the other hand, no one goes searching for confrontations like this. Do what you have to do to survive, but remember that you're not the only one trying to survive. Your attacker will be equally desperate not just to live, but to make sure you die. Assess your alternatives with care and use common sense, because reckless people die stupid deaths.

Bean Stalked?

Being stalked—or even thinking that you're being stalked—can be one of the most frightening things you'll ever experience. For this section, we'll focus on the traditional stalker—the one following you down a dark street, in a supermarket, in a mall, or anywhere. The kind that existed before the Internet and the culture of celebrity.

You don't know who this person is, but you do know that this person is following you.

What do you do? A lot of things, actually. But the one thing you *do not* do is confront the person. You don't know him or her. You don't know what the stalker wants or what the stalker is capable of. If you confront the person, say the wrong thing, make the wrong move, bam, you're in a situation like we discussed in the previous section: a gun or knife in your ribs.

So, what should you do? Here are some options:

➤ Find a cop. Pure, simple, direct. Stay calm when you talk to the officer. Report that "that person right over there" is following you. Point out the stalker. Make sure the police officer sees him or her. If that's not possible, give the police a detailed description of the suspect.

➤ If you're being followed in a car, don't pull the old "let's lose 'em" deal and floor it. That's just dumb. Your best bet is to drive normally, let the stalker follow you, and then proceed directly to the nearest police station. Chances are the stalker won't follow you into the parking lot. Give the cops as many details as you can about the car, the most important being the *license number*. Make, model, year, and color are also key.

➤ If the police aren't available, use your head. Stay public. Keep people around you. Do not allow yourself to be isolated.

➤ If the stalker: Is closing in and a confrontation is imminent, scream.

Your best bet at every turn is to involve the police. But if the stalker persists, think about change: your habits, your phone number, your e-mail. Carry pepper spray or some other form of defensive item (some states require a license to carry such items—do some research). And how about a camera? The police surely would love to have a picture of your number-one fan.

The bottom line is: Use common sense. Stay vigilant and stay public. Then call the cops.

Bound for Trouble

Only you know how you got there. But there you are, about to be tied up by a very dangerous individual. We won't create any vivid scenarios here. We won't discuss panic and adrenaline and the need to stay calm. What we will talk about is how to get out of ropes when you're all tied up.

If you're handcuffed, chained, or tied with elastic such as a bungee cord, the information in this section won't help you. However, if you're bound with rope, cord, cloth strips, or duct tape, it's possible to get free. The key is being discreet, because all of your preparations for escape will come as the attacker is tying you up. So stay cool, cooperate, and wait for your chance to escape. Here's how:

SOS

Some knots are designed to tighten as you pull harder. Beware that you don't inadvertently strengthen your bonds as you try to escape.

1. Inhale. Make your body as large as possible. But don't take a big, obvious breath. Fill your lungs slowly, gradually, and then breathe shallowly while they do their work.

2. Flex every muscle in your body. Again, the idea is to make your frame as large as possible. And again, the idea is to not be obvious about it.

3. When the attacker is finished, and hopefully leaves you alone, exhale and relax. You should feel the ropes give slightly.

4. Begin working your way out of the ropes with a combination of shoulder shrugging, wiggling, and stretching. Slow and steady wins this race. Big movements won't help you. Work your arms and legs against the rope systematically, gradually working your way out. It's rather like water eroding a riverbank. Results take time, but they do happen.

Obviously, if you have some sort of sharp instrument or a cigarette lighter, you could cut or burn your way out. Which is fine—if your captors are dumb enough to allow you access to such items.

Can you break some glass? A broken bottle, mirror, or window could be used to saw through the ropes (just make sure your captors don't hear glass shattering). Are you tied to a wooden chair? If it's old or rickety, you might be able to break it apart with a combination of muscle and weight. Bottom line: Use anything you can get your hands on to help you escape.

Adventures of a Lifetime

An interesting bar trick is lighting a paper match from a book of matches using only one hand. This becomes a useful survival trick in a bound-and-gagged situation (assuming you have a book of matches within reach). Open the cover and fold a match around the book until you're pushing the head against the striking area with your thumb. Then snap your thumb smartly to light the match. It's not easy and it takes practice. But like riding a bike, once you learn, it's with you forever. And who knows, it may come in handy someday.

Locked in the Trunk of a Car

Once again, we won't ask how you got there. But one day you just might find yourself locked in the trunk of a car. One of the more recent—and classic—Hollywood trunk episodes came in *Out of Sight,* when George Clooney rode a few miles pushed up against Jennifer Lopez in a trunk after a prison break.

Out here in the real world, none of us regular folk would be so fortunate to get locked up with either George or Jennifer, whomever you might prefer. No, we'd get stowed in the back alone, or with someone really annoying. Or even worse, with a dead body. That's just how it plays out for most of us.

Survival Kit

Some cars, such as the Honda Civic, have fold-down rear seats that open into the trunk and are held by a simple latch. You might want to wait until your captor is out of the car before going this route, however ...

Anyway, you're locked in a trunk. It's pitch black. Maybe you get some light from the taillights, but it won't be much. What do you do?

1. **Don't panic.** The fate that awaits you at the hands of your captor will be much worse than a claustrophobia-induced panic attack. So breathe normally, bottle the irrational fear, and become a survivor.

2. **Don't worry about air.** Car trunks aren't airtight. If you're in warm weather, however, it could get mighty hot. Conserve energy.

3. **Assess your surroundings.** If the trunk is completely empty and you have nothing in your pockets to help you, you'll have to go at the latch with your bare fingers (hey, better than nothing when it's life or death). Your best tool for escape is anything long and thin and metallic. A coat hanger works well. But even a tire iron would be useful (as a tool *and* a weapon). Catalog your new possessions and put them where you can reach them easily.

4. **Pop the latch.** Most car trunks have spring-loaded latches. Popping one from the inside is relatively easy with the right tool. The main objective is to get something behind the spring to release the tension.

5. **Be patient.** You'll be working in the dark with no instructions. Frustration just leads to useless emotions like hopelessness and panic. Stay focused. And of course, wait until the car stops moving to jump out.

In a way, popping the latch is the easy part. What do you do then? Well, you could be in a fix. You might not know where you are. You might be leaping out right in front of your enemy. The possibilities are endless. As always, stay calm. Be decisive. Be smart. And if all else fails, tell your attacker that his shoe's untied, kick him in the face when he looks down, and run like heck.

The Least You Need to Know

➤ Escape is always the first, best solution when being attacked.

➤ If you must defend yourself, use any means available to allow yourself to escape.

➤ Scream the entire time. It's best to scream "fire," since strangers are more prone to investigate.

➤ If you're being stalked, do not confront the stalker. Stay in a public place and get a detailed description. Then find a police officer.

➤ When being tied up, inhale and flex your muscles to make your frame as big as possible. When you relax, the ropes should have some slack which can allow you to work free.

➤ The trunk of a car is held closed by a spring-loaded latch. A slim metal tool such as a coat hanger can be slipped behind the spring to release the tension and pop the latch. Wait for the car to stop before jumping out.

Do Unto Others

We come to this final chapter as better people. We know more about emergencies, self-preservation, and how the world works than we did before we began—and that goes for the authors as well as the readers.

But there are some classic crises that have yet to be visited. They aren't easily classified. They aren't extensive enough to put in their own chapters. So we've gathered them here, realizing that they all have one thing in common an ordinary person helping another person who's in a bad way. Ordinary can quickly become extraordinary, however. All it takes is information—knowledge—and some guts. Stand and face the fire, survivor, for someone out there will need your help. Will you be up to the challenge?

We hope so. You'd certainly want a stranger to be up to the challenge if you were the one in trouble. Perhaps we could also use a chapter on karma ....

A Very Special Delivery

You hear the stories all the time. You see the scenes play out on TV and in movies as if this kind of thing happens every day. We're talking, of course, about delivering a baby without benefit of drugs, doctors, or hospitals. How many makeshift birthing places can you name? The back seat of a taxi is an old favorite. On an airplane. In the wilderness. Heck, Salma Hayek even delivered a baby on Hoover Dam at the end of the movie *Fools Rush In.*

These babies are always delivered in high drama, usually in act three and resulting in the obligatory happy ending. High drama is one thing, and certainly delivering a baby without a doctor is risky business for baby and mommy, but it doesn't have to be the crisis it's played out to be.

Why? Because you know the first rule of survival: Don't panic. Mommy needs to know that you're in this game to the end, whether you're a total stranger, her best girlfriend, or the proud papa himself. She needs to see confidence. She needs to know that she's doing well.

She needs a survivor.

Embracing Organized Labor

Obviously, the telltale sign of impending baby-dom is labor. Labor itself is nothing to be afraid of. A woman in labor, on the other hand, can be a blasphemy-spouting demon right out of *The Exorcist.* Relax. This is normal and natural.

For you male readers, don't even try to relate. You can't. Labor and delivery of a baby entail a fantastic and frightening process of nature that inflicts pain beyond the masculine imagination. Sure, there are drugs and epidurals to take the edge off. But in this chapter we're talking about delivery without doctors or hospitals. Which means no "mama's little helpers." It'll be pure pain, baby (or pure baby pain).

You're the one who must ignore the confusion, craziness, and cursing and guide that little fella/filly into the world. So back up, buttercup.

The usual signs of labor are ...

> ➤ **Loss of mucous plug and presentation of the "bloody show" (a small amount of blood that appears after the plug).** This is as gross as it sounds if the plug in question is not your own. Don't worry; it's part of the process. The mucous plug helps protect the baby from the outside world; that is, infection. Mommy will be shedding many things from her womb during labor and delivery. Such as ...

> ➤ **Water breaking.** The "water," or amniotic fluid, is what the baby lives in as it develops. Like the plug, the fluid protects the fetus. When the water initially "breaks," meaning the amniotic sac ruptures, only a portion of the entire

amount of fluid will pour out. This is still a generous amount. Don't be shocked by it. The rest of the fluid will come out with the baby.

➤ **Dilation.** The mother's cervix will open and the birth canal will dilate in preparation for the baby. A trained physician or nurse can tell with an internal exam how dilated the mother is. Ten centimeters is the magic number. However, you are not a trained physician or nurse. This information is here strictly for your information. Do not attempt to measure a mother's dilation if you don't know what you're looking (and feeling) for.

➤ **Contractions.** The bread and butter of labor. Uterine contractions force the baby through the birth canal. They start mild and build in intensity and frequency. The stronger the contraction, the more painful.

Under normal circumstances, it's time to go to the hospital when the contractions are five minutes apart. However, our working assumption in this chapter—for all subjects—is that there is no emergency medical service available. If there is, get that mommy to a hospital. Don't play hero.

But if it's just you and her and baby-to-be? Well … it's time for a special delivery … .

SOS

A woman's water does not have to break for her to be in full labor. Don't rely on this event as a signal of impending delivery. Your best indicator is the time between contractions.

Survival Kit

The way to detect a contraction—other than the mother telling you it's happening—is to feel for a hardening of the belly. In the middle of a good contraction, that pregnant Buddha will be hard as a rock.

Deliverance

Babies deliver themselves. Sure, mother's push. Doctors control the situation, help the baby, and deal with complications, if any. But the act of birth is as natural as breathing. Think about it. Humans were on this planet squeezing out babies long before there were schools training people to help out.

Granted, back then the mortality rate for both mother and child was astronomical compared to what it is today. But if a baby is positioned normally and all systems are go, the birthing process should be smooth (though hardly effortless). The key is to remember that everything you're seeing is normal and natural. Anxiety is expected; panic is dangerous. Be fascinated by the process, for it is truly miraculous.

Adventures of a Lifetime

Breathing exercises, such as Lamaze, help prevent a mother-to-be from pushing too soon. Controlled breathing also aids in concentration and pain management. Remind the mother of any training she may have had. If she hasn't had any, it's up to you to help. Tell her to find a focal point and concentrate on it. Inhale through the nose and exhale through the mouth. Do not let her push (she will want to very badly as her contractions intensify). Make the breathing a routine that you and the mother-to-be return to on every contraction. It will help both of you on many levels.

Here's how events should unfold:

1. Contractions will eventually come one on top of the other. Order the mother to push when those contractions hit. Don't worry, her body will be compelling her to push. Her pushing, along with the contraction, will move the baby along.

2. Have the mother hold the push as long as she can. She should continue pushing for as long as the contraction lasts. Then between contractions, she should concentrate on breathing.

3. Soon you'll be able to see the baby's head. If you see the child's butt or feet, you've got a breech delivery on your hands, which is a major complication (see the next section, "A Complicated Situation Made Worse").

4. Eventually, that one push will come that forces the baby's head out. Hold the head steady and keep the umbilical cord from wrapping around its neck. Don't stop now. Urge the mother on; she's almost there.

5. Once the baby's shoulders are out, the rest of the child should slide out with ease, along with a gusher of amniotic fluid. Be prepared. It's messy.

6. Clear the baby's mouth of any excess fluid. You don't have to smack the baby on the behind. It should start breathing on its own. A good healthy cry is exactly the kind of vital sign you want. If the baby doesn't cry, check to see if it's breathing. If not, you may have to begin CPR (see Chapter 4, "Lifesaving Skills 101").

7. Tie off the umbilical cord 2 or 3 inches from the baby's bellybutton. Twist-ties work, and so does string or a shoelace. Doctors use plastic clamps in the hospital, but do the best you can. After the cord is tied off, you can cut it near the tie

with a knife or scissors. The remaining cord will fall off the baby in about two weeks.

8. Wrap the baby in clean blankets and keep it as warm as possible. Then hand it over to mom, since she's the one who did all the work.

Ah, what a beautiful moment. What a beautiful baby. What a beautiful person you are for pulling this off (or out, you might say). But wait! You're not done yet:

1. Soon after the birth comes the afterbirth (hence the name). The placenta and just about anything else left inside the mother needs to come out as well. This is a simple process: Have the mother push one last time while you pull on the umbilical cord. The afterbirth should slide out easily. There will be some blood, so be prepared. This is normal.

2. Get mom and baby to a hospital ASAP. While you may have just delivered a healthy baby, both mom and baby still need medical attention (and a warm bed).

Congratulations! You've just done a good deed that should keep your karma paid up until the end of the decade. And you didn't even have to go to medical school.

Adventures of a Lifetime

Two common, very serious, and easily fixed complications after delivery stem from bleeding: the vaginal tear and oozing from a lax uterus. For a vaginal tear (as a result of no episiotomy), apply direct pressure with a clean, dry cloth. If the cloth becomes saturated, do not pull it off and use another. Simply add another one on top and maintain pressure on the area. For a lax uterus that continues to bleed, massage the abdomen (sort of like how Bugs Bunny massaged Elmer Fudd's head with hair tonic, with the fingers). This will coax the uterus to contract to its normal size and thus save precious blood.

A Complicated Situation Made Worse

As smooth as the birthing process can go, it can just as easily turn bad. Complications are especially fearsome in this situation, since you have no medical training to either identify them or treat them.

The most common complication is a breech birth. As we mentioned earlier, this happens when the baby is out of position, coming down the birth canal either buttocks first or feetfirst. The reason babies come out headfirst is that the head and shoulders are the widest parts. The baby's journey through is meant to dilate the cervix as wide as possible so the rest of the child passes through with ease. The problem with breech babies is that the head comes out last and the cervix may not be dilated enough for it to pass through. If the mother has been seeing her doctor regularly, the doc would know about the breech. There are methods of physically manipulating the mother to coax the baby to turn. If that fails, breech babies are usually delivered via Cesarean section (surgically).

Since you don't have medical training, you don't have an operating room, and you sure don't have any anesthetic, the breech will have to be delivered the old-fashioned way. Because one thing's certain: The baby is coming whether you want it to or not.

Your options are limited to …

➤ **Get to a hospital.** If that's impossible, it's time to do the best you can.

➤ **Watch the cord.** The width of the baby's head could squeeze the cord and cut off the blood supply to the baby, causing oxygen deprivation and brain damage.

➤ **Watch the neck.** If the baby's head is stuck, be very careful helping the baby out, for pulling could injure the child. The neck is an especially weak area on a newborn.

➤ **Coach mom.** She'll be in utter agony, but it's imperative that she continue pushing until that head is clear.

Medical attention is vital in this situation, because even if the baby is born successfully, breech babies are prone to further complications. But like we said, the child might not give you a choice. If you must deliver, help that baby out as much as you can. That little life depends on it.

Take My Life, Please

Are you a good salesperson? If you can sell courtesy to a cabbie, honesty to a politician, or stocks to a broker, you have the kind of personality it takes to talk someone out of killing him- or herself. If your verbal skills are more limited, you'll have to fake it. Why? Because someone's life is in danger—even though the danger is self-created—and because good people help those who need help.

There are two kinds of people who threaten to commit suicide: those who want to kill themselves and those who want attention. Treat them both the same way. After all, there's no way for you to know who's for real.

Adventures of a Lifetime

One very important part of negotiation training is managing your emotions. Yes, you must make contact, and yes, you must do your best to talk the person down. But inside, you should keep some emotional distance. Remember that you didn't put the person on the ledge. You didn't put the gun to the person's head. If the person does indeed jump or shoot, he or she probably would have done it even if you weren't there to help. This may be of little consequence after seeing someone die, but keep in mind that you're not a professional. If you did your best, that's all anyone can ask.

Some suggestions are ...

➤ **Stall until professional help arrives.** The police have professional negotiators for this kind of thing. You may just want to stall the person until the cops get there. Which is the smart thing to do. But if that's not an option ...

➤ **Make contact.** Introduce yourself. Start a conversation. You'll most likely receive threats in return. Stay calm and friendly. But persist.

➤ **Ask questions.** Why are you doing this? Why do you think you have no alternatives? Is hurting yourself really going to solve anything? Use a good line of questions to find common ground. Perhaps you both have lousy parents, bad marriages, or no money. Let the person know that he or she is not the only one with these problems.

➤ **Earn the person's trust.** This is the hardest part. Hopefully, after reaching common ground, this person will be willing not to just talk to you, but to listen to you as well. The moment the person thinks you're insincere, or jerking him or her around, or that you've been lying about caring, you've lost the trust and probably the person.

➤ **Keep the dialogue going for as long as it takes.** In the end, however, you must finally convince the person not to jump or shoot. You'll have to ask the person to step down off the ledge or to put the gun down. But promise that you won't drop him or her like a bad habit as soon as the threat is neutralized. You've earned his or her trust; don't abandon this person. "The gun is a bit of a problem, Fredo. It really makes me nervous. If you put the gun down, then we can really talk. I can't help you while you're holding the gun, Fredo." If Fredo puts the gun down, you absolutely owe him some face time.

Most suicide threats are just that, threats. People cry out for help, need attention, or simply enjoy seeing all the flashing lights on emergency vehicles. However, just because someone isn't serious about killing him- or herself doesn't mean that the person doesn't need help.

On the other hand, some people are *very* serious about killing themselves. If you're trying to talk someone down, this is a contingency for which you should be prepared, because things might not end the way you want. Just remember, if someone does jump or shoot, he or she was probably planning to do so all along, no matter what you said.

Ultimately, the decision to live or die is not yours to make. All you can do is your best.

Into the Ice

Everyone saw the movie *Titanic,* so we all know what happens when humans end up in freezing water. You get icicles in your hair and you get to kiss Kate Winslet buh-bye.

SOS

Do not try to pull the victim into the canoe. Even in the best of circumstances, it's very difficult trying to hoist someone into a canoe. The victim will most likely upset the boat, dumping you into the freezing water as well. Instead, *tow* the person to safety.

In Chapter 11, "My Little Deuce Coupe," you learned what precautions you should take to prevent your car (and yourself) from falling through ice. You know that if you see someone fall through ice, that poor soul has just minutes to live before hypothermia sets in. If too much time passes, the victim won't be able to help him- or herself even if he or she is still alive. Which means you have to act—and quickly. As always, however, an ounce of preparation can make up for a kilo of bad judgment. Luckily, you have options. Here are some useful ice rescue techniques:

➤ **Call 911.** In this day and age, chances are either you or an onlooker will have a cell phone. Call 911 first, then try to help the victim.

➤ **Spread your weight out over as great an area as possible.** This is the key to any ice rescue. The more concentrated your weight, the more risk you have of breaking through. Lie down as you approach the break, or better yet, use something that spreads the weight for you, such as a ladder laying flat on the ice.

➤ **Use a canoe or kayak to reach the victim.** This is perhaps the best of all ice rescue equipment. It's light enough to slide along the ice until you get close. Then if the ice breaks beneath you, you'll float. In which case you can paddle to the person's aid.

➤ **Use a rope.** Rope is a good rescue tool for obvious reasons. You can keep your distance while pulling the victim to safety. It's a good idea to first anchor the rope to a tree or car on shore. This prevents the rope from slipping out of your hands (never underestimate the cold) and also provides a safety measure if the ice breaks beneath your own feet in mid-rescue.

➤ **Use anything that floats.** Anything designed to float can have a line attached to it. Items include life vests, rescue rings, inner tubes (if anyone is riding one down a snow-covered hill nearby), and empty beer coolers. Secure it firmly and throw or slide it to the person in the water.

➤ **Form a human chain.** Several people can lie flat on the ice, holding on to each other by the ankles. If the ice collapses under the lead person, the people in the rear can pull the leader out.

➤ **Improvise.** Hockey sticks, ladders, belts, and tree branches all make useful rescue implements. Use anything that can help reach the person with the least risk to yourself, because you're useless if you fall in, too.

After you fish the person out, get the person warm and wait for emergency medical personnel to arrive. Hypothermia sets in when the body temperature drops below 95 degrees F. That's a mere $3^{1}/_{2}$ degrees below normal. Get the person out of wet clothes and into some heavy coats or blankets. Put the person in a car with a heater and drive to a hospital (unless the ambulance has already arrived).

Harsh Medicine

There are some remaining medical scenarios that aren't covered in basic first aid, although they all use certain first-aid techniques (see Chapter 4 for a rundown of basic lifesaving skills). These situations are extreme, high-drama deals that require a cool head and a quick mind.

Obviously, we run on the assumption that you're not a doctor or nurse. Which means if you mess around and try something fancy in any of these situations, you'll probably do more harm than good. So keep it simple, Hawkeye.

Wow. Sounds cool. What exactly are we talking about here that could be so ... *Rambo?*

Read on and find out.

Broken Limbs

Anyone can break a leg, even if you aren't an actor. But don't forget about fingers, arms, collarbones, ribs, and all their friends and neighbors in the human body.

Survival Kit

If a break is compound, where the bone pierces the skin, use direct pressure to control the bleeding. This kind of injury usually brings on shock, in which case treat the patient accordingly. *Do not* try to set the bone or "push it back in." Splint the limb normally and get some professional help pronto.

There are two basic rules when dealing with a broken limb:

1. **Don't try to set the break.** You're not a doctor. You could truly mess someone up. You'd be better off leaving the person there, going to medical school, and coming back after four years. Then you can set that bone until your heart breaks.

2. **Immobilize the break.** Use a makeshift splint—which can be anything you can find, such as a length of flat wood or a piece of an oar—padded with clothing. The main thing to remember is that the splint should be longer than the limb being splinted (the less movement, the better).

The bottom line here is simplicity. Get the limb splinted, and then get the person to a hospital.

Tracheotomies

Finally, one of the most dramatic rescue scenarios: performing the tracheotomy. Accomplished in memorable fashion—and under fire—by Father Mulcahy and Radar in an episode of *M*A*S*H*, performing the tracheotomy remains a dramatic procedure because you actually have to cut into someone's throat to pull it off. There's only one reason to do a tracheotomy: if the victim's air passage is blocked (maybe by a swollen or swallowed tongue) and the person can't breathe. A tracheotomy allows someone to breathe through a tube inserted in the neck.

SOS

Don't perform a tracheotomy unless it's absolutely necessary. We're talking about an invasive surgical procedure being performed by an amateur here. The situation must truly be life or death.

You'll need two things (at the absolute bare minimum):

1. A scalpel, razor, or sharp knife
2. A sturdy, thin cylinder such as a hollow ballpoint pen, an eye-dropper tube, or a plastic straw

Other helpful items are …

➤ Sterile bandages.

➤ Reasonably clean hands.

➤ Alcohol for sterilization.

If you're ready, here's the step-by-step deal:

1. The trachea tube must be inserted through the cartilage just beneath the Adam's apple. Run your finger along the Adam's apple until you find a distinct notch.

2. Make a half-inch horizontal (that's across) incision in this notch. You're trying to make a hole into the windpipe just large enough to fit your makeshift trachea tube. There will be some blood. Work through it.

3. Slip the tube into the incision, making sure that the patient now has a clear air passage.

4. If the patient is breathing on his or her own, you should hear and feel it through the tube. If not, you'll have to do a little mouth-to-tube resuscitation. Blow into the tube until the chest rises.

5. Pack bandages around the tube and get thee to a hospital.

Whew. We're spent. Obviously, these are all spur-of-the-moment, seat-of-the-pants deals that are rudimentary at best. Professional medical treatment is always your first, best option.

As for living a life of adventure, be careful out there. It's a hard, cold world worthy of a helmet. But like you, we wouldn't have it any other way.

The Least You Need to Know

➤ Delivering a baby is a natural process. If no complications exist, all you need to do is stay calm, coach the mother, and protect the baby as it is born.

➤ Breech deliveries need special care to ensure that blood flow through the umbilical cord is continuous and that the baby isn't injured during birth.

➤ When talking to a possible suicide victim, you need to earn his or her trust.

➤ Ice rescues can be aided with everyday objects such as canoes, ladders, ropes, life vests, and even empty beer coolers (with a line attached, of course).

➤ Never try to set a broken limb. Simply immobilize it with a splint and get the victim to a hospital.

➤ An emergency tracheotomy can be performed by making a small horizontal incision in the cartilage notch directly below the Adam's apple. Cut into the windpipe and insert a small, sturdy tube for breathing.

Glossary

albedo   An object's reflective power, the intrinsic light of the surface or body. Used in referring to light reflected off the moon or clouds.

arctic   A region in which the mean temperature of the warmest month doesn't exceed 50° F.

behaviorism   A school of psychology that takes the objective evidence of behavior as the sole consideration of research and bases its theories on behavioral events, not subjective mental states.

bench   An area of unstable land that forms where lava hits the ocean.

cannibalism   The eating of human flesh by another human being.

carotid   Either of two large arteries that pass up either side of the neck and carry blood from the aorta to the head.

cold deserts   Areas marked by extremely chilly temperatures; can be covered in a sea of never-ending snow and ice.

conflagration   A large, destructive fire that is often fueled by strong winds and can change local weather conditions.

coup or **coup d'état**   A sudden and decisive action resulting in a change of government illegally or by force.

Doppler radar   Advanced weather radar that is capable of looking at the heart of a storm and alerting scientists of severe weather conditions.

fault   A fracture in the Earth's crust along which one side of the fracture has been displaced in respect to the other side in a direction parallel to the fracture.

F-scale   Created by meteorologist Tetsuya Fujita, it is the scale of ranking for tornadoes from F0 to F6.

gorp   A mix of high-energy snacks like raisins, peanuts, dried fruit, nuts, and M&Ms.

jungle   Any type of tangled, impenetrable mass of vegetation or growth of thicket.

machete   A big, hefty knife used to remove underbrush.

peak experiences   Penetrating moments of happiness, love, clarity, and euphoria when people are totally alive and independent but understand that they are part of the world at large and are aware of truth, justice, and the global way.

pistol bite   An injury that occurs when an attacker's trigger finger is broken or ripped off in the process of being disarmed.

proteroglypha   Snakes with permanent "fixed" fangs in front of their teeth.

riptide   A powerful, fast-moving current or "river" in the ocean that usually runs perpendicular to and away from the shore.

seismic wave   A vibration within the Earth caused by an earthquake (and occasionally by an explosion or the impact of a meteorite).

shank   A prison term for a homemade weapon used for inflicting deep puncture wounds.

solenoglypha   Snakes with erectile "folded" fangs that are lifted into position.

spelunking   Exploring a cave, usually requiring protective clothing and climbing gear.

subarctic   A region in which the mean temperature of the four warmest months does not exceed 50° F.

tephra   Solid material ejected during a volcanic eruption and transported through the air.

trade wind   Any of the nearly constant easterly winds that dominate most of the tropics and subtropics throughout the world, blowing mainly from the northeast in the Northern Hemisphere, and from the southeast in the Southern Hemisphere.

tsunami   A great sea wave produced by submarine earth movement or volcanic eruption.

turbidity current   A current that flows down a slope and spreads out across the ocean floor.

warm deserts   An area where temperatures can reach above 55° C.

window of opportunity   The ideal time to take advantage of a situation and act. If you're under attack, this could be a distraction—a car horn, a person entering a room—that can cause an attacker to pause and give you a chance to escape.

Emergency Supply Kit List

Disaster Supply Kit

Whether you face a tornado, earthquake, or hurricane, there are certain supplies you should have on hand that will be valuable in most any situation. While relief workers will be doing their best to assist everyone, you might be on your own for hours or even days. By being prepared you will help make your life and the lives of your family just that much easier.

Tips for Assembling Your Disaster Supply Kit

When putting together your Disaster Supply Kit, be thorough but make sure that it's a collection that can be moved easily. An organized, well-thought-out kit can mean the difference between life and death for you and your family. Here are some other things to consider:

➤ Keep a smaller Disaster Supply Kit in the trunk of every car.

➤ Store items within the kit in airtight plastic bags.

➤ Use an easy-to-carry container (like a covered garbage can, backpack, or duffel bag) for the supplies you would most likely need for an evacuation. Label it clearly.

➤ Check with your physician or pharmacist regarding the best way to store prescription medications. Get copies of the prescriptions, and be sure to keep the medications in the kit up-to-date.

Disaster Supply Kit Basics

The following items should be stored in your Disaster Supply Kit. Keep the kit in a place where all family members have easy access to it.

➤ Portable, battery-powered radio or television and extra batteries

➤ Flashlight and extra batteries

➤ First-aid kit and manual

➤ Supply of prescription medications

➤ Credit card and cash

➤ Personal identification for each family member

➤ An extra set of car keys

➤ Matches in a waterproof container

➤ Signal flare

➤ Map of the area and phone numbers of places (shelters, hotels, relatives) where you could go

➤ Special needs, like diapers, formula, copies of prescriptions, hearing aid batteries, wheelchair battery, spare eyeglasses or contact lenses

Evacuation Supply Kit

Evacuation supplies should include things you might need if you find yourself forced to live away from home:

➤ Disaster Supply Kit basics

➤ Three gallons of water per person

➤ Three-day supply of nonperishable food

➤ Kitchen essentials: manual can opener; mess kits or paper cups, plates, and plastic/disposable utensils; utility knife; cooking fuel; household liquid bleach to treat drinking water; sugar, salt, pepper; aluminum foil; plastic resealable bags

➤ One change of clothing and footwear for each family member, including sturdy shoes or work boots, raingear, hat, gloves, thermal underwear, and sunglasses

➤ Blankets or sleeping bag for each family member

➤ Paper and pencil; needles and thread; pliers, shutoff wrench, shovels, tape; medicine dropper; whistle; plastic sheeting; A-B-C-type fire extinguisher; emergency preparedness manual; tube tent; compass

➤ Sanitation and hygiene items: toilet paper, towelettes, soap, hand sanitizer, liquid detergent, feminine hygiene supplies, shampoo, deodorant, toothpaste, toothbrushes, comb and brush, lip balm, plastic garbage bags, medium-sized plastic bucket with tight lid, disinfectant, household chlorine bleach, small shovel for digging an expedient latrine

➤ Games and books

Home Disaster Supply Kit

In addition to assembling your Disaster Supply Kit basics and Evacuation Supply Kit, gathering the following items will help your family endure the possibility of being confined in the home:

➤ Wrench to turn off household gas and water (this is a good thing to keep near shutoff valves at all times)

➤ A week's supply of food and water (it's important to replace your water supply every six months so it doesn't go bad)

Important Documents

For any disaster preparation, the following original documents should be kept in a safe deposit box with copies stored in a waterproof, fire-resistant portable container:

➤ Will, insurance policies, contracts, deeds, stocks and bonds

➤ Passports, social security cards, immunization records

➤ Bank account numbers

➤ Credit card account numbers and companies

➤ Inventory of valuable household goods, important telephone numbers

➤ Emergency contact information (friends and relatives who should be contacted)

➤ Lists of illnesses or drug allergies of all family members, including immunization records

Winter Survival Kit

Keep the following items in your car if you drive in winter weather:

➤ Blankets/sleeping bags

➤ High-calorie, nonperishable food

➤ Flashlight with extra batteries

- First-aid kit
- Knife
- Extra clothing to keep dry
- Large empty can and plastic cover with tissues and paper towels for sanitary purposes
- Smaller can and waterproof matches to melt snow for drinking water
- Sack of sand or cat litter
- Shovel
- Windshield scraper and brush
- Tool kit
- Tow rope or chain
- Booster cables
- Container for water
- Compass
- Road maps

Resources

Survival Preparation

Although this book is a one-stop shopping mall of survival information, you may want to further educate yourself. Here are some of the best resources we found while writing this book. Feel free to browse these Web sites while preparing for any natural disaster that may come down the pike.

EarthquakeStore (www.earthquakestore.com)

An online resource for everything you need, from valves to disaster kits.

National Weather Service (www.nws.noaa.gov)

National Weather Service, NOAA
1325 East-West Highway
Silver Spring, MD 20910

This site provides local and international weather forecasts as well as warnings and storm predictions.

United States Geological Survey (www.usgs.org)

A scientific organization dedicated to understanding the earth and natural sciences. One of their many goals is to help minimize loss of life and property due to natural disasters.

National Severe Storms Laboratory (www.nssl.noaa.gov)

An internationally known research facility studying all aspects of severe weather.

The Weather Channel (www.weather.com)

This site is the perfect source of information for weather locally or internationally.

The Disaster Center (www.disastercenter.com)

This site provides disaster-related statistics and historical data, and links to local, state, and national organizations involved in disaster warning, preparation, response, recovery, and mitigation.

Disaster Relief

I recommend familiarizing yourself with the following recovery resources. There is valuable information about local relief efforts and these organizations could be a god-send after the storm passes and your *Idiot's Guide* gets lost in Mother Nature's shuffle.

The American Red Cross (www.redcross.org)

Provides relief to those faced with a disaster. The Web site contains information for disaster victims, as well as a directory of local Red Cross numbers if you or someone you love is affected by a disaster.

Federal Emergency Management Agency (www.fema.gov)

FEMA
500 C Street S.W.
Washington, DC 20472

An independent agency of the federal government, FEMA's mission is to reduce the risk and loss caused by disaster.

Small Business Administration (www.sba.gov/disaster)

Provides financial assistance through low-interest loans to those hurt by a disaster.

Housing and Urban Development (www.hud.gov)

HUD
451 7th Street S.W.
Washington, DC 20410
202-708-1112

Aids in disaster-recovery assistance.

Books

This book is more of a wide-ranging primer in the survival industry and the books below are more specific and thorough. These fine authors can all be trusted to ensure you handle life's major foibles.

Wilderness Survival

Alloway, David. *Desert Survival Skills.* University of Texas Press, 2000. This practical handbook provides advice on short-term desert survival.

Brown, Tom. *The Tracker.* Berkley Publishing Group, 1996. The ultimate guide to animal tracking.

————. *Tom Brown's Field Guide to Wilderness Survival.* Berkley Publishing Group, 1989. Learn from the master everything you need to know about building shelters, animal tracking, edible plants, and even camouflage.

Jaeger, Ellsworth, and Lloyd Kahn. *Wildwood Wisdom.* Shelter Publications, 1992. Originally written in 1945, this book includes information on making fires, canoeing, using axes and knives, and building shelters from hand-gathered materials.

Montgomery, David R. *Mountainman Crafts and Skills: A Fully Illustrated Guide to Wilderness Living and Survival.* The Lyons Press, 2000. Geared toward both the novice and expert, this guide gives fully illustrated instructions on everything from how to make and use hunting tools, to making your own clothes and even building a fire.

Tilton, Buck, and Frank Hubbell. *Medicine for the Backcountry.* Globe Pequot Press, 1999. A guide to everything from injuries and illness, from blisters to cardiac arrest.

Weather

Hodgson, Michael. *Basic Essentials: Weather Forecasting.* Globe Pequot Press, 1999. Basic advice for any novice who wants to learn how to read basic shifts and patterns in weather.

Natural Disasters

Bluestein, Howard. *Tornado Alley: Monster Storms of the Great Plains.* Oxford University Press, 1999. A University of Oklahoma meteorologist helps to explain the truth behind tornadoes.

Davies, Pete. *Inside the Hurricane: Face to Face with Nature's Deadliest Storms.* Henry Holt and Company, 2000. A close look at 1998's Hurricane Mitch.

Rosenfield, Jeffrey P. Eye *of the Storm: Inside the World's Deadliest Hurricanes, Tornadoes, and Blizzards.* Perseus Press, 1999. An inside explanation of the world's deadliest storms.

Thompson, Dick. *Volcano Cowboys: The Rocky Evolution of a Dangerous Science.* St Martins Press, 2000. Follow these volcano hunters as they teach you the intricacies of these giant wonders.

Index

U

V